HOW COMICS TRAVEL

STUDIES IN COMICS AND CARTOONS

Jared Gardner, Charles Hatfield, and Rebecca Wanzo, Series Editors

HOW COMICS TRAVEL

Publication, Translation,
Radical Literacies

KATHERINE KELP-STEBBINS

THE OHIO STATE UNIVERSITY PRESS

COLUMBUS

Library of Congress Cataloging-in-Publication Data
Names: Kelp-Stebbins, Katherine Laurel, author.
Title: How comics travel : publication, translation, radical literacies / Katherine Kelp-Stebbins.
Other titles: Studies in comics and cartoons.
Description: Columbus : The Ohio State University Press, [2022] | Series: Studies in comics and cartoons | Includes bibliographical references and index. | Summary: "How Comics Travel looks at Metro, Tintin, Persepolis, and more to argue that modifications to graphic narratives between publication sites produce meaningful negotiations of translation, form, and print cultures"—Provided by publisher.
Identifiers: LCCN 2021046190 | ISBN 9780814215043 (cloth) | ISBN 0814215041 (cloth) | ISBN 9780814281963 (ebook) | ISBN 0814281966 (ebook) Subjects: LCSH: Comic books, strips, etc.—History and criticism. | Graphic novels—History and criticism. | Comic books, strips, etc.—Publishing. | Comic books, strips, etc.—Translating. | Literature and transnationalism.
Classification: LCC PN6714 .K45 2022 | DDC 741.5/9—dc23/eng/20211213
LC record available at https://lccn.loc.gov/2021046190

Cover design by Andrew Brozyna
Text composition by Stuart Rodriguez
Text composed in Palatino Linotype

For Constance, who taught me to break codes, and for Barbara, who taught me to break barriers

CONTENTS

List of Illustrations   ix

Acknowledgments   xi

INTRODUCTION   Graphic Positioning Systems   1

CHAPTER 1   The Adventures of Three Readers in the
                     World of *Tintin*   22

CHAPTER 2   Graphic Disorientations: *Metro* and Translation   69

CHAPTER 3   *Persepolis* and the Cultural Currency of the
                     Graphic Novel   104

CHAPTER 4   Border Thinking and Decolonial Mapping in
                     Michael Nicoll Yahgulanaas's Haida Manga   148

CHAPTER 5   *Samandal* and Translational Transnationalism   189

Bibliography   221

Index   245

ILLUSTRATIONS

FIGURE 1.1   Scott McCloud, *Understanding Comics*   28

FIGURE 1.2   Charles Burns, *Sugar Skull*   63

FIGURE 1.3   Charles Burns, *Johnny 23*   65

FIGURE 2.1   Joe Sacco, *Palestine*   72

FIGURE 2.2   Comparison of panel from Arabic, English, German, Italian, and US *Metros*   88

FIGURE 2.3   Magdy El Shafee, *Metro*   90

FIGURE 2.4   Chip Rossetti trans., *Metro*   92

FIGURE 2.5   Ernesto Pagano trans., *Metro*; and Iskandar Ahmad Abdalla and Stefan Winkler, trans.   94

FIGURE 2.6   Magdy El Shafee, *Metro*   97

FIGURE 2.7   Chip Rossetti trans., *Metro*   99

FIGURE 3.1   Marjane Satrapi, *Persepolis 1* and Satrapi, *Persepolis: The Story of a Childhood*   125

FIGURE 3.2   Covers of Marjane Satrapi, *Persepolis 1, 2, 3* and *4*   128

FIGURE 3.3   Cover of Marjane Satrapi, *Persepolis: The Story of a Childhood*   129

FIGURE 4.1   Michael Nicoll Yahgulanaas, *Carpe Fin*   168

FIGURE 4.2   Michael Nicoll Yahgulanaas, "In the Gutter"   176

FIGURE 4.3   Michael Nicoll Yahgulanaas, *Red: A Haida Manga,* full mural   178–79

FIGURE 4.4   Michael Nicoll Yahgulanaas, *Red: A Haida Manga,* page 83   182

FIGURE 5.1   Translation of Mazen Kerbaj, "Suspended Time Vol. 1: The Family Tree"   211

FIGURE 5.2   Assorted "flippy pages" from *Samandal*   216

ACKNOWLEDGMENTS

The writing of *How Comics Travel* took place on Indigenous land. Edward Said reminds us that culture and imperialism are, at base, always questions of land, "the actual geographical possession of land" (*Culture* 78). Dispossession of land and displacement from land are processes that use "narratives to dispel contradictory memories and to occlude violence" (132). A work about how books travel across and between different places should acknowledge the peoples historically displaced in discussions of land. I began writing this book on the villages and unceded lands of the Chumash people. Additional writing and research was undertaken on Kalapuya Ilihi, the traditional Indigenous homeland of the Kalapuya people. Wherever in the world this book finds you, know that the words in these pages were formed on Indigenous land.

I am grateful for the institutional support that I have received. This book was generously aided by a University of Oregon College of Arts and Sciences Humanities and Creative Arts Summer Stipend. Additional assistance was provided by the Oregon Humanities Center in the form of a book subvention.

Some sections from chapter 3 were previously published in "Global Comics: Two Women's Texts and a Critique of Cultural Imperialism," *Feminist Media Histories,* 4.3 (2018): 135–56. I acknowledge the University of California Press for their permission to use this material.

So many brilliant people have given time and care to this project. Rita Raley, Bishnupriya Ghosh, and Maurizia Boscagli all encouraged me to write about comics, and it has made all the difference. Lindsay Thomas, Alison Schifani, Mike Grafals, and Alston D'Silva offered advice and commentary that helped shape and reshape my research. Andy Warner suggested that I teach Mazen Kerbaj and reoriented my research for the better. James Cox gifted me *Red,* which became a key for how I conceptualize travel and graphic narrative.

My colleagues at the University of Oregon have been patient, gracious, and insightful in equal measure. I am grateful to Karen Ford, Tara Fickle, David Vazquez, and Fabienne Moore, who all gave wonderful feedback on the project. Deserving his own place of recognition, festooned with loving admiration, Michael Allan not only read and responded to the entire work, he has become family in Eugene.

I have had the great fortune to teach comics at three institutions at graduate and undergraduate levels. The insights and inquiries that my students have brought to this still-recent topic of academic study have tremendously enhanced my own scholarship.

Among the translation studies and comics studies communities, I am thankful for Andréa Gilroy, Emily Taylor, Anne Coldiron, Emmy Waldman, Hillary Chute, Dominic Davies, Haya Alfaran, and the many others who provided me space, opportunity, and time to speak some of these words aloud and be met by helpful rejoinders.

Of all the supportive scholars in Comics Studies, I am especially grateful to Susan Kirtley for sharing her wisdom and experience. As a woman in a male-dominated field, I would like to thank men who make this field more inclusive, and who treated my project like a necessary contribution to Comics Studies. Rocco Versaci and Charles Hatfield are two kind and sagacious comics scholars. Frederick Luis Aldama is a role model, and I count myself lucky that he has encouraged my work.

Editors, agents, and artists conversed with me and made my scholarship richer with their knowledge. To Edward Gauvin and Chip Rossetti, in the spirit of *traduttore traditore*: I am honored to represent your words, and if I fail them, the fault is mine. Thank you for making comics more accessible. Gary Groth took the time to answer questions about my "awfully arcane research project," and I am thankful for his assistance and for the incredible comics he has brought into the world. Thank you also to Jacq Cohen for more insights into Fantagraphics. This is not a book about superheroes, but if there is a superhero in *How Comics Travel,* it is Anjali Singh, whose conviction that there is an audience for comics about women of color inspires and motivates my research. Thank you to Leila Abdelrazaq, to Joe Sacco, and to Michael Nicoll Yahgulanaas. I am in awe not only of your art but of the ways that your lives shape your creativity, and of the drive for justice that underpins your creation.

More colleagues and friends have generously read through portions of this book and given me insight on making my way through some of its thornier concepts. Thank you to Eion Lys, Liz Thaler, and David Haan. I offer endless gratitude to Kacie Wills and Leila Estes, who are both my most trusted readers and my favorite people to write with.

Writing a book can be a lonely and maddening process. Without Jessie Goodell and Tien-Tien Yu, as well as Erin Whitaker, Shannon Micheel, Leah Kirkland, and Sally Dougherty listening to me work through my ideas while running so many thousands of miles, I would be far less sane. Without Joe Henderson and Rick Putnam coaching me, I wouldn't have run all those miles. Thank you to Neal Benson and Alyse Stone for finding me a place to write that is full of love. And thank you to Laura and Mike Allred for making me part of the comics *framily* and encouraging me to sing when I couldn't write.

I am grateful for my editor, Ana Maria Jimenez-Moreno, and for her patient and attentive support. With tremendous love, I offer thanks to my family, Barbara Stebbins, Larry Kelp, and Emma Kelp-Stebbins, for all of your benevolent responses and immeasurable help. Finally, thank you to Ben Saunders for making my career possible. And to Marcel Brousseau for making my life possible.

GRAPHIC POSITIONING SYSTEMS

Is the World of World Literature the World of World Comics?

The world is being redrawn. Lines that divide places and pages into discrete units likewise articulate relations of proximity and distance. Whether it be where the panel meets the gutter or where two nations rub against each other, a border is a meeting place. Yet, in an age of global pandemic, climate collapse, and massive human displacement, conventional epistemologies of place are in urgent need of new methodologies. Enter comics. This book contends that comics provide alternative mapping tools and methods for reading the world in its mutability. Instead of reading comics for how they bridge cultures and offer seemingly universal meanings, I propose a new methodological practice of reading transnational comics for difference. *Reading for difference* means not only looking at how comics are successfully translated both within and between national contexts but also examining points of disorientation and disjuncture among source and target texts. This approach, I contend, offers anticolonial, feminist, antiracist literacies that help us redraw the world as a means of reworlding.

How Comics Travel explores the challenges and benefits of thinking through the idea of world comics as objects of analysis and as tools for epistemological intervention. This project reflects a burgeoning interest in framing and defining comics as a global medium. As a testament to such efforts, in 2018 no less an authority than *The Cambridge History of the Graphic Novel* avowed that "at the time of publication, the idea of a world literature for the graphic novel is gaining momentum" (1). What would a world literature for the graphic novel look like? Rather than presuming the givenness of both world literature and world comics, I propose that we draw from long-standing debates in world literary studies to read world comics according to their differences from—as well as similarities to—world literature.[1] As a paradigm, world literature encourages readers to feel connected to other locations and cultures and to ignore the commercial practices that grant them or deny them access to foreign texts. Comics, on the other hand, are acutely indicative of the uneven flows of globalization as well as the fluctuating business of international comics. This book explores how divergent cultures of comics production, translation, reading, and circulation locate readers according to differential frameworks of expectation, understanding, commercial interests, and publishing industries.

The historical context for this book is based in market logics and academic critique. A marked increase in the production of graphic novels—as indicated by the existence of an entire edited Cambridge volume on their history—has led to overlap between spaces of comics and those of text-only books. In the US, literary publishers such as Pantheon and Norton have added many graphic novels to their lists in the last decade, and bookstores have also taken to shelving image-texts alongside text-texts. However, the commercial proximity and shared print form of the book should not conceal the visual, formal, and economic distinctions between comics and literature, especially in a worldly cast. As Michael Allan asserts, world literature "shares in common a normative definition of literature linked to a particular semiotic ideology" (7); that is, world literature assumes both a definite set of objects and a way of engaging them. Without discounting nuanced work that so many of the literary theorists cited in this book

---

1. Cf. Chute, "Comics as Literature?"; Hatfield; Versaci.

undertake to destabilize the boundaries of the literary and to suggest new reading practices, the binary of literacy and illiteracy remains. Comics, often satirized[2] as indicators of illiteracy, are not so cohesive in their anatomy, literacies, or milieu. Putting literary and translation theorists such as Emily Apter, Aamir Mufti, Rebecca Walkowitz, Pheng Cheah, and Rey Chow into conversation with comics theorists such as Thierry Groensteen, Bart Beaty, Rebecca Wanzo, Ann Miller, Hillary Chute, and Frederick Aldama, I argue that global comics both complements and challenges the precepts of world literature along three areas of divergence: translation, form, and print cultures.

Translation

As verbal-visual media, comics present new possibilities for theorizing translation. Scholars have drawn attention to the unacknowledged role that translation plays in world literature,[3] but its continued efficacy remains indispensable for expanding readerships beyond linguistic and national boundaries. Comics—as a hybrid medium—undergoes translation in ways that are incomparable to any other medium, even film, the closest cognate. Although works in translation account for only 3 percent of the literary production in the US, the share of comics in translation is closer to 30 percent. The case studies I provide demonstrate how words and images in comics create translational crises and opportunities for reading with a greater awareness of cultural difference. Comics such as Magdy El Shafee's *Metro,* which I discuss in chapter 2, force a translator to choose how much of the Arabic text to preserve and how to reformat panels and pages according to the orientation of right-to-left Arabic text and left-to-right English, Italian, or German text. Furthermore, although many comics scholars contend that images are universal in their meaning, the images in comics, which are sometimes altered in translation but

---

2. Or outright condemned; see Hatfield 34–36.

3. See Venuti, "World Literature" 180: "World literature cannot be conceptualized apart from translation"; Apter, *Against World Literature* 3: "many recent efforts to revive World Literature rely on a translatability assumption"; Spivak's indictment of "the arrogance of the cartographic reading of world lit. in translation" (*Death of a Discipline* 73); as well as Casanova's succinctly pragmatic "translation, despite the inevitable misunderstandings to which it gives rise, is one of the principal means by which texts circulate in the literary world" (*World Republic of Letters* xiii).

rarely completely redrawn,[4] are always prone to the cultural specificity of visual interpretation. Panels in comics are thus sites of encounter between translatable and untranslatable registers.

Form

The concept of global comics also demands a rethinking of the cultural relations underlying form. The novel, which serves a key role in the development of world literature, maintains a formal monopoly in publication circuits. As a relatively recent development, the *graphic novel* represents a move toward formal standardization of comics that is both heterogeneous in its deployment—not all comics everywhere are published as graphic novels—and an inexact response to formal heterogeneity of comics—some comics are more or less adaptable to the graphic novel format.[5] Comics in the US have a vast array of formal incarnations—strips, floppies, webcomics, graphic novels—while mainstream *bandes dessinées* in francophone countries are uniformly published in *album* format with distinctive formal standards (hardcover and larger trim sizes than comic books). As detailed in chapter 1, although Hergé's *Tintin* albums are some of the most popular comics worldwide, their lack of success in the US is often attributed to the unfamiliar, large shape these books presented for American readers.[6] However, when smaller-sized versions were printed by Little, Brown & Co., readers complained that the art was ruined by the resizing.

Given the importance of shape and size to the narrative and artistic content of comics, these questions of form and the relationships between formal traditions in different locations go well beyond literary trends like "the aesthetics of bookishness." As described by Jessica Pressman, many literary texts in the twenty-first century indicate a renewed attention to the book as an art object as a way to respond to the speculative "death of the book" in the digital age. Yet even

---

4. Although translations under copyright will generally preserve the artwork, there are numerous cases of artists changing or revising their own work for translation or even reproduction, as well as a large community of fans and entrepreneurs who practice different types of piracy as well as scanlation. See also Reyns-Chikuma.

5. See Lefèvre, "Importance of Being 'Published'"; Rota, "Aspects of Adaptation"; and Gabilliet, "Disappointing Crossing."

6. An article in the *New York Times* referred to the books as "oversize comic books" (Elsworth), in a neat bit of intercultural translation.

the examples Pressman describes, full of images or engaging visual elements, do not approach the level of inseparability between form and content that comics possess as a spatially determined and constrained medium. Thus, when considering how comics travel across national borders, we must grapple with formal translation: Will readers disregard a foreign-looking format like the albums of *Tintin*? Will they see a slim, two-volume graphic novel and recognize the alternative French comics volumes, *Persepolis,* according to a domestic formal register established by Art Spiegelman's *Maus*? As I describe in chapter 3, this formal translation was undertaken by US publisher Pantheon, which not only published both *Maus* and *Persepolis* for US readers but also changed the number of volumes of *Persepolis* from four, as it had been printed in France, to two, as *Maus* had been printed in the US—irrevocably altering the narrative divisions in the two versions of *Persepolis,* while brokering its formal translation.

Print Cultures

Global comics also trace new circulation models for print cultures. Unlike literary projects such as Goethe's *Weltliteratur* (world literature),[7] comics do not always reflect national traditions and divisions, owing both to comics' association with lowbrow culture in many areas and its transnational origins. *Tintin* comics were inspired by comic strips from the US, republished in Mexican newspapers, and brought back to Belgium by Léon Degrelle, a Belgian reporter covering the Cristero War (Assouline 17). Alternately, when *Metro* was originally published in Egypt, Hosni Mubarak's government banned it for obscene content, and its author—himself a Libyan émigré—was arrested. The ban on *Metro* became a selling point for its Italian and German translations and contributed to its publicity in the US. These examples demonstrate the variegated peregrinations

---

7. Johann Wolfgang von Goethe's invocation of a "universal world literature" takes the nation-state as its a priori condition of possibility, even while advocating for the bridging of national divisions. As quoted at the outset of Franco Moretti's "Conjectures on World Literature," Goethe's statement that "national literature doesn't mean much: the age of world literature is beginning" positions national literature as textually and historically anterior to world literature, just as Marx and Engels write "from the many national and local literatures, a world literature arises" (54).

of comics, the role of transnational economies in comics distribution and production, and the diverse cultural and ideological implications of the multimodal medium. Because comics employ visual as well as verbal idioms, their national origins or boundaries differ from other text-based media: thus, *Tintin* transported the aesthetic and narrative patterns of US strips like George McManus's *Bringing Up Father* into the Franco-Belgian marketplace, generating the singularly European *ligne claire* style—a style named by Dutch artist Joost Swarte decades after its development in Belgium. On the other hand, *Metro* was banned in Egypt precisely because of its importation of Western visual storytelling and use of "offensive images." Between these two examples, a counterpoint of differential reading suggests that corollary to a so-called borderless world are diasporic, colonial, postcolonial, and decolonial worlds of fragmentation, displacement, and stoppage (Miyoshi).

Differences in the World

The recognition of the differences between literature and comics furnishes an intellectually fecund space for imagining global media. A welter of recent theoretical revisions of world literature indicate possible stakes for world comics—cultural imperialism, neoliberalism, target optics—as well as potential models of literacy—contrapuntal reading, planetarity, symptomatic reading, distant reading, the world republic of letters, untranslatability, texts born translated.[8] Most pressingly, an ethical approach to world comics must resist the abundance of seductive testaments to the universality of comics.[9] Such generalizations are understandable as endorsements of the importance and range of a frequently maligned, juridically challenged, and financially tenuous medium. Yet such assertions are detrimental to the study and appreciation of comics through their obfuscation of its heterogeneity. If world comics can develop as a way of reading for difference, its scope will be far greater and richer than a reading program invested in seeing sameness always and everywhere. Rather

---

8. See Said's *Culture and Imperialism*; Spivak's *Death of a Discipline*; Chow's *The Age of the World Target*; Moretti's "Conjectures" and "World-Systems Analysis"; Casanova's *World Republic of Letters* and "Literature as a World"; Apter's *Against World Literature*; and Walkowitz's *Born Translated*.

9. E.g., Elder. See Neil Cohn's *Who Understands Comics?* for a nuanced critique of assumptions regarding the universality of comics.

than insisting that comics are intelligible identically everywhere, world comics can insist on the points of (un)translatability, cultural specificity, formal or commercial difference, and map out a wider, more diverse, and more democratic terrain.

Reading for difference is not limited to the differences between or among comics; nor does it resolve solely along nationally limned comparative lines. Rather, as Chow stipulates in her conception of a more just comparative literature: "To do its job properly, this kind of comparative practice must be willing to abandon inclusionary taxonomizing habits and ready to interpret cultural narratives symptomatically, as fragments that bear clues—often indirect, perverse, and prejudiced—to a history of ideological coercions and exclusions" (85). Thus, the readings that accompany various chapters frequently seek out disjunctures and erasures in the comics they examine. For example, the approach to world comics enacted in this book *does* examine *Metro* in terms of its unique history and the sites of friction and untranslatability that the text provides in its various forms and transnational movements. The book *does not* take *Metro* as synecdoche for Egyptian comics *in toto,* as distinct from and opposed to, say, French bande dessinée.

Differences inhere not only between national traditions but also within traditions that may be national, but also international, or transnational. Reading for difference requires the "border thinking" espoused by Walter Mignolo, which insists on critically engaging the logic of coloniality underpinning the project of modernity (*Local Histories* ix)[10] so that a study of world comics may initiate productive studies of the sites of difference in its own construction, seeking limits and points of contention over the very terms *world* and *comics.* As Shane Denson contends:

> The act of reading a graphic narrative involves the reader in a process of articulation, which prior to (and as a condition of) "expression" also implies both a drawing of distinctions between parts and, simultaneously, an act of joining them together—that is, a double determination of borders, both as points of contact and of separation. (271)

---

10. Mignolo describes border thinking as "the necessary epistemology to delink and decolonize knowledge and, in the process, to build decolonial local histories, restoring the dignity that the Western idea of universal history took away from so many people" (*Local Histories* x).

Is *Metro* an Egyptian comic because it was originally published in Egypt, or is it a transnational comic because it has spent more time in print elsewhere? Should we study *Metro* according to traditions of African comics, or should it be grouped with Arabic-language comics to distinguish it from francophone or other linguistic groups of African comics? These questions about the "world" of world comics denote the sites of difference that expand its historical and geographic points of inquiry.

To conceptualize world comics as a way to contest hegemonic and colonial worlding is to be mindful of the historical situation of world literature, which has, in Aamir Mufti's description,

> functioned from the very beginning as a border regime, a system for the regulation of movement, rather than as a set of literary relations beyond or without borders. Put somewhat differently, we might say that the cultural sphere now generally identified as world literature, far from being a seamless and traversable space, has in fact been from the beginning a regime of enforced mobility and therefore of immobility as well. (9)

With Mufti's account looming, how might we describe comics without circumscribing them within immobile boundaries and producing a catalog of nation- and language-based examples? Why not study world contours through a methodology that considers seemingly heterogeneous events in the historical weft of graphic narrative?

I see in the profusion of titles by fellow travelers along this disorienting terrain attention to the kinds of differences that determine how comics might be located in the world. Aldama's forthcoming *World Comics: The Basics* uses a world systems approach to consider how forms and works derived in one country flow into global systems of exchange. Dan Mazur and Alexander Danner's *Comics: A Global History, 1968 to the Present* highlights points of intersection among its three main areas—Europe, Japan, and the US. Dominic Davies's *Urban Comics: Infrastructure and the Global City in Contemporary Graphic Narratives* hews closer to an area studies approach informed by a focus on urban centers. The collected volumes *Transnational Perspectives on Graphic Narratives: Comics at the Crossroads* and *Postcolonial Comics: Texts, Events, Identities* employ transnational and encounter-based modes of approaching their objects. Further, Nina Mickwitz, Candida Rifkind with Davies, and Nhora Lucia Serrano, among others, have all produced book-length scholarship that consider comics in relation to refugee and migrant narratives and positionalities. Comics may be global, urban, transnational, postcolonial, and displaced, and simultaneously all of the above.

In this work, I employ all these terms to indicate that comics are above all worldly insofar as they describe practices of reading and seeing that simultaneously make and remake the world. Comics are also global, as they circulate through economic systems that send texts drawn in Philadelphia to be printed in China before being sold in France, or through platforms that circulate scans through databases originating in and routed through divergent nodes along networks of reproductions of reproductions. Between the oft-theorized[11] antipodes of world and globe, I frame comics as unconfined within the conditions of either, but rather, in their medial hybridity and cultural heterogeneity, as a means for destabilizing the borders of both.

Differences in the Comics

Prevailing wisdom assumes that comics, by their formal nature, facilitate a universal semiotics united around transcultural and uncomplicated imagery. For instance, Derek Parker Royal asserts that "comics, by necessity, employ stereotypes as a kind of shorthand to communicate quickly and succinctly" and then avows that "given its reliance on symbols and iconography, comic art speaks in a language that is accessible to a wide audience, transcending many of the national, cultural, and linguistic boundaries imposed by other media and giving it a reach that is as democratic as it is immediate" ("Foreword" ix). Yet the idea of a democratic stereotype is a contradiction in terms that conceals the struggles for representation enacted in media flows. Rebecca Wanzo analyzes how stereotypes are used to uphold racial inequalities and to construct "black bodies as lesser human beings and citizens" (20–21). By shifting the critical focus from examining the universality of comics to questioning how comics enact resistances to universality—sites of untranslatability—I demonstrate that the transnational reach of stereotypes does not indicate democracy but instead indexes the production, policing, and dissemination

---

11. For brief summaries of a long debate: Cheah, "World Against Globe:" and *What Is a World*; Ganguly 19–24; Mignolo, *Local Histories* 39–43.

of local knowledges as global designs. Rather than a transcendent shorthand, a stereotype marks a struggle for representation, wherein certain groups are empowered with the ability to use and properly understand the knowledge that the stereotype represents.

Comics index struggles for representation not only in their content but also in their formal existence in the world. This book does not presume the fixity of discrete objects termed *comics* in anglophone areas, bandes dessinées in francophone regions, *manga* in Japanese-speaking regions, *manhwa* in Korean-speaking regions, *manhua* (or even *lianhuanhua*) in Sinophone areas, *fumetti* in Italian, *historietas* or *tebeos* in Spanish, and other variations (*komiks, comicbunch*, etc.) (Groensteen, "Definitions" 94–96). As literally translated, these drawn strips, inappropriate images, puffs of smoke, little [drawn] stories, and "I see you"s together map out a world system of "untranslatables," as Apter describes "a translational humanities whose fault-lines traverse the cultural subdivisions of nation or 'foreign' language, while coalescing around hubs of irreducible singularity" ("Untranslatables" 584). Yet these markers of local histories concurrently gesture toward the flip side of pluralistic terminology: Apter allows that while "planetary inclusion" is often the goal for lexical diversification, it can "paradoxically reinforce dependence on a national/ethnic nominalism that gives rise to new exclusions" (581). So Thierry Groensteen remarks how the "generalized semantic imprecision in the lexical field of American comics" was "exported to the whole world" under the terms "strip" and "comic" ("Definitions" 94). These uneven economies of objects and terms also lead to cross-contamination and reformulation among international comics. Comparatively, as I explore in my final chapter, Arab comics, in search of an appropriate nomination, risk obsolescence in lists such as the preceding one. However, the founders of the first trilingual comics journal published in Lebanon propose *salamander* (*Samandal*) as an apt translation for comics.

Similarly, while I employ the term *comics* in a rather roughshod fashion to account for an excessively diverse set of artistic products, such a totalizing discursive act, despite its heuristic motive, gives rise to a spate of questions over hegemonic terminology and the flattening of divergent cultural practices. Are *Tintin* albums comics because they employ the hybrid mixture of words and images used in the US comic strips that inspired them? Or are they bandes dessinées because that is the term used to describe them in their country of origin? Are they still bandes dessinées in translation? As anticolonial and feminist theorists contend, words matter, and discursive specificity is always engaged in the politics of recognition—how we come to know what comics *are* and how their borders are delineated. While it is tempting to diversify our reading lists by including a wide range of cultural products under the category of comics, this move toward inclusivity risks erasing the historical and geographic differences implicated in transnational circuits of comics.

Differences between types of image-text are mirrored by differences in scholarly approaches to their analysis. US studies of comics tend to rely heavily on reading practices developed by Scott McCloud, and they have only recently begun to incorporate European theoretical approaches drawn from semiotics and communications theory. McCloud focuses primarily on the gaps or gutters between panels, a rift that he claims necessitates closure on the part of the reader in order to create meaning from the otherwise separate components (*Understanding Comics* 63). Disjuncture between panels and between semantic elements or verbal and visual inscription is essential to the study of comics, yet many theorists have taken issue with the lack of attention McCloud pays to other functions of the page.[12] A long-standing Franco-Belgian theoretical tradition asserts the central role of the tension between various scales and modalities of reading. In 1976 French semiologist Pierre Fresnault-Deruelle published his seminal article insisting that the linear readings of panels—McCloud's unilateral emphasis—while invested with fictional depth, are disrupted by the simultaneous appearance of the page as tableau.[13] On any comics page there is a vacillation between the "three-dimensionality" of the narration or sequence and the "two-dimensionality" of the page as assembled tableau, operating in compositional unity of expression. As a way of trying to ground this divergence between approaches, Belgian scholar Jan Baetens draws from French theorists Pierre Masson and Harry Morgan (the pen name of Christian Wahl) to suggest that US emphasis on the comic strip may be the reason for increased attention in US scholarship to linear over tabular/tableau-centric reading ("Hommage"). Baetens does credit US scholars Hatfield and Chute with taking up the subject

12. For example, Frome 82–87; Groensteen, *Comics and Narration* 70–71, 73–74; Cates 91, 97–98, 103 n23; Hatfield 36–37, 70.

13. Fresnault-Deruelle, "Du linéaire au tabulaire" 20. Fresnault-Deruelle's formulation of "tabulaire" allows for other forms of "tableau" beyond the shape of the page.

of tabular reading in the form of temporal consideration but notes that the anglophone field has not reached the full range of rhetorical analytics posited by francophone theorists including Fresnault-Deruelle, Thierry Groensteen, and Benoît Peeters.

In many ways, what might seem like a minor discrepancy—a focus on narrative linearity over full-page consideration—is itself an indication of the impulse of many US scholars to situate comics fully within the field of the literary over and at the expense of the field of visual studies or alternative media studies. It is a theoretical perspective in keeping "with the 19th-century middle-class tradition that conceived of culture exclusively in terms of the book reigning over all the other arts," as media theorist Bernhard Siegert explains (10). Instead of championing the literariness of graphic narrative, how might one read comics in order to re-examine the process of differentiation already at work in constituting the opposition between literature and nonliterature or even between word and image? How might comics challenge the self-apparency of the truth claims of image and text?

By combining literary and visual arts, comics create what Groensteen dubs an "unnatural alliance" ("Why Are Comics" 8) simultaneously debasing the aesthetic value of both disciplines. Groensteen points to the historical separation of text and image as being "an integral part of occidental culture" (8). For Groensteen it is the hybrid nature of the comics form, imbricating both the logocentric and visual, that goes against "the ideology of purity that has dominated the West's approach to aesthetics" (9). In Groensteen's description, comics provide a resistant approach to the imperium of Western aesthetics and offer ways to read image and text *differently.* In the chapters that follow, I read for difference *within* comics, examining how image and text produce friction within the spatial composition of the page; *among* comics, exploring how different sites of production dovetail and diverge in their approaches to comics production; and *between* comics, ascertaining how translations or revisions can lead to entirely different texts with entirely different literacies.

Methodology

Thinking about how comics travel is, in this book, a geographical concern insofar as I question the processes by which comics objects move across national borders and what happens when they become entangled in different marketplaces and readerships. More conceptually, the comics studied in this book travel according to theoretical ways of reading the world and to practices of reading in the world. My subtitle relates through parataxis terms that work in concert to delimit, to expand, to challenge, and to reinterpret world comics. Publication and translation are both a priori and co-constitutive processes attending the radical literacies this book considers. My project resists an approach to world comics in which scholars from the US and other Western nations describe the world of comics by selecting representative "foreign" works in order to map aesthetic or narrative trends. *How Comics Travel* provides an alternate model by which to study world comics, cognizant of and invested in tracing the unequal systems of power and access that create the conditions of possibility for transnational media flows. At the same time, this book looks at the ways in which imperial or colonial systems of culture and valuation factor in to the critical appraisal of world comics, as in, for example, the reception of Marjane Satrapi's *Persepolis,* which positions it as both an authentic Persian artwork and an example of the universal appeal of comics.

Instead of using national categories to structure the book, I look at constellations of actants and issues woven together in the warp and weft of comics around the world. Reliance on stable and divisive geographic sectors of comics development has inflected much work in the field. McCloud segments comics into exactly three geographic areas with their implied concomitant appellations: comics in the US; manga in Japan; and bande dessinée in Europe (76–80). This T-O map of world comics has proved persistent. Tim Pilcher and Brad Brooks's book, *The Essential Guide to World Comics,* provides an overview of many works from different global regions, paradoxically relying on translations of many works yet asserting that "sequential art speaks directly to us without the need for translation" (14). Seemingly without critique, they frame global comics commerce in imperial terms, describing how US superheroes "dominated the global comic book market" until recently, when "the cultural tide has turned and a new empire has risen; the manga, which has turned to tables on US comics" (15). Methodologically, the research undertaken for *How Comics Travel* instead maps out a new and conceptually emergent framework that is both transnational and anticolonial.

My conceptual approach is indebted to the scholarly work of others invested in tracing how colonialism and transnational exchanges impact comics studies. Because of the long history of francophone comics scholarship and the seriousness with which bandes dessinées are treated critically, there are a number of books in French and English that consider the worldliness of comics from a Franco-Belgian perspective while accentuating the colonial implications of such a project. Mark McKinney has written about the "colonial heritage of French comics" (*Colonial Heritage*) and postcolonial negotiations of contemporary transnational comics (*Postcolonialism*). In *Redrawing French Empire in Comics,* McKinney provides a valuable theoretical model in the form of the *affrontier*—"a boundary . . . that divides and connects" imperial and colonial cultures "and around which individuals and groups confront each other" (3)—and its role in colonial and postcolonial representation. Likewise, Philippe Delisle tracks the role of bande dessinée in the reproduction and circulation of colonial ideology (*Bande dessinée*); Jean-Paul Gabilliet conducts historically engaged research into transatlantic migrations of comics as well as the national modes and values that inflect comics production ("Disappointing Crossing"); and Ann Miller attends to the importance of location in the representation and transgression of cultural and national frames ("*Les héritiers*").

A number of anglophone books also recognize the borders of the world as sites of encounter and exchange through which comics are mediated. Mazur and Danner begin their *Comics: A Global History, 1968 to the Present* by acknowledging the ever-present "cross-cultural and transnational influences" in the development of comics (7), in order to "provide a broader-than-usual map" (8) of the history and development of comics. Binita Mehta and Pia Mukherji characterize their edited volume *Postcolonial Comics: Texts, Events, Identities* as "a timely intervention within current comic-book area studies that remains firmly situated within the 'US-European and manga paradigms' and their reading publics" (4). *Postcolonial Comics* purposefully collects scholarship on comics from a range of geographic locales in order to "critically examine the issues at stake in representing the assembly of postcolonial conditions" (15). The volume *Transnational Perspectives on Graphic Narratives* similarly eschews treatment of Anglo-American comics, Franco-Belgian bande dessinée, and Japanese manga as "self-contained phenomena," instead focusing on "the ways in which graphic narratives have been shaped by aesthetic, social, political, economic, and cultural interactions that reach across national boundaries in an interconnected and globalizing world" (1). The editors, Daniel Stein, Shane Denson, and Christina Meyer, acknowledge local or national traditions of content and form that comics take on in various instantiations, while pointing to "border-crossings, interstitial relations, and cultural and material exchanges between traditions" (3). The objective of their project is to trace how "the multidirectional transactions uncovered by a transnational perspective problematize the foundational role of discrete national units" (3). As the editors argue, amid the transnational transactions of comics, "the particular is . . . rendered internally multiple as the traces of exchange are discovered *within,* and not merely *between,* national cultures, traditions, and identities" (3, emphasis in original). Other anthologies, such as *Comics as a Nexus of Cultures: Essays on the Interplay of Media, Disciplines and International Perspectives* (Berninger et al.); and *Crossing Boundaries in Graphic Narrative* (Jakaitis and Wurtz), indicate the shared scholarly interest in approaching comics "as hybrid form, not simply in identifying the tension between images and words, but in emphasizing its engagement with other genres and cultural forms" (Jakaitis and Wurtz 21). While these volumes do not share my focus on translation, they do insist on the complexity of location in all studies of media and culture.

The Politics of Location

Following Adrienne Rich's exhortation that feminist readers take responsibility for where we are reading from (219), it is necessary to give a theoretical framework for the sorts of designations I make between cultural practices, as well as for how I situate myself according to the comics I select for the project. As a scholar working within the academic system of the US, I focus on comics available in English in the US; however, this selection criteria is based on tracing precisely the trajectories and material histories that brought these works—or some versions of them—to my sites of reading and valuation. I argue that these comics are not reducible to a singular point of origin or to a standardized national practice.

My approach to these objects is grounded in translation, postcolonial, and feminist transnational theory. Susan Bassnett and Harish Trivedi outline how translation studies recognizes inequalities and power differentials among works:

> translation studies research has followed a similar path to other
> radical movements within literary and cultural studies, calling into
> question the politics of canonization and moving resolutely away

> from ideas of universal literary greatness. This is not to deny that
> some texts are valued more highly than others, but simply to affirm
> that systems of evaluation vary from time to time and from culture
> to culture and are not consistent. (2)

Looking both at recognizable (*Tintin, Persepolis*) and less recognizable
(*A Tale of Two Shamans, Samandal*) world comics through the frame
of formal and linguistic translation, I extend Bassnett and Trivedi's
insistence on translation studies as a mode of circumventing canoni-
cal valuations.

Pursuantly, this work comports with the ethical project of Tejaswini Niranjana's *Siting Translation,* which "outlin[es] the importance of the translation problematic for the post-colonial project"
(49). Describing this book as a postcolonial project is at once a politics and a heuristic. As Mignolo states, the discourse of postcoloniality "brings to the foreground the colonial side of the 'modern world
system' and the coloniality of power imbedded in modernity itself"
(*Local Histories* 93). This discourse also demands that historical geographies be brought to the fore of conversations about creative and
knowledge work. Nonetheless, as Sara Ahmed reminds us, postcoloniality can only ever operate as "a failed historicity," one that "allows
us to investigate how colonial encounters are both determining, and
yet not fully determining, of social and material existence" (*Strange
Encounters* 10). As a failed historicity, postcoloniality does not gesture
toward a single shared past; it reveals that "history is not the continuous line of the emergence of a people, but a series of discontinuous
encounters between nations, cultures, others and other others" (11).
Postcoloniality then functions meaningfully as a historically oriented
mode of foregrounding place, but not as a stable bounding of temporal or even geopolitical span.

As demonstrated by Haida artist Michael Nicoll Yahgulanaas's
Red—analyzed in chapter 4—one must work to avoid reading in a
way that replicates settler colonial imperialist practices of recognizing, dominating, and explaining *others*; further, one must resist over-
categorizing imperial entities like the US as homogeneous, unilateral
locations. Instead, this book also attends to what Inderpal Grewal
calls *Transnational America.* Grewal disputes totalizing theories about
US power and its territorialization, asserting that the US persists as a
hegemon of both "centralized and decentralized power through neoliberal regimes, technologies, and rationalities" (21). For Grewal, the

"global," as a Euro-American fantasy, "is not and never was quite global" (22). I follow Grewal's lead in tracing the "heterogeneous and multiple transnational connectivities" (22) that bring some but not most comics into economies of world media and that resonate with but do not replicate the economies of world literature.

In visualizing these alternate connectivities of relation and displacement, we glimpse the potential for world comics to furnish the counter to world literature in a fashion similar to Mufti's vision of the people's library. As Mufti describes it in *Forget English!: Orientalisms and World Literatures,* "the people's library embodies the desire not just for different books—than those enshrined in national curricula or literary cultures or in globalized commercial publishing, for instance—but for different ways of reading, circulating, valuing, and evaluating them" (7). It is precisely in this capacity, as a people's library for reworlding, that I designate the radical literacies offered in these chapters.

Radical literacies imply practices that reroot and reroute the process of reading according to different political, locational, and material contexts. Throughout the book, I characterize resistance, *détournement,* translation, reformatting, decolonial mapping, and flipping as radical literacies, and thus *potential* ways of reading comics. Resistance—which I examine in the form of a Congolese student's lawsuit against a *Tintin* album—is, as Wanzo notes, a way to "direct the gaze at . . . producers and consumers of racist caricature" (27), to draw attention to the injury of racist stereotype and to thus recreate the work as a "*manifestation* of injury" (220, emphasis in original). Détournement, a term for misappropriation or hijacking, is described by Guy Debord and Gil Wolman as a form of "extremist innovation" that uses elements taken from "the literary and artistic heritage of humanity" and recombines them in revolutionary ways (15).[14] Translation provides yet another form of reading that reorients literacy according to the tensions between codes of signification (Hatfield 36); thus, in translating comics such as *Metro,* readers reveal divergent cultural values and interpretive frameworks. Reformatting is its own type of translation dependent on cultures of publishing work.

---

14. Describing D. W. Griffith's *The Birth of a Nation* in terms equally applicable to *Tintin au Congo,* Debord and Wolman assign the film tremendous formal importance due to its technical innovations yet note that it is a racist film that should not be shown without a *détourning* that might remind the viewer of the horrors of imperialist war and racial hatred.

Decolonial mapping—in the form of Yahgulanaas's Haida manga—
is a related concept that reads comics according to experimental,
changeable, and culturally situated practices. Flipping is a material
maneuver by which comics multilingually *world,* or open a space for,
transnational subjectivity, expression, and political life.

A Map to Travel Through

The chapters conjugate *world* in its many verbal connotations, each
considering comics' worlding through a different conceptual framework. Thus, the first chapter examines the visual imperialism of *Tintin* comics as a totalizing worlding in the age of the world picture.
Chapter 2 recognizes the multiple contests of worlding manifested
in translations, which—in their dissonance—provide a system much
like Apter's world system of "untranslatables" or Édouard Glissant's
"mondialité" or "worldness." In Glissant's discourse, worldness is
opposed to globalization in its insistence on relations, differences,
and creolizations (86); as I explore, the multiple translations of
Magdy El Shafee's *Metro* generate intricate relations and heterogeneous cultural grammars. Chapter 3 draws from Spivak's call to produce an "alternative historical narrative of the 'worlding' of what is
today called 'the Third World'" ("Rani of Sirmur" 247) by revisiting
the publication and translation process of *Persepolis.* Chapter 4 asks
how Yahgulanaas's decolonial Indigenous manga offer maps of the
world that disrupt settler colonial toponymic and demarcating systems. Finally, chapter 5 considers the emergent comics practices of
Samandal as tools for unlearning empire and creatively shaping alternative worlds.

Beginning with *Tintin* is an audacious gambit, in light of the
overabundance of critical texts and popular attention the series has
received. The twenty-four volumes of *Tintin,* published during the
period 1929–86, have been translated into over 110 languages and
circulated throughout six continents. They present a subject fundamentally engaged in the practice of ethnographic knowledge production, wherein "foreign" culture is identified and represented as such
in paradigmatically clear lines. I shift my focus from the contents and
technical conditions of the series to more pointed analysis on *who*
reads *Tintin* and *how,* as framed by postcolonial and postmodern theory. For this endeavor, I triangulate three readers: US comics theo-

rist Scott McCloud, Congolese student Bienvenu Mbutu Mondondo, and US comics artist Charles Burns. These three constellate different literacies contingent on cultural contexts as well as racial categories. Together, McCloud, Mondondo, and Burns model comics reading as a multidimensional and emergent practice.

Chapter 2 examines the translation processes that accompanied the publication of Magdy El Shafee's *Metro. Metro,* the "first adult Arabic graphic novel," was originally published and distributed in Cairo in 2008 and then quickly banned by Hosni Mubarak's government. In the following years, *Metro* was translated into Italian, English, German, and French; it has now spent more time in publication in other languages than in the language of its original printing. For Western readers, *Metro* in translation appears as an authentically Oriental, yet recognizably Western, object—the graphic novel—that, because of its banning, appears to be oriented toward the revolutionary zeitgeist. However, for all its indisputable transnational appeal, *Metro*'s formal aspects create points of conflict in its translations.

Chapter 3 looks at how publishing economies position comics according to expectations of reception and valuation. As Grewal and Caren Kaplan argue in their discussion of transnationalism, "Critiques of Western reception can deconstruct the aesthetic and political mystiques that govern the marketing and distribution of cultural artifacts from the 'Third World'" (16). Further, as these theorists explain, understanding the role of reception in the manufacture of economies of global cultural objects—such as world literature—furnishes an inroad for demystifying the West as a cohesive or pure and unhybridized vantage point. When a reviewer or scholar describes Marjane Satrapi's *Persepolis* in terms of how the text visually translates Iran for a Western audience, what is lost in reception? The extant discourse on Satrapi's work rests almost entirely on the assumption of a stable referent deemed *Persepolis* that acquires meaning through cultural negotiations between Iran—the author's birthplace and a major setting in the works—and the West. However, displacing the location of the text from its original site of publication in France and the networks of translation and distribution that attended its success risks complicity in a mode of Orientalism whereby knowledge of the "East" is extended through Western products and consumer tendencies. This chapter shifts the geographic territory of analysis from one East-to-West transit to another, from Iran-to-"the West" to France-to-the US.

Chapter 4 considers cultural syncretism and decolonial practice in Michael Nicoll Yahgulanaas's Haida manga. Bringing together Haida artistic techniques and the Japanese form of manga, Haida manga intervenes in comics traditions, visualization paradigms, and the book as a commodity object. Yahgulanaas's transcultural works complicate layout practices considered conventional to comics, retraining a reader of comics to recognize borders, contact zones, and sites of translation as spaces full of meaning and contestation. For example, Yahgulanaas's book *Red* is composed of a series of pages segmented by Haida formlines into panels of curving, labile connectivity. These panels eschew the expected rectangular partitioning in favor of Haida linework that poses a rebuke to colonial knowledge systems whereby the whiteness of the comics gutter metonymically recalls the *terra nullius* of settler colonial imagination. Yahgulanaas's investment in the diegetic, formal, cultural, and commercial borders of comics reverberates across the preceding chapters and suggests radical new reading practices for world comics.

Chapter 5 highlights the radical and experimental politics of the Lebanese trilingual comics journal *Samandal.* Begun in 2007, *Samandal* credits itself as "the first trilingual, amphibious comics magazine open to submissions issued in the Middle East." The amphibious element refers to its situation between worlds of word and image, high and low, and traditional and experimental. I argue that *Samandal*'s multilingual object orientation compels readers to recognize not only where they are reading but also where they *are not* reading. Unlike global translations of *Metro* that attempt to negotiate between source culture and target culture with minimal friction, *Samandal* visually plots and materially enacts frictions among different reading cultures. The magazine's trilingual printing necessitates a trilingual format; readers must physically flip *Samandal* between stories in order to orient themselves to the page. The act of flipping *Samandal* while reading forces a reader to confront the physical orientations of literacy. This physical and cognitive situating is not limited to bodily orientation, however; it also reflects the politics of production. *Samandal*'s languages and linguistic orientations draw the reader's attention to the histories of violence underlying their co-presence in the work.

As their own contiguous yet delimited spaces, these chapters follow local lines of inquiry while creating throughlines that shuttle between and among each other. The book begins by asking how comics *world*: what tools and practices do they supply for reimaging and reimagining the world? By the final page, a multitude of possible tools—from maps of water to salamanders—and tactics—from détournement to flipping—are offered to describe an assemblage of world comics. This world is neither static nor unilateral, and as you read through the places of the following pages, you will encounter an ever-expanding and shifting atlas of reading for difference. Safe travels.

CHAPTER 1

THE ADVENTURES OF THREE READERS IN THE WORLD OF *TINTIN*

Introduction: World Comics through Three Readings of *Tintin*

How do comics *world*? If images constitute ways of worldmaking, as Nelson Goodman formulates, then comics, through their imagistic multiplicity and image-text hybridity, hardly constitute a dominant vision along the lines of Heidegger's world picture. Given their—albeit globally heterogeneous—relatively lowbrow cultural positions, as well as their fragmentation of any singular view of the world, the diverse array of objects loosely referred to as "comics" seem to have much more in common with what Bishnupriya Ghosh would dub "apertures to the popular." As Ghosh claims of *Global Icons,* these "mass-mediated images are precisely the widely and cheaply available means for apprehending global interconnections" (11) to the extent that some participate "in worlding, in conjuring a shared globality" (41). Yet, as this book contends, it would be a false start to make any global assumption about both world comics and comics in the world. Where then, to begin?

Within the field of global comics, one series stands out in its scope and worldliness. Debuting in 1929, *Les Aventures de Tintin,* or *The Adventures of Tintin,* is unparalleled as an artifact of world comics and provides a fecund source for inquiry and analysis. Created by Hergé (Georges Remi), *Tintin* comics have sold over 230 million copies worldwide and have been translated into more than 110 languages.[1] The scope of their influence is likewise demonstrated by the scores of secondary works published on both *Tintin* and Hergé,[2] as well as by the emergence of the transnational identity category of Tintinologist, or Tintin expert.[3] Taking *The Adventures of Tintin* as an urtext of world comics, this chapter analyzes what the series reveals about the lines connecting and delineating local and global readerships, how these lines are technically effected and reproduced, and how the global designs of colonialism and modernism determine how comics travel the world.

Tintin is patently synonymous with travel: a series about the adventures of a peripatetic hero, it has itself traversed the globe as printed material and ideological content. The transnational flows of *Tintin* books in the economy of world comics so parallel the indefatigable protagonist's own fictional international journeys that one may interpret the observation by Tintinologist Philippe Goddin that "Tintin travelled every corner of the globe" to refer equally to both fictional character and textual corpus (*Reporters* 87). However, the global influence of *Tintin* extends beyond its representational capaciousness and marketplace saturation. The manners of making *Tintin*—the formal and technical components of the comics' production and reproduction—established a number of conventions for Franco-Belgian bande dessinée as well as for transnational graphic narrative. Of creator Hergé's *ligne claire* (clear-line) style, comics scholar Paul Gravett attests that "no other aesthetic model has exerted such a significant and ongoing influence on comics, in Europe and beyond." Ligne claire describes a style that "gives equal weight and consid-

---

1. As of 2020. This information comes from https://www.tintin.com, the official site of the copyright holder, Moulinsart.

2. When *Tintin: Bibliographie d'un mythe,* a book-length annotated bibliography of secondary texts on *Tintin,* was published in 2014, the authors noted more than 500 such texts (Roche and Cerbelaud).

3. Although *Tintinologist* is standard, Pierre Fresnault-Deruelle instead refers to himself and like-minded scholars as "Hergéographers" ("Moulinsart Crypt" 122).

eration to every line on the page" (Pleban). Yet, as I explore in this chapter, these clear lines do more than distinguish background from foreground within panels; they are instead a medium for ideological expression. Luc Sante describes ligne claire as enclosing every "particule of the visible, no matter how fluid and shifting, in a thin, black, unhesitating line":

> The style makes the world wonderfully accessible, in effect serving as an analogue to its hero's mission: Just as Tintin, a mere boy, can travel the world and navigate its dark passages and defeat its oppressors without himself succumbing to corruption, so you, too, whether you are seven or seventy-seven . . . can confront the overwhelming variousness of the perceptual universe and realize its underlying simplicity without sacrificing your sense of wonder. ("Clear Line" 30)

Theorist Bruno Lecigne argues that ligne claire trains its reader to understand the world as a legible text[4] while concealing the mechanism that generates this legibility. As an interpellative subtext, which conveys to the reader an authorized and authorizing reading of the world, ligne claire is thus exemplary of what Rebecca Wanzo calls "visual imperialism," or the "production and circulation of racist images that are tools in justifying colonialism and other state-based discrimination" (4). The visual, formal, and material cohesiveness of *Tintin's* world is, as this chapter will explore, belied by difference.

To frame difference as a problematic, this chapter convenes three divergent readers of *Tintin*. The use of these readers is inspired by Edward Said's traveling theory in its insistence on how ideas are shaped according to the differential calculus of power and context (*World* 226). Scott McCloud, the foundational theorist of US comics studies, serves as an ideal reader, or, to adapt Mary Louise Pratt's formulation, a "reading-man": a reader who, in his identification with and appraisal of *Tintin*, seeks to "secure [the] innocence" and "anti-conquest" neutrality of Hergé's project, while at the same time asserting its cultural prowess and knowledge power (7). As an American, McCloud geographically connotes the westward course of

---

4. "That which the maximum legibility gives for reading is not the real world, nor even an idea of the world, as in a direct connection, but on the contrary, the idea that the world *is legible*" (Lecigne 40, emphasis in original). Translations by the author unless otherwise noted.

empire, as well as the oft-desired and rarely attained US market for European comics in the age of neoliberal globalization. In his proselytizing of *Tintin* to the US, McCloud invests in *Tintin* as the epitome of the formal properties of comics. His formal reading overlooks the inherent politics of racialization or the technical histories of representation that inform ligne claire. McCloud thus normalizes ligne claire and its stereotypical processes as a lingua franca for comics creation and assumes a white subject, as represented by Tintin, as the universal subject.

In contradistinction, Bienvenu Mbutu Mondondo, a Congolese émigré to Belgium, provides a protest, a reading that rejects the authority and normalization of *Tintin* as visual imperialism. By bringing his case against *Tintin au Congo* to a court in Belgium,[5] Mondondo lobbed a postcolonial challenge to the authority of *Tintin*'s formal and aesthetic regime as well as its erasure of the Black subject. Mondondo's case provides a direct rebuke to McCloud's reading; he indicts the stereotypical rendering of Africans as a form of racism, identifying the depiction as a production of what Marie-Rose Maurin Abomo calls "La Nègrerie en Clichés" (154, 158). Furthermore, Mondondo proposed a new paratext to qualify the content of the book. By grounding his critique in European law as a way of reading for difference and investing his own legal body in the complaint, Mondondo rematerialized the mechanisms of *lisibilité* occluded by McCloud's attention to surface.

Finally, another US artist, Charles Burns, represents a postmodern engagement with *Tintin* that undoes the authority of Tintin's worldview while also amplifying the alienation of *Tintin*'s formal and material properties. In Burns's détournements, the stable, nationalistic identity of Tintin is itself revealed to be a white mask (one the reader can also potentially wear, a mask of paper). By deterritorializing the formal and material components of *Tintin,* and by pirating his own *Tintin*-esque series, the Nitnit trilogy, Burns nods to the ambivalence of colonial discourse always already threatening the authority and cohesiveness of *Tintin.* As Tom McCarthy notes, anxiety over "the culture of the copy" is "what Hergé's work was always about" (156–57), and Burns's own copies—and copies of copies—aesthetically, formally, and materially position *Tintin* as a transnational agent

---

5. For a complete chronology of Mondondo's case, see Pasamonik, *L'Affaire Tintin.*

of Western imperium while playfully undercutting the exclusivity, if not the significance, of the series' claim on global culture. Burns's copies, compared with Mondondo's legal challenges, also reveal the disjuncture between the postmodern and the postcolonial as modes for confronting the coloniality of power and the progress narrative of modernism. Considering Burns and Mondondo as contrapuntal readers to McCloud's reading-man, this chapter ultimately comes to rest in the perennially open question of Kwame Anthony Appiah, "Is the Post- in Postmodernism the Post- in Postcolonial?" As Appiah notes in that essay, postmodern culture, including readings such as Burns's, "is global—though that emphatically does not mean that it is the culture of every person in the world" (343).

The readings of McCloud, Mondondo, and Burns thus triangulate the ways in which *Tintin* functions as a global comic. The different subject positions drawn together through these divergent readings provides a framework for mapping how comics *world,* or how they open and delimit a space for subjectivity, for expression, for political life. *Tintin* not only uses comics forms to compel a reader's belief in the correspondence between the series' clear-lined fiction and their own lived reality; it further interpellates a reader to believe in recursive colonial stereotypes of race and culture. Arguing that this identificatory process cannot be separated from the technical substrates of comics, I seek to trace the genealogies of print culture that cohere in Tintin's colonial phantasmagoria. Following Wanzo's critique of visual imperialism and Nick Mirzoeff's concept of the "complex of visuality" (*Right* 5), I approach *Tintin* by unfolding the logic of stereotype. In this instance, stereotype does not refer exclusively to portrayals of different peoples within *Tintin*; it describes the exigence of iterability and visual authority vis-à-vis media technologies and print cultures.

A stereotype, in its basic, technical definition, is a system of movable type, remodeled for maximum reproduction. However, prior to its casting, each stereotype consists of so many possibilities of moving furniture, leading, and type, of which the stereotype represents but one permutation, itself subject to error, degradation, revision, and disuse. As McCloud's, Mondondo's, and Burns's divergent readings show us, the symbolic stereotype—as in the reproducible caricature—is contingent on mediality and context. McCloud demonstrates an acceptance and belief in the rationality of *Tintin* as stereotype, as a legibly reproducible worldview in which racial and ethnic others are clearly distinguished. Yet underlying this view of the world is a technical genealogy of material parts and social interpretations that come together in conjunction with imperialist political economies. Moving from McCloud's reading-man promotion of *Tintin* to Mondondo's civil complaint as an apotheosis of global discontent with *Tintin*'s worldview and then finally to Burns's reworking of *Tintin*'s stereotypology, the chapter shows how even this most worldly and legible series reveals the fissures and inequalities within world comics.

"Lines to See" and "Lines to Be," or Ligne Claire, Black Skin, and White Masks

McCloud provides his telling gloss on the "'clear-line' style of Hergé's *Tintin*" in his magnum opus *Understanding Comics: The Invisible Art.* In the last panel of page 42, McCloud describes ligne claire as consisting of "very iconic characters" and "unusually realistic backgrounds." Continuing on to page 43, two panels present McCloud's interpretation of the style, showing a white character against a detailed background in the first, and the same character—now whited out—against a background—now blacked out—in the second (see figure 1.1). The text accompanying the first, richly detailed panel explains that the clear line allows readers "to *mask* themselves in a character and safely enter a sensually stimulating world." Meanwhile, the second panel, with its white figure against a black background, provides what one assumes, through iconic parataxis, to be an appositive of sorts: "One set of lines to *see.* Another set of lines to *be*" (43, emphasis in original). Unmentioned in this visual calculus is that the transformation of the detailed background and iconic character in the first panel into a white shape on a black background in the second panel reduces all lines to one line—the line separating the character from the background, or the line separating white from black. The convergence of the lines into a single black/white division correlates to the ambiguity of the parallel textual construction, with its mixture of transitive and copulative verbs. Perhaps one set of lines is see*n*; perhaps it is the means of see*ing.* Regardless, the *being* is clear, and clearly white.

Here, McCloud's reading artfully, if uncritically, reduces *Tintin* to binaries: a white subject against a black background. This two-panel example furnishes a lucid illustration of the distinction between read-

THIS COMBINATION ALLOWS READERS TO **MASK** THEMSELVES IN A CHARACTER AND SAFELY ENTER A SENSUALLY STIMULATING WORLD.

ONE SET OF LINES TO **SEE.** ANOTHER SET OF LINES TO **BE.**

FIGURE 1.1. Scott McCloud, *Understanding Comics,* page 43

ing difference and reading for difference. Although a preposition may not seem so significant, it distinguishes a practice of consumption—reading difference—from one of critical inquiry—reading for difference. As McCloud promotes it, *Tintin*'s complex of legibility is, at face value, a mode for training a reader to consume difference as naturalized binaries of seeing and being, subject and background, and black and white. By internalizing these binaries, as mediated by ligne claire, the reader in McCloud's formulation is hailed as a reading-man, able to see the world, and to be in the world, through an innocent process of self-identification with white and black lines. Thus, although McCloud does not explicitly address Tintin as a white European colonial hero, his explanation of ligne claire extends beyond the pages of *Tintin* to encompass and embrace a worldview of visual imperialism.

Against McCloud's uncritical practice of using Tintin to read difference as a means for knowledge power and self-identification, I posit the practice of reading *for* difference. An act of reframing and anticolonial resistance, reading *for* difference is a way of thinking about the global not simply as it is imagined by texts such as *Tintin* but also from the world of its imagining. As such, it is a materialist critique that investigates the perspective from which *Tintin*'s view of the world arises, bringing forth that which has been the vanishing point—the white mask made of paper—through which the world is seen, but which is not itself seen in its materiality or mechanics.

When reading *for* difference, I ask how *Tintin*'s legibility is constructed through a heterogeneous media framework, replete with revisions, edits, and omissions. I also seek out the points of disjuncture and ambiguity at work in *Tintin*'s visual logic. This work would be unrealizable without the rigorous scholarship already undertaken by so many theorists in their contrapuntal readings of *Tintin*'s colonial legacy and influence. Numerous scholars[6] provide critical readings of *Tintin* that reveal what the clear lines suppress, and that explicate "when the lines are not so clear," as a recent volume on *Tintin*'s creator Hergé stipulates.[7]

Reading for difference elucidates *Tintin* as what Mirzoeff calls a "complex of visuality," or an "imbrication of mentality and organization . . . forming a life-world that can be both visualized and inhabited" (*Right* 5). As such, *Tintin* functions as a "visualized deployment of bodies and a training of minds, organized so as to sustain both physical segregation between rulers and ruled, and mental compliance with those arrangements" (5). This is to say that the potential for seeing and being that McCloud identifies in *Tintin* is already enmeshed in a "set of social organizations and processes" and correlated to a "psychic economy" that cannot simply be sublimated into what McCloud calls "audience involvement," "viewer-identification," and "world popular culture" (Mirzoeff, *Right* 5; McCloud 42). *Tintin* precisely enacts what Mirzoeff identifies as an "imperialist complex . . . of visuality and countervisuality" in that *Tintin* develops a graphic language that correlates to "the shaping of modernity from the point of view of the imperial powers" (*Right* 196). The "imperialist visuality" that Mirzoeff defines as a "means of ordering biopower" according to "the hierarchy of the 'civilized' and the 'primitive'" (196) produces the visual imperialism described by Wanzo. Imperialist visuality cum visual imperialism are not bound by a particular imperial power or geographical delimitation. Rather, the "production and circulation of racist images that are tools in justifying colonialism and other state-based discrimination" (Wanzo 4) attain currency precisely through their reproducibility in contexts outside the specific imperial structures they depict. Hence, as Philippe Delisle stipulates of *Tintin* and the entire Franco-Belgian school of comics production, the "vision of dominated peoples that it cultivates" extends beyond

---

6. See, e.g., Delisle, *Bande dessinée*; McKinney, *Colonial Heritage*; Miller, "*Les héritiers*"; Dony, "Writing and Drawing Back"; Frey, "Contagious Colonial Diseases."

7. Sanders.

the specific colonies of French and Belgian occupation or control: "Stereotypes about Africans, Asians, and Oceanians can be found in bandes dessinées that in no way depict colonies" (*Bande dessinée* 51).[8] McKinney similarly reads the celebrated duo of *Le secret de la Licorne* (1943) and *Le trésor de Rackham le rouge* (1944)[9] as texts that do not explicitly show colonized peoples but that champion colonial inheritance and contribute to "the imperialist, eurocentric mapping of the world" (*Colonial Heritage* 7). In this context, McCloud's reading of *Tintin*'s formal design as an invitation for self-identification is a call for assimilation not merely to a historically colonial but to an actively colonizing Eurocentric worldview that travels to readers and delivers "iconic characters" and "realistic backgrounds" as stable referents for the world.

Writing in the US in the early 1990s, McCloud demonstrates how the "being" afforded by ligne claire enables the visual world of *Tintin* to transcend its moment of composition. Writing in the UK in the early 2000s, novelist and Tintinologist Tom McCarthy claims that "everybody wants to be Tintin: generation after generation," indicating that the white mask offered by Tintin and claimed by McCloud seems a universal inheritance (106). These white male authors both ascribe to Tintin an identificatory and even ontological potential that appears all-inclusive and transcendent of history, albeit imaginary on the part of the reader. Such thinking precedes McCarthy and McCloud: in 1984 author Jean-Marie Apostolidès argued in *The Metamorphoses of Tintin* that it is precisely because of the "barely flesh and blood" character of Tintin that "everyone can readily identify with his 'full-moon' face and project onto it all their desires" (10). However, Apostolidès qualifies the capaciousness of Tintin, saying that he invites reader identification "because he himself embodies a certain ideal: he incarnates Western Christian values at a precise moment in history" (10). Apostolidès's analysis is a rejoinder to any ahistorically identitarian reading of *Tintin* in that Apostolidès discerns Tintin's stereotypical milieu as a mode for establishing the worldview of the colonial Belgian state, and/or the "technologically advanced West" (33). In this light, a reader's act of "mask[ing] themselves in [Tintin]" is an act of identifying with the white Belgian subject, who

---

8. As an example, Delisle cites the first adventure, *Tintin au pays des Soviets*, which features caricatures of Chinese people.

9. *The Secret of the Unicorn* (1959) and *Red Rackham's Treasure* (1959) were the basis for Stephen Spielberg's film adaptation *The Adventures of Tintin* (2011).

is colonialist, or more generally, with the white European, who is an enlightened liberal subject.

Juxtaposing McCloud's identificatory reading of *Tintin* with Apostolidès's historical critique of the character shows *Tintin* operating at the level of Barthesian myth.[10] In "the eyes of the myth-consumer" such as McCloud, the ideology structuring the visual economy that allows for the ready separation, identification, and consumption of others is understood "not as a motive, but as a reason" (Barthes 129). A reading-man of *Tintin* sees its graphiation not as a system of (hierarchical) values but as an inductive representation (Barthes 131). In this regard, McCloud reads *Tintin* as a "global sign," or, as Barthes conceptualizes it, "the first term of the greater system which it builds and of which it is only a part" (113), with the greater system being an imperialist complex of visuality that structures comics readers' "viewer-identification" in terms of colonial semiotics (McCloud 42). In testament to this complex, Hergé biographer Pierre Assouline remarks that "the adventures of Tintin . . . reflect not only a world, its history and geography, but a whole society with its codes and rituals; that they come to constitute an international language is their great accomplishment" (xi). Tintinologist Philippe Goddin asserts, "Tintin is a language in himself" (*Reporters* 217), and others have espoused the coherence and mythic quality of the oeuvre: it is "everlasting," "timeless," "global," "immortal" (Serres). Correlate to the idea of *Tintin* as global sign and system, McCloud's reading also reveals Tintin to be what Walter Mignolo calls a "global design," in that *Tintin*'s complex of visuality references "European local knowledge and histories" in the forms of Franco-Belgian literary—graphic—techniques that compose a "classificatory apparatus" (*Local Histories* 17). As such, *Tintin* enacts the "coloniality of power" by inscribing the "colonial difference"—or the "conversion of differences into values"—and "projecting [such Franco-Belgian colonial values] onto universal history" (17, 160, ix). As a global sign, or a global design, *Tintin* exemplifies the process by which the imperialist complex of visuality overdetermines the world of world comics.

However global or transcendent, the myth of *Tintin* can be read contrapuntally by attending to its local conditions of possibility. In the identitarian reading proposed by McCloud, the legibility of *Tintin* is predicated on ligne claire's binary between "iconic char-

---

10. See also Baetens and Frey, "Modernizing Tintin."

acters" and "realistic backgrounds," whereby a reader may "be" a character and, in so doing, "see" the "world." A closer look at the discursive and material conditions of *Tintin*'s production and reproduction, however, makes it possible to "dereif[y] and complicat[e]" the binaries of character and background—and of seeing and being— by revealing another dichotomy, namely what Shu-Mei Shih terms "the binary division between the West and the non-West" (22). The "mask" of legibility that *Tintin* provides is an ideologically driven, efficient framework for reproduction that, while first indicative of the colonial Belgian state, has come to endow global comics with techniques of recognition that far exceed "character" and "background." As Shih asserts of global literature, these techniques are responsible for producing "'the West' as the agent of recognition and 'the rest' as the object of recognition, in representation" (17). I emphasize four techniques of *Tintin* comics—the album format, the abandonment of the typeset *récitatif,* the *ligne claire* style, and habitual revision—as components of *Tintin*'s complex of visuality, determining how—and for whom—the "safe" characterization and "sensually stimulating world" of *Tintin* were constructed.

The Album

Global comics, however mythic, are forged with local materials. *The Adventures of Tintin* began in a weekly supplement of the Belgian newspaper *Le Vingtième Siècle* in 1929.[11] The appearance of Franco-Belgian comics or bandes dessinées[12] in newspapers was standard at the time. Less standard, although not unheard of, was the collection of many strips (*bandes*) into a book or *album* format. Usually hardcover and approximately A4 in size, the album may now seem synonymous with Franco-Belgian comic book production, but in 1929 it was still relatively rare. Publication formats change over time, but the album remains the standard for a single-story French-language comic book.[13]

---

11. The paper's director, Father Norbert Wallez, wanted "to give a new life to the journal" and "had the idea to launch a weekly illustrated supplement for children: a page of the journal folded into quarters" (Hergé and Sadoul 15).

12. Laurence Grove points out that this term does not become standardized until long after the appearance of many of the most influential francophone "BDs" (15–16).

13. See Lefèvre, "Importance" 99–101; Beaty 44–69.

The French series *Bécassine* is generally considered the first bande dessinée published in album format beginning in 1913 (Dine 195), yet it was *Tintin* that definitively established its use. Belgian comics scholar Catherine Labio goes so far as to describe the album as "initially an offshoot of Hergé's codification of *Les aventures de Tintin*" (84). *Tintin* albums were published from the outset of the series, beginning with *Tintin in the Land of the Soviets* (1930). These durable, collected formats immediately appended the newspaper printings of the narrative arc. As Matthew Screech notes, the "high quality hardback albums[ ] transformed infantile ephemera into lasting, aesthetic objects" ("Introduction" vi). Delisle traces the formula of the album to *Tintin* while describing this material development as an "inescapable vector at the heart of Franco-Belgian production" (*Bande dessinée* 8–9). According to some, *Tintin*'s cross-market mobility, its success in album format, "was its most significant contribution to the History of Comics" (Lofficier and Lofficier 15). The doubled printing formats meant that *Tintin* was doubly marketable, simultaneously available in the newsstand and the store. Compared with the newspaper, the album engenders longevity (it lasts longer than a newspaper), commercial valuation (it costs more than a newspaper), and the autonomy of media technology (the comics no longer share space with entirely textual stories).

Between the newspaper and the album, two media flows are yoked in order to facilitate and authorize *Tintin*'s reproduction. This dual format allows for a bivalent worlding: Tintin could centripetally present the world to the Belgian state through the newspaper and centrifugally travel the whole of francophone (and, later, even more languages) Europe through the album. In *Imagined Communities*, Benedict Anderson insists on the importance of the newspaper for a specific type of world-building: "the very conception of the newspaper implies the refraction of even 'world events' into a specific imagined world of vernacular readers" (63). Just as "Hergé authenticated Tintin by making him a reporter for *Le Petit Vingtième*, the newspaper in which the strip itself appeared" (Screech, *Masters* 18), the worldliness of the newspaper strip gave it an authority over the world of its dissemination:

> The character, Tintin, was a journalist, a special envoy sent to the furthest corner of the world, a correspondent charged with reporting his impressions of his journeys to those at home. He was an

observer, authorized to relay the picture he had of the country in which he found himself. (Goddin, *Reporters* 29)

While Goddin describes a character that seems innocuous enough in his fictionality, Delisle grounds Tintin's mission in terms of his colonial location. Tintin as fictional character and *Tintin* as print media emphasize the newspaper's import for nation-building and imperialism. As Delisle states, "despite the development of nationalisms," the period 1930–60 corresponded both to "the golden age of Franco-Belgian bande dessinées" and European "colonial domination especially in Africa" (*Bande dessinée* 8). In its verbal visualization of "the furthest corner of the world," *Tintin* could report for an intended audience of Belgians while being capacious enough to support a far broader audience.

As an image-text designed for reproducibility in multiple platforms, *Tintin*'s local and global circulations exemplify the tension that Charles Hatfield refers to as "text as experience vs. text as object" (58). The dual newspaper (later magazine) and album format is essential to *Tintin*'s establishment of its relevance *in time* and *in space*. At the level of story, *Tintin* was the first bande dessinée to proleptically construct album-worthy narrative arcs. *Tintin* stories followed a journey out into the world and traced its return, marking the borders of the story according to the time of the voyage. *Tintin* was therefore instrumental in creating the standard of single-story albums, using the colonial patterns of travel literature[14] as the basis for their punctuation. At the level of publication format, *Tintin* harnessed the co-productive print technologies of newspapers and albums to give unparalleled authority to its contents. These stories of Tintin's encounters with others in the world were both "timely"—arriving with current world news in *Le Vingtième Siècle*—and "timeless"—collected as single-story albums.

From a spatial perspective, the young Belgian reporter who travels to foreign locations in order to report back to his audience of Catholic readers was—little by little—delocalized or relocalized while

---

14. Michel de Certeau delineates the travel account into three stages: (1) the outbound journey, "the search for the strange . . . illustrated by a series of surprises and intervals (monsters, storms, lapses of time, etc.) which at the same time substantiate the alterity of the savage, and empower the text to speak from elsewhere and command belief"; (2) "a depiction of savage society"; and (3) "the return voyage" (*Heterologies* 69–70).

Hergé and his editor, Father Norbert Wallez, sought a larger audience for the comics. When the strips were syndicated by other European newspapers and magazines, localizing textual elements were substituted: "Liège" became "Paris" in the French *Coeurs Vaillants* version of *Soviets* (Goddin, *Art Vol. 1* 66–67), and in the Portuguese syndication of *Tintin au Congo,* in *O Papagaio,* "Congo" became "Angola" (Goddin, *Art Vol. 2* 50). Thus, in its ephemeral, newspaper and magazine circulation, *Tintin* could be reworked for a local readership, and, as McCloud asserts, readers all over Europe could see themselves (and "their" places) in the series. Meanwhile, albums were edited over time: Delisle tracks how colonial sites like "the Belgian Congo" became "less and less Belgian" as the albums were revised over the decades (*Bande dessinée* 14). Most albums were eventually reworked to add color and standardize length. However, *Tintin au Congo* was edited in its 1942 black-and-white reprinting so that references to *Le Petit Vingtième* and to Antwerp could be removed (21). Then, in 1946, the colorized album, despite retaining the titular reference to *Congo,* was stripped of all other references to the Belgian colony, favoring an "image of a rather vague colonial Africa" (23) ready to be sold to a range of imperial readers.

Examining the material instrumentality of comics is part of the project of demystifying *Tintin*'s relationship to Belgium's imperial world in space and time. For example, in some of the early panels of *Congo,* Tintin and Snowy visit the department store Bon Marché in order to equip themselves for their colonial travel. McKinney makes the point that comics such as this were instrumental in bridging the distance between Europe and its colonies, "in part by circulating in both spaces" but also because they fostered colonial familiarity through their use of visual rhetoric (McKinney, *Colonial Heritage* 16).[15] In its visual narrative, *Tintin* sells the empire at the same time that it establishes its own reproductive existence within the empire's economic and material flows.

---

15. Assouline comments: "The newspaper *L'Essort colonial et maritime* praised Tintin for its fantasy by reminding its readers that true propaganda begins in the schools: 'You will laugh till tears come to your eyes because the Congo presented by Herge will make you forget about the other one, the one you saw'" (29). This reference to "the one you saw" is likely actually a reference to Albert Londres's *Terre d'ébène,* written about the *French* Congo, indicating the substitutability for European readers between colonial locations.

The album made a discrete, consumer object of Tintin's worldly adventures. It simultaneously asserted the divisibility of the world into bordered cultural zones—as noted by each titular venture (*Land of the Soviets, Congo, America, Tibet,* etc.)—and the divisibility of the series into authoritative objects. Harold Innis argues in his seminal text *Empire and Communication* for a correlation between the particularities of media and the methods that are used in the imperial management of vast expanses of space and time (138). Although commercial objects, *Tintin* comics have come to function as imperial media in their command of space and time. Through the use of different materials, methods, and markets of reproduction, the album and newspaper created widespread and durable economies for *Tintin*'s encounters. While first widely disseminated as ephemeral newspaper or magazine strips, *Tintin* achieved longevity as albums, the form in which it is still read today. By printing albums, publishers *Le Vingtième Siècle* and, later, Casterman asserted the monetary and cultural value of *Tintin*—it would not simply become yesterday's papers—as well as the conditions of possibility for legally authorized versions and uses of Hergé's creation. *Tintin*'s simultaneous claims to currency and timelessness are integral for the authority of its worldview, yet inextricable from its techniques of reproduction.

Text and Image

Before the development of the album as a consumer object, another local innovation had transformed francophone comics. Preceding and following the publication of *Tintin,* convention dictated printing a caption beneath panels to explain what happens in the pictures (Grove 32). In francophone comics of the early twentieth century, these explanatory texts were generally typed, producing an aesthetic dissonance between registers of inscription and of reproduction. Although *Tintin*'s abandonment of this system may seem obvious to a contemporary reader, the move away from an image-text disjuncture was not inevitable. Theorizing the shift from the separate caption to the word balloon, Thierry Smolderen cautions against teleological assumptions regarding the development of the language of comics. As Smolderen asserts, the transparency with which contemporary readers consume comics does not entail the naturalness or simplicity of the language of comics: "what its transparency suggests is that we are able to read it fluently" (137).

Both Smolderen and Benoît Peeters credit Swiss artist Rodolphe Töpffer with conceptualizing the mixed image/text language of comics, explicitly in his introduction to *Monsieur Jabot* (1837), wherein Töpffer explains the inextricability of image and text in his narrative for the sake of cohesion and legibility (Peeters, *Lire* 103–11; Smolderen 34–51). However, as Peeters claims, Töpffer's lesson would be forgotten because of advances in printing and a shift toward typescript text beneath images in graphic narratives of the late nineteenth and early twentieth centuries. This seemingly small change in where and how the text accompanies the image created a fragmentary relationship between the components of the narrative, challenging the fluency of reading. For Peeters, the use of typed script meant that francophone bandes dessinées leading up to and past 1900—*Mossieu Réac* (1848), *Bécassine* (1905), *Pieds Nickelés* (1908), and so forth—favored a predominantly *verbal* form, while comics in the US, following Richard F. Outcault's use of speech balloons in "The Yellow Kid and His New Phonograph" (1896), favored a predominantly *visual* form.[16]

Hergé became an innovator in francophone graphic narrative as a result of his implementation of intrapanel narration, in the form of word balloons and small notes (*bulles* and *ballons*), instead of extrapanel narration (typed *récitatifs* and *legendes*). Even in his *Totor* (1926–27) series, which preceded *Tintin* by three years, a typed legend beneath each panel bears the bulk of the narrative, while humor is generated from the sometimes dissonant tonal registers of image and text. Hergé qualifies *Totor* and its ilk as "illustrated text" or "drawings with captions" (Hergé and Sadoul 13), noting that he sometimes risked inserting exclamation points or other types of visual dialogue within the panels of *Totor* but relied on the print legend for the narration. Peeters characterizes the development of bande dessinée as a "succession of amnesias" (*Lire* 116) from which Hergé awoke to remember Töpffer's lesson as it was already being transatlantically practiced by American artists Rudolph Dirks, George McManus, and Winsor McCay. Smolderen, for his part, conceptualizes the separate American development of dialogue balloons as an unprecedented creation of an audiovisual stage on paper, informed by phonographic media (136–47). Beginning with "The Yellow Kid and His New Phonograph," word balloons in modern comic strips came to eschew an indexical relationship to an "authored text"; instead, they acted to

---

16. Peeters posits that the rise of visually narrative comics first in the US and then in Belgium might be explained by the lack of a consecrated literary tradition in these countries, as opposed to France or the UK (*Lire* 118).

"entangle the sound image produced by the character in the kinds of spatial relationships and mechanical forces that define visible objects and bodies" (147).[17] Hergé subsequently developed *Tintin* by shifting away from the use of the more literary extrapanel *récitatif* and *légende* toward the concrete visuality of intrapanel narration. Peeters describes the formal development in semiotic terms:

> Influenced by American comics, the author has moved on from the illustrative concept seen with [his earlier strip] *Totor* to that of a new language where text and picture complement each other without repeating themselves. (*Hergé* 26)

Tintin was not the first modern Franco-Belgian bande dessinée to use word balloons or *phylactères*.[18] However, by excising the typed text below the images and using balloons to express discourse, *Tintin* was decisive in developing the coherence and autonomy of bande dessinée form. Rather than articulating between divergent manual and machinic print systems, spatially separated into discrete areas of the page, *Tintin* unified the reading areas within one spatial unit and technical system of reproduction. In the shared space of all images and texts, neither asserted definitive authority over the representational aspects of the story, and both were necessary in order to fully understand the narrative. Coincidentally, typesetting, as used in the printing of récitatifs and legendes, gave way to handwriting, creating a closed system of *graphisme*. The similitude of lines in text and image composed a complex of visuality that signified the world in a single semiotic system of line.

The novelty of this unilinear system is evident at the outset of the first *Tintin* adventure. The first panel is filled with handwritten text, explaining to the reader that *Le Petit Vingtième*, in order to stay abreast of foreign affairs, is sending one of its top reporters to Soviet Russia. The primary text is accompanied by a note: "N.B. The edi-

---

17. The inspiration of contemporary American comics on Hergé is well documented: Hergé procured comics by US artists that were translated into Spanish, and published in Mexican newspapers, from his colleague Léon Degrelle, who was covering the Cristero War for *Le Vingtième Siècle* at the same time that Hergé was working as a photographic reporter and cartoonist for the newspaper (Assouline 17; Hergé and Sadoul, 15; Cf. Peeters, *Hergé* 37).

18. That distinction is generally given to Alain Saint-Ogan's *Zig et Puce* (Delisle, *Bande dessinée* 13).

tor of '*Le Petit Vingtième*' guarantees that all these photographs are strictly authentic, taken by Tintin himself, aided by his faithful dog Snowy!" (Hergé, *Soviets* 4). Despite its joking tone, McCarthy interprets this panel as the sign that *Tintin* would depart from light-hearted comics fare by laying claim "to social and political insight." As he explains, the expository text in the panel signals how the cartoon format needed to "invoke notions of documentary rigour" while "making no attempt to disguise" the ultimate fiction of the story (4).[19] Yet, the first adventure of *Tintin* is important not just for *what* its panels say but for *how* they say it, in the sense that they undo the disjuncture between machine-produced word and hand-produced image, literally drawing all the compositional elements into synthesis.[20]

The style and thickness of lines in *Soviets* are identical not only for drawn images and written text but also for the outlining of panel borders, or frames. By delimiting what is framed—and how—panel borders profess the interiority of a composition. Unifying image, text, and frame in a single form of line, *Tintin* consolidated a meaning system specific to comics, whereby narrative was streamlined to move from panel to panel with no outside semiosis, less like an illustrated story, and more like film, which Hergé sought to remediate (Peeters, *Hergé* 23, 38). Where the typeset *légende* had produced a schizoid vacillation between reading the text beneath the caption and looking up at the images, *Tintin* effected a single-panel unit that compelled bande dessinée readers to read verbally and visually within the same frame. Furthermore, while the légende structure constrained the mobility of panels, by tethering each image to its correlate text, the concrete image-text panel is easily moved, recropped, or even excised. This plasticity facilitated the reproduction of *Tintin* in album form, and the re-editing and revision of albums for new editions.

19. Alternately, Peeters reads this as an "in-joke" referencing the duties of "reporter-photographer that Abbot Wallez had initially assigned to the young Hergé . . . duties that he never actually managed to fill" (*Hergé* 35).

20. Upon syndicating *Tintin* strips in 1930, the French magazine *Coeurs Vaillants* added a conventionally typeset legend beneath the strips, fearing that readers would not be able to understand Tintin's new "language." However, "the addition of these legends to pages whose layout was not designed to include them made reading the pages almost impossible. . . . the two characteristics were fundamentally incompatible" (Peeters, *Hergé* 38). See also the description in Hergé and Sadoul: "That same year, *Coeurs vaillants* undertakes the publication of *Tintin au pays des Soviets,* but begins to print an accompanying explanatory text with each image. Hergé protests" (15).

Tintin in the Land of the Soviets inaugurated Hergé's development of an increasingly autonomous comics form that encapsulated
the world within a universalizing verbal-visual line. As an imperialist complex of visuality, *Soviets* asserted Belgian global mobility and
political superiority through a hand-drawn "imbrication of mentality and organization" that neither needed nor permitted an outside,
despite its debt to flows of global comics from the US and Mexico
(Mirzoeff, *Right* 5). However, shifting focus to the medial conditions
of newspaper comics production reveals a technological exteriority
closer to home, in the sense that *Tintin*'s "lines to *see*" and "lines to
be" universalized the world not merely as standardized image-text
but as mechanically reproducible image-text (McCloud 43). Or, to put
it another way, the "strictly authentic," hand-drawn "photographs"
announced at the beginning of *Soviets* actually *are* photos (4).

Ligne Claire

A complicated history—Belgian imperial annexation and colonial
expropriation of the Congo, the devastation of World War I, Hergé's
"Catholic and traditionalist" schooling and youthful "adventure[s]"
in scouting, "conflicts everywhere" in Belgium "between French and
Flemish speakers . . . socialists [and] Catholics," the creep of postwar
fascism and anticommunism (Peeters, *Hergé* 5–27; Assouline 3–14)—
informs the imagination of *Tintin*'s early narrative, but it is the technology of photogravure printing that conditions the image of *Tintin*'s
clear line. According to Didier Pasamonik, the universal verbal-visual
line innovated by Hergé for *Soviets* not only concretized the signifying
codes of the page; it was practicable for the print conditions of photogravure (qtd. in Peeters, *Hergé* 30), which was developed at separate
junctures in the nineteenth century by William Fox Talbot, Charles
Nègre, and Karel Klíč and became the state of the art for commercial printing in the early twentieth century (Stulik and Kaplan). Both
Pasamonik and Peeters attest to the exigency of photogravure for the
development of Hergé's ligne claire style (qtd. in Peeters, *Hergé* 30).
Prior to creating *Tintin,* Hergé had worked as a photo engraver at
Le Vingtième Siècle, and he understood the mechanics of photogravure, which uses a technology similar to photography, whereby acid
and gelatin are used to transfer an image to a plate (Smolderen 119).
Planned for photogravure, *Tintin* was drawn for maximal reproduc-

tive efficacy. Clear lines, no shading, and the banishment of all ambiguity would come to dominate Hergé's ligne claire style.

Thus the reference to photography that launches *Tintin* in the first panel of *Soviets* refers not only to the diegetic content of the panels but also—whether intentionally or not—to the printed page of *Tintin,* which is not, in itself, a drawing, but a kind of photograph of one. *Tintin*'s seemingly "[un]remarkable debut" panels establish the comic's capacity for worlding not only through hybrid use of text and image but also through metareference to its reproducibility (Peeters, *Hergé* 35). With text and image unified for photogravure, neither maintains what might be its traditional authority in other media contexts; instead, they share the same plane of presentation. As Peeters declares:

> Georges Remi's experience with photo-engraving had proven decisive, stamping on his mind the simple and obvious fact that a press drawing is made to be reproduced; therefore it must be readable, effective, and clear from the start. (*Hergé* 30)

Although Hergé's style would become established as what is now known as ligne claire in subsequent stories, programming *Tintin*'s earliest adventures for their means of reproduction influenced the rest of his career. Assouline contextualizes the clear-line style thus:

> Hergé's aversion to shading and toning down the colors stemmed from the days when such techniques were prohibited by the poor-quality paper. It coincided with his tendency to focus on only the essentials, with just one goal: maximum comprehension. Hergé played the card of absolute clarity to the point of transparency. (155)

As Peeters notes, the terms that Töpffer had used to validate the uniform and inextricable simplification of text and image in his early picture stories would be nearly identical to those that Hergé would use almost a century later to qualify ligne claire (*Lire* 106). The "Tintin style," as Hergé, called it, dictated that graphic elements must "be neither too simplified nor too detailed, that each of them stays in its place and is based on the whole" (Hergé and Sadoul 45). Beyond facilitating protogravure, the outcome of *Tintin*'s calculated stylistic simplification—Hergé's "privileging" of "line drawing," as Peeters describes it—is its "gain in readability [lisibilité]" (*Lire* 106). Ligne claire catalyzes the worlding of *Tintin* by refocusing the constraints of its reproduction into a rhetorical strategy. The clarity of style that facilitates *Tintin*'s publication also advances its universality, its syndication in foreign markets, its exponential reproduction, and, ultimately, its global influence.

The semiotic effects of ligne claire have, in turn, been capaciously and globally analyzed. As mentioned above, in *Les Héritiers d'Hergé,* which examines ligne claire's influence on myriad comics, Lecigne argues that the clear-line style trains its reader-viewer to understand that the world is legible while concealing the mechanism that generates this legibility (40). Lecigne asserts that legibility does not function as realism. Rather, as is evident in Hergé's later works and in the revisions of earlier *Tintin* albums, lush ornamentation is added to the backgrounds in order to suppress a reader's recognition of its artifice. Moreover, Hatfield stipulates that *ligne claire* does not simply suppress potential illegibility in the world; it appears to denature the comics object as such, in that it "seems to deny the materiality of the comics page, relying on precise linework and flat colors to create pristine and detailed settings into which simply drawn characters are inserted" (61). Implicating these effects in the gestalt of *Tintin*'s thematization, Miller explains that the simplifying, universalizing rhetoric of ligne claire promotes the reader's identification with "the apparent mastery of Tintin." In her view, it is not only events in Hergé's storytelling but the graphic style of the comic that aligns the reader's sense of control with the protagonist, whose focalization is "emphasized through the harmony of the *ligne claire,* which seems to offer the 'single, primary, literal meaning' sought by the conscious mind, which blocks out the variable and multiple meanings generated by the unconscious" (*Reading* 206). In the light of such rhetorical and psychological appraisals of ligne claire's semiosis, the confidence that McCloud shows in the "mask" of *Tintin* is idealistic, if not willfully hallucinatory (43).

However, if the clear line hides its own artifice, as Lecigne asserts, or "blocks out" alternate meanings, as Miller argues, then the question remains what is behind or beyond ligne claire's mask? From a medial-technical standpoint, ligne claire is a method of ensuring the meaning of a message by managing the "fundamental relationship . . . between communication and noise" in the practice of photogravure, wherein Hergé inscribed verbal-visual stories as uniform lines in order to prevent errors and ambiguities inherent in the process of transferring an image from page, to photo, to plate, to publication (Siegert 21). Insofar as "communication is the exclusion of a third, the oscillation of a system between order and chaos," and technicity conditions rhetoric (Siegert 23), then ligne claire's totalizing style enacts an ideology of control, of mediating a world "neither too simplified nor too detailed" so as to mask complication and confusion (Hergé and Sadoul 45). As technicity conditions rhetoric, it also processes politics. In this regard, French semiologist and visual theorist Pierre Fresnault-Deruelle considers Hergé's style to be a global design, arraigning "*ligne claire* as a process of cataloging or labelling from which any hybridity, *métissage* or ambiguity is excluded" (*Hergé* 8). More pointedly, McKinney indicts clear-line as an imperialist complex of visuality, declaring that "ideology, historical context and form are inextricably intertwined in the ligne claire drawing school of Hergé . . . its clear-ness, its legibility, is to a considerable degree an imperialist, orientalizing, eurocentric manner of reading the world" (*Colonial Heritage* 10). While analyses such as these have inspired Apostolidès to declare that "there is no innocent reader [of *Tintin*] any longer" (qtd. in Mountfort 34), we may still question the worldliness of a reader who does not doubt the assimilation of the world within one untroubled line. Between simplicity and detail, ligne claire masks the noise of empire.

Revisionism

Translatio imperii: Empire carries across time and space, revising its complex of "visuality against countervisuality," rearticulating the "claim to authority" in its "configurations of . . . material systems" (Mirzoeff, *Right* 5–8). Having established above some of the relays between local histories and global designs that materialize *Tintin*'s complex of visuality, a question emerges: how can *Tintin* travel through space and time, such that despite debuting in a Catholic newspaper supplement for children in Belgium in the late 1920s, it commands global attention up to the present day, encouraging white Western anticonquest readings such as McCloud's and postcolonial countervisual critique such as Mondondo's, and be one corpus? The answer? *Tintin* is not one corpus. Or, if it is one corpus, it is not inviolable but instead plastic and rhizomatic, constantly under revision, reformatting, repackaging, and remediation. *Tintin*'s revisions correlate with its travels into other complexes of visuality, as when Hergé excised Black characters at the request of his first US publisher, Golden Press (Owens). Also, echoing its formal development, *Tintin*'s revisions respond to technical predicates, as when, in 2006, the hand-lettering of translations of the series was replaced by a digital text meant to imitate hand-lettering. While the former case reveals cracks in *Tintin*'s global design, whereby Hergé acquiesced to the authority of "US censors" in order to expand *Tintin*'s empire (Owens), the latter case indicates that *Tintin*'s ethnographic opportunism is matched—and potentially explained—by its industrial pragmatism. To justify the adoption of a standardized *Tintin* font for all "foreign" language versions, a Casterman representative cited the "evolution of technology," and reasoned that

> books used to be printed from offset films and for Comics and Graphic novels the texts were normally hand-made. Now the printers work from computer files and the lettering for comics is now performed on computer. (qtd. in jock123)

Despite enmity from Tintinologists—particularly fans of the English translations lettered by Neil Hyslop—this late shift in *Tintin*'s reproduction—which undoes Hergé's unilineal textuality and seems to flout his love of lettering—is itself only an evolution in the series' imperialist custom of reworking its visuality.

As *Tintin* became more capacious, the world it created and claimed through its album format, unified image-text layout, and ligne claire style underwent an iterative process of deletion and revision in order to remain coherent. McCarthy asserts:

> The books are both full of erasure and subject to it themselves: as Hergé transferred the stories from their original newspaper and then magazine versions to the album format in which we now read them, he reworked them, covering up material he considered out of date or below par. (30)

Albums created authoritative versions of the stories but also could be reworked any time a translation or a new printing was undertaken. Hergé and his many unacknowledged collaborators[21] reviewed

---

21. A number of insightful texts have sought to rescue the labors of Hergé's collaborators from obscurity (Lecigne; Assouline; Mouchart; Mouchart and Rivière; Bourdil and Tordeur). As Assouline states, Hergé would not give credit to the oth-

the albums, changing numerous aspects to bring the series into an ever-more synthetic unity of style and content (Soumois; Assouline 148–83). In addition to these copious, minute changes that Hergé and his uncredited colleagues undertook, the albums were all reset to a length of sixty-two pages as the agreed-upon "norm for Tintin books" (Farr 25). Color was added to early black-and-white albums, controversial or distasteful historical elements were excised, and the time-frame of the works was manipulated to establish a specific *Tintin* "world time." Consequently, after revisions, Tintin reads a book on German rocket engineering in World War II, despite the war's nonexistence in the *Tintin* oeuvre. More famously, Tintin's colonial geography lesson to Congolese students in *Tintin au Congo* shifts, in revision, from instruction on the great "fatherland" of Belgium to a simple arithmetic lesson.

Repeatedly changing *Tintin* albums drove the oeuvre's visual economy into constant modernization and global expansion. However, the earlier *Tintin* albums did not disappear, resulting in a bibliographic palimpsest of worlding. For example, *Tintin in the Land of Black Gold* was redrawn no fewer than four times, each version evincing further attempts to manage difference. The story began its serialization in *Le Petit Vingtième* in 1939, but work was interrupted by the Nazi invasion of Belgium. Originally set in Palestine during the British Mandate, *Black Gold* contained references to Zionism that were subsequently removed from panels set for syndication in *Coeurs Vaillants* in occupied Paris (Soumois 213–15). Hergé resumed work on the story in 1948, revised it in 1950, and again in 1971, removing over time all references to the British Mandate in Palestine. Haifa became Khemikal of Khemed, and British troops were redrawn wearing vaguely "Arab"-looking uniforms (Soumois 213–24). There is violence in these erasures, wherein colonialism is first hidden and then mystified. The history of Palestine is eradicated through simple commutations of toponym and costume. *Tintin*'s processual commodification and management of difference in the revising of *Black Gold* reveal the discrete entities and political borders of Palestine/Israel to be too unwieldy and politically charged after European colonizers have withdrawn.

Tintin's branching corpus itself became a problem of intellectual property management. For example, after *Tintin in the Land of*

---

ers who worked on his books, "in his view their work belonged to him because they were paid to follow his directions. He found it normal to take credit for their ideas" (202).

the Soviets was not reissued along with most of the early works, a number of pirated editions began circulating. Hergé was reportedly offended by the poor quality of the drawings, while Casterman was offended by the threat to their market share. In 1973 Casterman published a single volume collecting *Tintin*'s first three adventures (*Soviets, Congo, America*) in an attempt to "eliminate the market for counterfeit books" (Assouline 205). This omnibus did not stop the flow of pirate editions, which, as Peeters recounts it, left only one recourse, "to publish a true facsimile edition of the original *Tintin in the Land of the Soviets*" (Peeters, *World of Hergé* 27). Finally, an official reprint of *Soviets* was published in 1981. However, the true facsimile of *Soviets*, intended to disenfranchise "pirated editions of 'Soviets,' which had acquired a false authenticity" (Goddin, *Reporters* 208), also complicated the canon, as the album was not revised verbally or visually, marking its anachronism among the other multiply revised albums. However, with so many *authentic* changes over the decades, the anachronism of any *Tintin* album is only a revision away.

Ironically, the album format, image and text synthesis, and clear-line style that made *Tintin* so fit for travel, circulation, and distribution also made it ripe for piracy. The proprietary nature of each work is the subject of constant anxiety (and litigation) on the part of publisher Casterman and copyright holder Fondation Moulinsart. Even these designations were put under revision following a 2015 ruling in a Dutch court that Casterman, not Moulinsart, owned the rights to the series.[22] This anxious ownership shows a tenuous commercial border patrolling *Tintin*'s local and global transit, strained by Casterman's and Moulinsart's protectiveness of *Tintin*'s world, and its command of the world comics trade. If *Tintin*'s imperium is as fragile as it seems capacious, it would match Gayatri Spivak's analysis that imperial worlding "reinscri[bes] a cartography that must (re)present itself as impeccable" ("Rani" 263–64). Therefore, although the world of *Tintin* is under relentless surveillance—such that Bart Beaty has accused Moulinsart of policing "the Tintin copyrights even to the

---

22. The ruling occurred after Moulinsart sued a Dutch Tintin fan club for using original *Tintin* images to illustrate their newsletter (Cascone). Despite the ruling, in 2019 Moulinsart "asserted its leadership over Casterman" by publishing a new digital version of *Tintin au Congo* under its own imprint, *Éditions Moulinsart* (Detournay, "Pour le 90e anniversaire"), furthering long-standing speculation that Moulinsart was planning to sever financial ties with Casterman (Detournay, "Tintin quitterait Casterman?").

point of discouraging academic study of the Tintin books" (qtd. in Cascone)—litigiousness is an anticonquest—legal—method of indemnifying *Tintin* against peripheral challenges to its empire. Assured of safe travel on the map of *Tintin,* however, many readers have come to see, and to see themselves to be, the peccancy beyond the mask.

The World of *Tintin* and Its Discontents

A stereotype is valued for its reproducibility, which in turn enables its mobilization. As Delisle and many others establish, one of the legacies of *Tintin*—particularly in relation to its second volume, *Tintin in the Congo*—is the tradition ["lignée"] in "the Franco-Belgian school" of mobilizing "the colonial stereotypes" (*Bande dessinée* 8). As I will show, this tradition has not gone unchallenged. Mirzoeff declares, "Any engagement with visuality in the present or past requires establishing its counterhistory." Thus, it is not enough to champion the hybrid form of comics without taking seriously their use of caricature and stereotype, and the ways in which such techniques are "always already opposed and in struggle" as they work to naturalize difference (*Right* 6). In this regard, *Tintin* functions as a case study for showing how recognition becomes naturalized. As argued above, the ideologies of *Tintin* all too easily appear at the level of depoliticized signified if the series is read as representing difference without attention to how comics actually encode difference. To attend to this role is to consider visual imperialism in terms of its historicity and technicity.

Critics have taken issue with *Tintin*'s blatant colonialism, Eurocentrism, and racism, yet debates over the series, the character, or creator Hergé's specific stance vis-à-vis racism seem to lead only to a discursive impasse.[23] The "implicit and explicit imperialism of the albums" (Frey, "History" 301) has heretofore been examined mostly in the diegetic aspects of the *Tintin* series, with critical dispute occurring on an album-by-album level. Some *Tintin* scholars like Apos-

---

23. Tintin's *mission civilisatrice,* as Ann Miller and Jean-Marie Apostolidès note, changed over the forty-seven years of his oeuvre. While the specific stance Tintin adopted changed from album to album, the moral and cultural superiority of his position never waned. Alain Reys specifically calls Tintin the good conscience of the bourgeoisie, "colonialist when it is necessary, decolonialist when it befits" (qtd. in Miller, "*Les héritiers*" 307–9).

tolidès argue that it is as early as the fifth adventure in the series, *The Blue Lotus* (1936), that Tintin demonstrates opposition to (Japanese) colonialism and "really opens up to a non-Western world, [for] the first time [letting] himself listen to the Others rather than simply impos[ing] his own values on them" (Apostolidès, *Metamorphoses* 26). On the other hand, Paul Mountfort argues that the same album is "unable to shake off an Orientalist gaze" (34). Further, Mountfort claims that Hergé's "most damning" offense lies in *The Shooting Star* (1942) because of the inherently antisemitic caricature of the villain Blumenstein (later changed to Bohlwinkel), which he created for the collaborationist newspaper *Le Soir,* under Nazi occupation (42). On yet another hand, Frey has argued against scholars who see the post–World War II albums *The Seven Crystal Balls* (1948) and *Prisoners of the Sun* (1949) as increasingly mature ("Contagious" 178). Frey reads these two works together as an exercise in neofacism, where the fear of race-mixing is transferred from a no longer acceptable Semitic target to Incas. For Maxime Benoît-Jeannin, Hergé's racist paternalism is evident in the series' unchanging caricatures of Africans, which extend through albums from 1931's *Tintin au Congo* to 1958's *Coke en Stock* (78).

Maurin Abomo notes of *Tintin in the Congo* that its combination of text (in all its manifestations) and drawings, as well as its specific division and organization of the page, coalesced into an ideogrammatization. This ideogrammatizing system is a cultural technique that creates a machine for reading others: the colonial comic. In other words, the production of *Tintin au Congo* creates a system for the clear demarcation between those who are read—the objects of the colonial fantasy of *nègrerie*—and those who read—subjects interpellated by the complex of visuality. In reading the comic, a colonial subject and a reading subject are simultaneously and coterminously produced. Through the mastery of reading—facilitated by the marking and design—this subject becomes a superior reader, one whose superiority is inscribed in and by his difference from the objects of his reading, objects (i.e., colonized Africans) stigmatized by their own misreadings. Abomo points out how the "Congolese" of *Tintin* struggle with language, political organization, costumerie, and so forth. However, as argued above, the coloniality of *Tintin in the Congo* is not reducible to its content; it is a fulfillment of the complex of visuality by which the content is instrumentalized. By melding verbal and visual regimes and normalizing the disjuncture between fanciful images and the historical plenitude of toponyms and "petit nègre," *Tintin au Congo* produces a graphically novel colonial reading subject.[24]

Hergé is neither the first nor the last comics artist to use caricature or stereotype in narration. Derek Parker Royal argues that graphic narratives routinely valorize a specific ethnic group and mark "the Other" as such (Royal, "Introduction" 8). The relegation of detail or ambiguity in the service of plot is standard for the form. Iteration of characters and settings favors easy recognition; thus, the basic formal structures of comics are prone to normalization of stereotypes (Royal, "Introduction" 7). If the first panel depicting Tintin's encounter with the Congolese in *Congo* is shocking in its "visual stereotype of the ape-like African" (Rifas 230), then by the final page this caricature has become standardized by its reiteration. As Mountfort shows, in *Tintin* such normalization constitutes the "progressive dehumanization" of marked "Others," which "immerses the reader in a fully-fledged cultural myth" (Mountfort 35). Wanzo argues that racist caricature "has typically functioned as propaganda supporting *white* supremacy" (31, emphasis added). Even if the "frame the caricature inhabits sometimes suggests a challenge to bigotry" (31), Wanzo asserts that this framing requires a reading that thematizes the "white gaze" (218) as the intended recipient for these images. Visual imperialism is a process wherein "white people literally and figuratively create black subjects that are left out of the nation" (218), just as McCloud delineates blackness as outside the reader's figuration of being.

Many readers have critically framed *Tintin*'s visual imperialism in order to read Hergé's works for difference. Historian Nancy Rose Hunt investigates the colonial and postcolonial production and circulation of Congolese comics and comics in Congo as a means of interrogating *Tintin*'s iconicity and placing "the colonial-minstrelsy rubric of Tintin within a larger context" (97). Questioning both the oft-repeated claim that *Tintin in the Congo* was most popular among Congolese and Zairian readers and the "canard [that] *Tintin au Congo* had once been so detested that it was banned [in Congo]," Hunt discovers this discursive construct's relation to "the Hergé-Casterman enterprise to prove the acceptability of *Tintin au Congo* to postcolonial Congolese" (111, 93). Furthermore, Hunt discerns the complex

---

24. Frédéric Soumois describes the creation of a "'géographie' congolaise élémentaire" that aids the reader's understanding of how to read space thanks to its fantastical elements "exotiques" (33).

relationality of Congolese readers to *Tintin,* which enshrines "the colonized world" of a European imaginary that compels "native colonial Africans . . . [to identify] themselves with the hero [Tintin], not with the degraded savages" (96, 111). Hunt notes that the self-identification offered by *Tintin*'s "colonial screens of blackness" reifies "a colonial gaze," a sublimation of the "ever-lurking white look" that stereotypes the Black body (111–13). Thus, *Tintin* provides either the "possibility of identifying with the [white] hero" or—as Hunt quotes Kaja Silverman, referencing Franz Fanon—"'identify[ing] with an image that provides neither idealization nor pleasure'" (111).

In 2011 Nadim Damluji completed his project of traveling to "the places where Tintin traveled, where the comics are actively marketed, and where there is a budding or strong contemporary comics culture" ("Introduction"). A companion piece to Damluji's *Hooded Utilitarian* column, "Can the Subaltern Draw?," his Tintin-tracking project, chronicled at https://tintintravels.com, reflected his desire to "understand how artists have historically resisted Hergé's Orientalist depictions and how contemporary comics creators have managed to create vibrant political communities using the same medium." Damluji received a grant to travel to Belgium, France, Egypt, the United Arab Emirates, Taiwan, and China. In each location, Damluji chronicled the reception of *Tintin* as well as the comics scene in the area. One example of Damluji's remarkable findings is Egyptian magazine *Samir*'s "bootlegging" of Tintin comics twenty-three years before they were officially translated into Arabic. Damluji reveals how "illegal" translations of *Tintin* in *Samir* "put Hergé into dialogue with—instead of opposition to—his Arab counterparts" ("Samir Magazine"). Damluji catalogs how Hergé—drawing from a geographic and cultural distance—often used squiggly lines to represent Arabic and other scripts,[25] an analysis that aligns with other examinations of how the speech of non-European characters in *Tintin*—the Congolese, Indigenous North Americans, African pilgrims, and so forth—is rendered as pidgin or broken French.[26] Drawing heavily from Edward

---

25. See also Bentahar, who qualifies these as "squiggly lines that were supposed to be Arabic and not meant to be understood by readers in the original French" (43).

26. As Farr reports of the album *Coke en Stock / The Red Sea Sharks*: "It offered Hergé scope to prove that he was not racist . . . However, his well-intentioned portrayal of the trapped African pilgrims liberated by Tintin was to backfire." Farr recounts Hergé's stunned response: "Oh there, once again, I am a racist. Why? Because the blacks speak pidgin!" In his "amendment" of the offensive speech,

Said's critique of Orientalism, Damluji's travels led him to argue that *Tintin* produces normative visions of Asia and Africa predicated on a colonial imaginary of the inferiority and alterity of non-Western Europeans.

Hunt's and Damluji's projects reveal *Tintin*'s systematic and aesthetic dispossession of the civilization of non-European others to be a process of mystification carried out from the metropole. By visiting sites that Hergé did not see, yet made consumable, Hunt and Damluji offer alternate worldings that expose the fallacies behind *Tintin*'s oft-noted realism. Some readers have gone so far as to object to the continued commercial circulation of *Tintin.* The centenary of Hergé's birth, 2007, saw numerous such condemnations amid renewed attention to *The Adventures of Tintin.* While so-called Tintinophiles staged tributes and events celebrating Hergé's life and career, other global readers protested the colonial phantasmagoria of *Tintin in the Congo.* In the UK, human rights lawyer David Enright successfully petitioned for the English translation to be affixed with a warning label and removed from the children's sections of bookshops in Great Britain. In the US, Brooklyn Public Library patron Laurie Burke requested that the book be removed from circulation; it was subsequently placed in an appointment-only special collection.[27] Meanwhile, Congolese national Bienvenu Mbutu Mondondo, a student who had lived in Belgium for many years, brought a claim against the book—specifically against Moulinsart and Casterman—in Belgian court, stipulating that it violated Belgium's antiracism legislation.[28]

In the same year, three reading subjects used an encounter with *Tintin* to orient three different interventions into commercial, institutional, and juridical discourses. While, in their respective nations, Enright and Burke emerged as politically correct readers, Mondondo lost his case in court,[29] where his reading was adjudicated as a misreading. The Belgian court found against Mondondo and his co-plaintiffs, stipulating that Hergé's 1931 book was paternalistic but not

the characters are still not depicted as speaking the same French that Tintin does; instead, Hergé improves their grammar but "adopts the American practice of dropping letters" (152–53).

27. Her Request for Reconsideration of Library Material noted that "culturally we have progressed beyond" (qtd. in Cowan) the racist depictions of *Tintin in the Congo.*

28. Mondondo was joined in his suit by Le Conseil Représentatif des Associations Noires.

29. Delisle cites this schism as one that indicates longstanding division between the Anglo-American and francophone worlds ("Reporter" 267).

racist because "given the context of the era, Hergé could not have been motivated by such intention" (Le Monde.fr and AFP). The decision against Mondondo was upheld on appeal, with the court citing Voltaire as another text that would be considered racist but must not be banned. Underscoring Mondondo's perceived folly, Alain Berenboom, one of two lawyers representing Moulinsart and Casterman, added to the court's canon of unbannable racist world literature, claiming that banning *Tintin in the Congo* would be akin to opening a Pandora's box, leading to bans on "Dickens . . . Mark Twain, the Bible" ("Student Sues Publishers"). Constellating *Tintin* among these great works of literature, Berenboom denies the central component of what makes both *Tintin* and pursuantly Mondondo's claim distinct: visuality.

Using Belgium's 1981 antiracism law as their basis, Mondondo and his co-plaintiffs entered a primary and secondary injunction for what Mirzoeff would call the "right to look." As Mirzoeff explains, the right to look is visuality's opposite (2): it lodges a claim to "a political subjectivity and collectivity" as a form of countervisuality (1), "challenging the law that sustains visuality's authority in order to justify its own sense of 'right'" (25). If visuality, in the form of *Tintin*'s cohesive worlding, claims authority to naturalize the visual evaluation of human difference as a prerequisite for colonial modernity, then Mondondo claims the right to look as an autonomous reader, and to reject *Tintin*'s forms of segregation and classification by *intervening* in their proliferation, and thus their legibility. Of the two primary claims in Mondondo's suit, the first demanded the cessation of all commercial exploitation, circulation, and printing of *Tintin au Congo*. Explaining his rationale during an interview with Pasamonik, Mondondo characterizes the images in the album as "unacceptable" and explains the personal injury he felt: "I filed the complaint because I felt that there was an attack on my image" (Pasamonik, "Bienvenu"). In his language, Mondondo asserts the harm of visuality, not simply—as Berenboom would have it—racism.

When Pasamonik, in the course of the interview, uses the same logic as Berenboom, arguing that banning great literature would encompass so many "worldly" works, Mondondo locates his specific right according to local history and in keeping with his secondary injunction. As noted in the suit and its appeal, the cessation of commercial exploitation—that is, ceaseless reproduction—was followed by a secondary request, for *framing*. In the event that the court refused to order the total cessation of sale and reprinting of *Tintin au Congo,* Mondondo asked that the album at least be *revised* with a warning or a preface explaining the work as an "affirm[ation] of colonial prejudices of the time" (Pasamonik). Using the decision by the British publisher Egmont—compelled by Enright's complaint—as a model, Mondondo averred that the outcome in England (the cessation of the sale of *Tintin in the Congo* to children and its affixing with a warning label) established a certain right to look according to "the equality of the races" that had been previously unthinkable in Belgium (Pasamonik). In the event that it was properly framed, Mondondo also allowed that *Tintin in the Congo* might lead to an otherwise suppressed discussion about colonialism in Belgium, but only if it were "critical" (Pasamonik). In relation to such a scenario, Wanzo provocatively suggests that caricature and stereotype might be means for antiracist and decolonial ends. However, she declares that such iconography must be read through a framework that acknowledges how "Black caricature always deals in pain because historically it has been a way of inflicting injury." Furthermore, Wanzo advises that critical uses of caricature and stereotype should ask whether a given work's "narrative and visual structure that it shapes may be doing work other than, or something more than, the injury" (220). The present version(s) of *Congo* and Moulinsart's long-standing efforts to suppress its historical context demonstrate that critical discussions such as these will not be taking place from its side.

Both of Mondondo's claims to the right to look—either a full intercession in the commercial profit from the reproduction of racist caricature *or* the historical framing of the colonial injury—were denied by the court in an unsurprising rejection of his reading and of his "autonomy to arrange the relations of the visible and the sayable." In its ruling, the court furnished its own reading, which re-established the value and innocence of *Tintin* while denying Mondondo a place "from which to claim rights and to determine what is right" (Mirzoeff, *Right* 1). The court justified its ruling by citing Belgian legal precedents and cultural needs, acclaiming *Tintin in the Congo* as "above all a testimony to the shared history of Belgium and Congo at the given time" (La cour d'appel). In a unique conflation of the character of Tintin and the character of the album itself, the judgment even interprets the plot of *Congo* to support the case of *Tintin,* opining that Tintin is presented as an ideal hero to emulate, and that everyone is sad when he leaves the Congo. In its reading of *Congo,* the court not only performs an uncritical McCloudian consumption of difference, it also mirrors a scene in the original work itself, wherein Tintin educates Congolese children on how to read a map of Belgium, "votre patrie." Thus, the verdict produces a colonial mise-en-abyme in which a graphic imperial agent named Tintin teaches colonial subjects in the Congo how to read a map-image of their Belgian "fatherland" within an image-text named *Tintin* that a Belgian court uses to educate a Congolese student émigré in Belgium on how to read colonial patrimony.[30]

Media coverage of the trial, particularly in Europe, tended toward condescension and even outright hostility toward Mondondo. The cover of the Belgian weekly *Télémoustique* featured a caricature by Pierre Kroll in the style of *Tintin in the Congo*'s Congolese characters (specifically le roi de Ba baoro'm) exclaiming over the book—which he is reading upside down—"Ça y en à raciste!" ["Dat's racist!"]. Kroll's application of *Tintin*'s iconography is a reminder that the *post-* of postcolonialism does not mean *past,* insofar as the work of historical reckoning continues. Through his suit Mondondo sought to "clear a space," in Appiah's terms, from the colonial stereotypology of *Congo* by "appeal[ing] to an ethical universal" that would include Belgium in a larger project of reckoning with coloniality and racism—a project shared, incidentally by England, and more distantly, by the US (342, 353). In its declamation of Mondondo's misreading, it is the court, in fact, that misreads Mondondo's case as an attack on Belgium's cultural heritage or European literary tradition rather than as an allegation that visual imperialism should be marked as passé or relegated to the past to clarify shared antiracist values in the postcolonial present. Although Mondondo's challenge failed to amend the imperialist complex of visuality represented by *Tintin in the Congo,* his "space-clearing gesture" is a testament to readers "who will not see themselves as Other" in the face of the stereotypes of global comics (Appiah 348, 356).

Nitnits and Other Tintins, or *Tintin* and the Pirates!

If the *post-* of Mondondo's postcolonial stance indicates "challenges to earlier legitimating narratives," then his resistance is obliquely

---

30. Note that the court also justifies the images in the album by asserting that they might be readily compared to "photographs from the 1930s," wherein one would be "struck by the similarity of the situations" (La cour d'appel).

shared by the *post-* of postmodernist critique of *Tintin* (Appiah 353). Appiah asserts that postmodernism, in its ungroundedness, has not readily been "the basis" for the "reject[ion of] Western imperium" in Africa or amid the African diaspora (353). In a general global context, however, postmodernist tactics have magnified the comics medium while mocking Hergé's message in a proliferation of pirated *Tintins*. Modernism, Appiah contends, "saw the economization of the world as the triumph of reason" (346). The commitment of *Tintin*'s publishers and copyright-holders to produce and protect authorized versions of *Tintin*'s corpus is thus a decidedly modernist symptom of a rational economy wherein Tintin symbolically masters the world that *Tintin* encompasses in commodity form. Yet the authorized object conditions the possibility of the unauthorized object. Since its inception, illegitimate *Tintins* have undermined *Tintin*'s economy, forming their own material and symbolic global flows. Some of these are traced over the "original" *Tintin* albums and recopied; some are drawn anew, with varying degrees of likeness to the original pages. This counterfeit economy has spanned eras of analog and digital distribution. In 2011 an iPad App entitled "Tintin: The Complete Collection," retailing for the price of $4.99 (US), was revealed to be "nothing more than some hastily assembled photocopies [with] many of the pages sized incorrectly for the iPad, but . . . not even sized consistently incorrectly, and due to shoddy scanning work, [with] colors [that] aren't even always consistent within a single book." On the *IFC blog* where this "fraud" was reported, the author contends not that the poor-quality pages are not actually copies of *Tintin* adventures but merely that they are not licensed and thus "bogus and created using pirated material" (Sitterson).

Some pirated *Tintins* follow the Situationist practice of détournement.[31] Using the characters, ligne claire style, or actual pages and panels from a *Tintin* album, authors create "new" *Tintin* adventures, much to the chagrin of the corporations guarding the myth. One of the first Tintin détournements immediately followed the liberation of Belgium in 1944. The Belgian paper *La Patrie* published *Tintin au Pays des Nazis* ("Tintin in the Land of the Nazis") in order to criticize Hergé's work for the collaborationist paper *Le Soir*. A subsequent story showed Tintin leading a division to discover the secret to man-

31. As McCarthy points out, Guy Debord's *Situationist International* featured a "'détourned' version of *The Crab with the Golden Claws*," replacing the word "Crab" with "Capital" (186).

ufacturing the V2 rocket before the Germans can use it; this strip was titled "in the manner of Mr. Hergé, who is indisposed due to the Liberation" (Assouline 106). Thus, as Appiah notes of postmodernism, the piracy of *Tintin* "revels in the proliferation of distinctions that reflects the underlying dynamic of cultural modernity" (346), resuscitating the differences, shadows, and ambiguities repressed by the modernist taxonomy of reason through which *Tintin* transcends its own historical context.

A thorough accounting for all of the détournements of *Tintin* would take volumes beyond even existing collections such as Alain-Jacques Tornare's *Tint'Interdit: Pastiches et Parodies.* Pastiches and parodies of *Tintin* occur in manifold countries and languages, with myriad attitudes toward Hergé's originals. McCarthy breaks such détournements down into three categories: pornographic, political, and "art" (186). In the last category, McCarthy hails French artist Jochen Gerner's *TNT en Amérique*—wherein pages of *Tintin in America* are completely covered in black save a few words and symbols—as a form of symbolic "burial." Gerner's work goes beyond responding to the "meaning" of *Tintin* to focus on the form, challenging the limits of legibility of the album page. Such tactics demonstrate how the same discrete, moral, clear, attributes that make the world of *Tintin* effective as myth also make it open to perversion. Certainly ligne claire, in becoming a style so emblematic of European culture, has been an apt technique for deformation. Lecigne heralds Jacques Martin and Bob de Moor, both colleagues of Hergé, as *héritiers d'Hergé* who unwittingly revealed the artifice at the heart of ligne claire. Uncredited as artists on *Tintin,* the men famously created an imaginary page from an unwritten adventure and left it on Hergé's desk, provoking outrage. Their interoffice détournement threatened the sovereign borders of the world of *Tintin,* demonstrating that Hergé's clear line was merely a style to be imitated (Lecigne 49). A number of later *héritiers,* such as the Belgian artist Jijé, the French artist Yves Chaland, and the Dutch artist Joost Swarte—who coined the term *ligne claire*—would appropriate the style not for détournements but for their own characters and adventures.

Other détournements focus on exposing *Tintin*'s ideological conceits. Swiss artist Exem's *Zinzin, maître du monde* or Québécois artist Henriette Valium's "Nitnit in Otherland" both fulfill this role, subjecting the main character to all manner of sordid affairs in order to undermine the innocence of the series. In a similar vein, South African artist Anton Kannemeyer's reworking of *Tintin au Congo* for *Bitterkomix* uses much of the same imagery from the original, yet subtly revises it to show the violence underlying *Tintin*'s paternalism. For example, Kannemeyer (as Joe Dog) redraws one scene from *Tintin au Congo* as *Pappa in Afrika,* substituting African children for the dozen antelopes that Tintin accidentally shoots, believing each to be the same antelope. Describing *Pappa in Afrika,* Christophe Dony characterizes the work as an example of postcolonial "writing back" "whereby artists adopt and adapt colonial traditions and discourses" ("Writing and Drawing" 22) "as a mode of contesting and revising ideological, political, and narrative authorities" (25). Dony's celebratory reading of Kannemeyer's "difficult" (33) works relies on the ability of the white artist to use derogatory "golliwog iconography" (33) as an appeal to postcolonial justice. In Dony's analysis of Kannemeyer's détournement, the racist iconography can be preserved yet used for antiracist ends. *Pace* Dony, I assert that although *Pappa in Afrika* is a provocative postmodern deconstruction of *Tintin*'s visual imperialism, it is not antiracist, as it relies on the continued injury of the Black caricature for its rhetorical effect.

I focus on US artist Charles Burns's détournements of *Tintin* because Burns mobilizes comics-specific elements without reproducing wholecloth their stereotypical colonial idiom. Burns's Nitnit trilogy is, as Jan Baetens and Hugo Frey have argued,

> a springboard to a broader, more general interpretation of the work (in this case the reworking of the Tintin model to achieve a disquieting merger of observer and observed, reality and dream, body and mind, culture, imagination and troubled social relations). ("'Layouting'" 200)

McCloud's reading uncritically consumes the binaries that Baetens and Frey set out as they are visually constructed in *Tintin*; Mondondo challenges these binaries directly; Burns "reworks" them. Considering how Burns mobilizes and adapts medial practices from the *Tintin* series provides a less cohesive but more historically attuned view of Tintin's mythic world.

Some comics theorists view all of comics production—with its low cultural standing, reproducibility, and spatial poetics—as, if not outright postmodernism, aligned with "postmodernism's critical ethic" and located within "the context of postmodernism" (Chute, "Popularity" 357). However, Appiah's description of how postmodernism inheres in art is especially telling in this context: "there is an antecedent practice that laid claim to a certain exclusivity of insight, and . . . 'postmodernism' is a name for the rejection of that claim to exclusivity, a rejection that is almost always more playful, though not necessarily less serious, than the practice it aims to replace" (342). For world comics, this antecedent practice is *Tintin's* visualization of the world, and the rejection of exclusivity is lodged by Burns's use of formatting, swiping, denaturing clear line, and self-plagiarizing.

Formatting

The Nitnit trilogy was originally published in three serialized albums, beginning with *X'ed Out* (2010), followed by *The Hive* (2012), and, finally, *Sugar Skull* (2014). Burns's use of the serial album format for his work suggests a transatlantic mistranslation of sorts, as the appearance of albums among American graphic novels is irregular. Burns describes an uncertain response to his use of the album format from readers familiar with his earlier series *cum* graphic novel *Black Hole,* describing their response as "'what's that? what happened?'" Burns qualifies this reaction, by speculating, "I think the fact that there's more serialized books in France and Belgium—you know, it was based on the album format, which certainly doesn't really exist in the US" (Guilbert). An album in the US marketplace does not evoke the familiarity that made *Tintin's* oeuvre so cohesive and authoritative elsewhere in the world. Indeed, as Jean-Paul Gabilliet asserts, the "failed cultural acclimatization" of *Tintin* to US audiences in the late 1950s and early 1960s is at least partly due to the album format's large shape impeding sales ("Disappointing Crossing" 257). Similarly, Gabilliet notes name recognition as a system limited by class and culture, asserting, "to the overwhelming majority of North American mainstream comics readers, Tintin and Asterix are names associated, if at all, with esoteric foreign comic-strip traditions" (263). Despite today's market featuring American graphic novels of varying shapes and sizes,[32] the volumes of Burns's Nitnit trilogy operate

---

32. For example, Art Spiegelman's *In the Shadow of No Towers* and Chris Ware's *Acme Novelty Library Annual Report to Shareholders* have used the approximate shape of the broadsheet to gesture to the origin of comic strips in the supplements of US newspapers.

in a material register immediately apparent to European audiences familiar with the *album* format but, conversely, as Gabilliet declares, relatively foreign—or specifically not recognizable as a standard format—to US audiences.

The Nitnit albums' cloth bindings, coupled with their covers' fonts and imagery, invoke *Tintin* works. However, the dark coloration of Burns's artwork, and his use of a non–ligne claire chiaroscuro style, ambiguate this recognition. Further, as a "concession to [his American] publisher" (Guilbert), Burns allowed Pantheon to publish a collection of all three Nitnit albums as one large volume, called *Last Look,* more evocative of a large-format US graphic novel. This omnibus was not made available in European markets; Burns assumed an affinity there for the discrete albums, saying, "in France or Belgium or Germany or Italy, I think everyone can understand: well, here's a series, and they fit together and you read them and re-read them and you go back to them and see how they fit together" (Guilbert). This transatlantic commercial distinction concedes that the trilogy of albums are "out of place" in the US market, requiring an assimilation to the graphic novel format. At the same time, the series' US origin makes it foreign in Europe, regardless of its appropriate size and shape. The commercial and cultural asymmetry of transnational formatting is explored in even more detail in chapter 3, but Burns's Nitnit series provides a useful primer in how an artist, rather than pursue an authorized global standard for their work, can use formatting to make comics that will be playfully out of place wherever they are in the world.

Swiping

The Nitnit trilogy's visual translations of *Tintin* extend beyond reference to parodic resonance and subversive reiteration. On *X'ed Out*'s cover, the pattern of the mushroom from Hergé's *The Shooting Star* now adorns a gigantic egg; *The Hive* and *Sugar Skull* have covers that use a melange of *Tintin* imagery, from the stalactites depicted in *Explorers on the Moon* (1954) to the rocky promontory of *The Black Island* (1938). The collected volume *Last Look* features a mask that Doug, the protagonist of the stories, wears to become his alter ego, Nitnit. The Nitnit mask floats, looming over a landscape with white blanks for eyes. This mask, resembling Tintin, unwittingly thematizes and inverts McCloud's interpretation of *Tintin* as a safe and sensually stimulating mask, by directly—if unseeingly—gazing back at the reader-consumer. Within the books, other skewed referents from *Tintin* proliferate. The intercom figured in the Tintin adventure *The Secret of the Unicorn* becomes a motif recurring throughout the series, featured in *X'ed Out* as the central image of the endpapers and later presented in a triptych next to a panel showing a circular orifice in a pink wall and a panel showing a storm drain emitting a stream of dark-red substance. The "intercommunication" between the world of Tintin and the world of the Nitnit trilogy is made grotesque in these iterations, where the intercom as a familiar technological device is rendered less legible by every repetition. Where Tintin relied on a knowledge of such communication devices and codes to decipher the ambiguities or mysteries of foreign locales, the symbol of the intercom is repeatedly denatured in *X'ed Out,* exemplifying the hazards of transmission. In *Tintin,* the iteration of stereotypes or familiar forms cohere to form a rational narrative discourse, but in the Nitnit trilogy, icons and shapes recur in disjuncture from the narrative, interpolating visual stoppages, strings of signification, and literally disturbing flows in the story.

In his study of Burns's art, Benoît Crucifix examines Burns's long-standing use of "swiping" as a comics practice, even before his explicit engagement with *Tintin.* A "swipe" in comics terminology is the widely used yet often maligned practice of copying the work of another artist in the form of a panel or an entire page. Showing that Burns's oeuvre is full of swipes that metareflexively comment on comics as a medium of reproducibility, Crucifix asserts that "the very practice of swiping expresses an attachment to comic book culture and an iconophilic collecting, gathering and redrawing of visually striking images" (318). Burns uses swiping throughout the Nitnit trilogy not only to reference comics history but to combine and transform transnational comics genres as an experimental process of production. Crucifix traces how the storyline of protagonist Doug—and especially that of his alter ego, Nitnit—"is composed of panels swiped by Burns's preferred canon of *Tintin* and romance comic books" (325), resulting in a nonlinear and fragmented narrative "based on a densely braided network of recurring images" (323). Alongside Crucifix, Jan Baetens and Hugo Frey declare that Burns "reprograms" ("Modernizing Tintin" 111n3) *Tintin* imagery through a "deviant and demythifying appropriation of the Tintin character and style" resulting in the "most complete attempt to destroy *and* reinvent Tintin" (107). They explain his use of swipes through the structure of virology, noting how Burns "relies on the insertion of small capsules of Tintin-like material that proliferate as dangerous cells through the work that hosts them" (109). As all three theorists assert, Burns swipes to destabilize the legibility of the image on its own or as a narrative unit, and to make indiscernible any authenticity regarding the image as a "Tintin pastiche or Burns original" (109).

There is yet another mode in which Burns's swiping subverts its source. Intertextuality is a bivalent system of renegotiation predicated on a two-way feedback network. Baetens and Frey confirm as much by reading Burns's swiped images as a "structure capable of launching new interpretations" ("Modernizing Tintin" 108) that could "remythif[y] Tintin" (111). Applying this logic to material practice, one can accordingly read Burns's swiping as a reproduction of Hergé's own research practices, with a difference. Because Hergé drew the world without leaving Europe until later in his life (Assouline 178), he relied on myriad *colonial swipes*: Postcards, prospectuses, articles, and the Musée Royal du Congo in Tervuren all became material for Hergé's own iconophilic redrawing (Delisle, *Bande dessinée* 15–16; Delisle, "Le reporter" 270; Hergé and Sadoul 45). Michael Farr references Hergé's "constantly swelling archive files" as the symptom and source of his swiping: "He was almost obsessive about keeping material that could on some occasion be of possible use. As a result his files bulge with information of every kind, from picture postcards to furniture catalogues" (8). Comparing Hergé's and Burns's swipes allows for an anticolonial reading of the Nitnit trilogy wherein Burns's playful swiping of *Tintin* uncovers Hergé's more serious imperialist complex of visuality, which treats the world as picture, full of visual objects ripe for the swiping. The swiped imagery in the Nitnit trilogy and its narrative ambivalence indicate Burns's postmodernist rejection of the exclusivity of *Tintin*'s visual referents drawn as if from the real and assembled as seamless clear-lined graphic narrative.

Denaturing Clear Line

As detailed above, *Tintin*'s innovative use of image and text drawn together in ligne claire style established an ideologically motivated means to draw the world together in story. The cohesion of ligne claire ensures Tintin's legibility: "Tintin should be recognized whatever the context, that is what is meant when the 'clear line' is spoken of" (Goddin, *Reporters* 217). The Nitnit trilogy ambiguates this recognition by fragmenting its narrative between two styles of alternating authority. As Baetens and Frey contend, clear line is not only a style of drawing, "it is also a form of storytelling that relies on the readability of both the images (easy to decode and immediately recognisable) and the readability of the storyline (easy to follow, while permanently full of small twists and surprises)" ("'Layouting'" 194). In the light of this definition, the Nitnit trilogy "undermines both page composition and storytelling, which lose their Clear Line transparency" (197). The trilogy's narrative revolves around the protagonist, Doug, who shifts between a chiaroscuro world, richly shaded with Burns's usual feather-lines,[33] and a ligne claire otherworld where he becomes his alter ego, Nitnit (see figure 1.2).[34] Between these two graphical worlds the trilogy is marked by the oversaturation of imagery. As analyzed above, Burns's vivid panels *oversignify* in the context of the narrative, offering too many connections and possibilities to allow one clear message. The stylistic fragmentation between ligne claire and chiaroscuro makes it harder to determine which panels are meant to be read according to codes governing representations of diegetic reality and which according to those of fantasy. This obscurantist code-switching heightens the reference to *Tintin* and to Tintin's ability to clearly read other cultures. It is suggested through Doug's transposition into the Nitnit character that the world of *Tintin* may be just as imaginary as that of Nitnit.

---

33. Of his own style, Burns notes: "I try to achieve something that's almost like a visceral effect. The quality of the lines and the density of the black take on a character of their own—it's something that has an effect on your subconscious. Those lines make you feel a certain way. That kind of surface makes you feel a certain way" (Chute, "Interview").

34. Jean-Paul Gabilliet qualifies the entirety of Burns's style as a confusion between ligne claire and what Gabilliet dubs *ligne noire*. For Gabilliet, Burns's entire oeuvre similarly stages the miscegenation of ideological and symbolic registers connoted through these distinct styles: "Tintin was as absent from American homes as it was omnipresent within those of Europeans. Hence the remarkable uniqueness within the trajectory of [Burns]: of all the American artist of his generation, Burns is the only one to have constructed a graphic identity based on a fusion between the clarity of the Hergéen line and the darkness of the brush inking of a number of comics produced within the 1903s and 1950s" ("Sutures génériques").

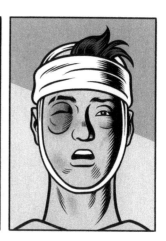

FIGURE 1.2. Charles Burns, *Sugar Skull*, n. pag.

Although the images in the clear-lined Nitnit sections are brighter and bear a resemblance to *Tintin*'s panels, their position in the trilogy's narrative destabilizes their claims to clarity or legibility. Doug wears a Nitnit mask in certain chiaroscuro panels to perform his "cut-up" poetry à la William S. Burroughs. Yet Doug's mask becomes his face when he enters the clear-lined otherworld of his imagining. The "masking" cited by McCloud as an essential component in *Tintin* becomes monstrous in Burns, a form not of safe self-escape but of imprisonment within the self without recourse to an outside. When Nitnit enters the ligne claire world, it visually recalls the foreign bazaars of Hergé. However, this "Interzone" is populated *not* by familiar ethnographic caricatures but by creatures uttering unintelligible signs whose appearances blur the distinction between human and nonhuman. Doug's—Nitnit's—encounters with the "Others" of this world reframe Hergé's imagined "Others" as creatures of the Western cultural imagination.

Hergé draws Tintin as a subject "in the differentiating order of Otherness" (Bhabha, "Remembering" 117), but Burns challenges this claim to cultural location. As postcolonial theorist Homi Bhabha describes the process, Tintin becomes a subject, as does the audience that identifies with him, through encounters with those who must be recognized for their difference from the seeing subject. Tintin's travels establish who we—the good readers of its visual economy—are *not*. Tintin's travels make otherness readable and manageable; as Goddin states, "the adventures of Tintin unify the diversity of the world" (*Reporters* 224). Nitnit's travels, however, involute the "order of Otherness," locating it as an internal aspect of subject-formation rather than as a reality of the "world." Doug/Nitnit's identification as subject "is always the return of an image of identity which bears the mark of splitting in that 'Other' place from which it comes" (Bhabha, "Remembering" 117). Confronted by the Nitnit trilogy, the totality of Hergé's visual corpus is made to display its seams amid "the atmosphere of certain uncertainty that surrounds the body" and which "certifies its existence and threatens its dismemberment" (117). Nitnit's oversignified panels and fragmented narrative pose contamination, or a lack of secure borders—clear lines—between the subject, its others, and modes of visually containing and consuming difference. No more safely disclosing a sensually stimulating world, Nitnit's mask portends a hazardous, frightening, uncertain world that undermines the narrative stability of reader and referent in turn.

Self-Plagiarism

By destabilizing the codes of *Tintin*'s authority, Burns's work also destabilizes the authority and familiarity of its legible world. The fragmentation of the Nitnit trilogy is perpetuated further in Burns's pirating of his own work. In addition to *X'ed Out, The Hive, Sugar Skull,* and *Last Look,* Burns released a number of "unofficial" components of the work: *Johnny 23* is a limited-release "pirate" version of *X'ed Out,* published in 2010 by French publisher Le Dernier Cri. *Incubation,* published in 2015 by Pigeon Press in Oakland, California, collects rough sketches in pencil and pastels. *Vortex,* published in 2016 by French publisher Cornélius, collects spoof covers and fragments of stories never used in the trilogy. Both *Vortex* and *Johnny 23* use a foreign-looking cipher, but the latter is structured as a graphic narrative throughout. It is formatted in a smaller, horizontal trim size, which "evokes the Chinese bootleg versions of *Tintin* in the *lianhuanhua* format ubiquitous in China" (Crucifix 325). Not sold in American bookstores, available only via mail order, *Johnny 23* is now out of print. Pirate *Tintins* flourished in locations where the authorized album was not available or too expensive; *Johnny 23* instead creates a demand for a "deauthorized" version in the market where *X'ed Out* is readily available, signaling shifting flows in the economy of world

FIGURE 1.3. Charles Burns, *Johnny 23*, n. pag.

books. Moulinsart's desire for commercial and material authority over "official" *Tintin*s is inverted in Burns's establishment of an alternate economy built on the desire for the unofficial, secondary versions in which no single publishing entity can claim ultimate provenance over all of the works.

Many panels in *Johnny 23* appear to be directly taken from *X'ed Out,* but they are composed in a different order and layout, reminding a reader of Hergé's own process of revising and recomposing panels between newspaper, magazine, album, and revised album printings. In *Johnny 23,* the text within panels is composed of a mono-alphabetic cipher of American English (see figure 1.3), gesturing toward the position of American English as the ultimate key of all language in the age of globalization.[35] The reader must become like the detective Tintin, breaking the code to gain knowledge over

35. The casting of American English as the universal code can also be read in reference to Hergé's decision, when accused of racism in *Coke en Stock,* to replace the "Petit Negre" spoken by the Muslim pilgrims with a style drawn from French translations of "romans américains" (Goddin, *Reporters* 259).

the narrative. Yet, once the intrepid decoder begins "translating" the invented characters, it is evident that this encoded text is not as "familiar" as the anglophone reader may have initially surmised. *Johnny 23*'s form and "text" is constructed in a mode allusive to Burroughs's cut-up methods, deterritorializing the "uncoded" phrases, and again disrupting the seamlessness of the narrative or its composition.[36] The verbal messages in panels seem to have little relevance to the image content. Some of the lines are song lyrics (e.g., "Nothing can become of nothing" from Lydia Lunch's "3X3" or "Always crashing in the same car" from David Bowie's so-titled song; 40), some are direct quotes from or references to Burroughs's work (e.g., "your dull dirty naked lunch"; 38), some appear to be references to Burns's other work (as in the reference to Eliza, a character from his *Black Hole* series / graphic novel; 7). The proliferating piracy and disjuncture between verbal and visual codes in *X'ed Out* and *Johnny 23* thus draw from the material, iconic, and stylistic aspects proper to *Tintin* in order to denature or deform the clear borderlines of its authority.

Burns distributes thin cardboard Nitnit masks at some convention appearances and with certain copies of his work. Coupled with the bemusing ciphers in his détourned offprints, Burns reveals McCloud's metaphorical "mask" to be literally and figuratively paper-thin. In the chiaroscuro of Burns's work, all of *Tintin*'s deliberate ease of recognizing, reading, and consuming the world is made strange, difficult, laborious. The Nitnit trilogy and its pirate offspring clearly engage in what Appiah calls a space-clearing gesture (348) through the "construction and the marking of differences" (342) elided or obfuscated in *Tintin*'s production. However, the Nitnit trilogy's visual *tressage* of pollution, miasma, and fecundity does not so much distance readers from visual imperialism as illustrate that in *Tintin*'s "broad circulation of cultures . . . we are all already contaminated by each other" (354). As Burns's work, via Appiah's theorization, reminds us, there is no "autochthonous *echt*-African culture" (354), but there is also no Belgian or US culture without Africa. Rather, it is in the co-constitution of each place that inequalities are masked, protested, or reimagined.

---

36. This form itself recalls the OuBaPo works with Tintin, especially those by Francois Ayroles and Jochen Gerner.

World Comics in Three Dimensions

Comics present immersive worlds with little recourse to an outside. As we have seen in *Tintin,* sometimes the surface of the page seems more real for its being only surface. Yet the worlding of comics does not occur in isolation of frameworks beyond the panel frames. Even in a style as pure as *Tintin*'s, "it is noteworthy that the world without shadows portrayed through the conventionalized and diagrammatic realism of the *ligne claire* can nonetheless betray the presence of repressed material" (Miller, *Reading* 214). The cultural construction of media is predicated on shifting assumptions of visual and discursive legibility.

In the system of ligne claire as well as that of récitatif-less comics and revised albums, a fullness is offered to the subject, a plenitude at the level of line, panel, and book. This fullness appears natural, and conceals the many lines that were erased in the process, the many strips and panels that were spliced together for the album and then edited and reprinted. What the media technology of *Tintin* offers to the reader is a sense of clear material boundaries. These boundaries also inhere in the adventures that reassert the clear lines between other places and peoples. The toponyms and ethnographic markings that denote specific races and places are thus always already naturalized within the system. Regardless of any debate as to whether *Tintin* is racist to the "Congolese" or "Saudi Arabians" or "Japanese," the series manifests the creation of a system in which these markers are ultimately interchangeable or prone to revision and completely bereft of the complex historical and material circumstances of their fabrication. The problem of recognition precedes the specific content of any album and lies in the visual economy, the system of mapping others that is both unquestionably accepted and promulgated by *Tintin.*

McCloud's reading, in its collapse of the boundaries between the lived world and the seen world—the world on paper and the world in which the paper is held—reveals Mirzoeff's "complexes of visuality" (*Right* 4): overt structures of political power and authority that operate through regimes of seeing. Comics are rarely considered as significant apparatuses for such regimes, but Wanzo's work reminds us that comics partake in visual imperialism in ways that are all the more effective for the inattention paid to them. Cultural constructions such as race, legibility, and the legibility of race should be traced in comics' playful medial instantiations. It is in adolescent forms that proclaim the innocence of the discourse and the audience alike that protean techniques for reading the world are inculcated.

Critical readers like Mondondo embody the truth that *Tintin*, for all its transnational influence, is not read the same by everyone, everywhere. With their iconic register, comics simultaneously enable cross-border recognition without recourse to translation—as the enterprising individual who recast *Tintin* in Angola understood—and complicate this recognition—as Mondondo's "misreading" exemplifies. Rather than a transcendent shorthand, a stereotype marks a struggle for representation, wherein only certain groups benefit.

Obliged to assign a monetary value to his suit, Mondondo asked for the sum total of €1. Moulinsart and *Tintin*'s publisher Casterman both countersued Mondondo for €15,000 each for "vexatious proceedings." Having dismissed Mondondo's suit, the court also dismissed Moulinsart's and Casterman's countersuits. Although the court decided against Mondondo's claim, the same juridical body evaluated Mondondo's claim as having *some* value to the extent that it did not merit compensation for those corporations that felt their time had been wasted. Mondondo's gambit, his intervention in the economy of world comics, forced those who benefit from the unmarked continuation of visual imperialism to account for their readings. Mondondo compelled Moulinsart and Casterman to justify their readings in court and drew attention to the disparity between those who profit from such readings and those who suffer from them.

The following chapters ask how comics, by making visible questions of translation and medial production, provide tools to rethink world literacy. Mondondo's case highlights the necessity for thinking of media in three dimensions and moving beyond the representational aspects that may compose a dominant culture's interpretation. If we think of the space of the page as but one component of the encounter that a reader makes with a media object in a historicized, geopolitical context, how might we implicate other components of that encounter in new considerations of the local and the global?

CHAPTER 2

GRAPHIC DISORIENTATIONS

Metro and Translation

A Passage to Cairo

In its etymology, the verb *translate* denotes spatial movement, and it signifies both a placement and a displacement. To carry something across, either from one language to another or from one geographic site to another, engenders a new and uneven relationality between sites. In this chapter, I examine the friction generated in comics translation. More specifically, I look at the divergent transnational editions[1] of Magdy El Shafee's *Metro* that proliferated after its banning in Egypt, observing how each edition differently interprets the roles and relations of the images, texts, and maps in the graphic novel. These interpretations reveal a great deal about audience expectations, relational geographies, and ways of reading comics. Ultimately these translations exemplify the ambiguity at the heart of translation scholar Lawrence Venuti's "domestication" versus "foreignization"

---

1. Transnational in a number of ways, but specifically in that the editions are linguistically rather than nationally determined: e.g., the English translations are circulated through the UK, Canada, and the US; the German translation is produced by a Swiss publisher, etc.

dialectic. Even as Venuti allows that these terms are not binaries, but instead ethical and variable "attitudes,"[2] the translations of *Metro* evince greater instability than an attitude might afford. Among the Arabic, Italian, German, and English editions, the graphic elements frequently work in tension with or direct opposition to each other, complicating the situation of a reader to the linguistic, pictorial, and locative aspects of the Cairo underground.

Metro provides a salient case study owing to its unique publication history; its formal combination of maps, images, and linguistic elements; and its realism. The plot of *Metro* follows a fictional story of a bank robbery that exposes political corruption, yet its setting in Cairo in the early twenty-first century is replete with detailed drawings of the city and accurate subway maps. The combination of fictional plot and nonfiction setting creates a unique challenge for translation in terms of how to balance these two registers. Relatedly, the place-based aspect of the work entails cultural negotiations of the local and the global. *Metro* employs comics formatting in ways that are specific to Cairene linguistic orientation and also drawn from external visual referents, especially a layout from Maltese American author Joe Sacco (Edwards, *American Century* 57–58).

Sacco's *Palestine* could not—by any stretch—be considered a book about Cairo. *Cairo* (as a verbal and visual denotation) only appears in roughly 1 percent of the work—or three of 285 pages, to be exact. The word *Cairo* and the pictorial representation of Cairo as a setting share only two of these three pages. And yet, I begin my analysis of El Shafee's *Metro* with Sacco's *Palestine* because of the way it orients a reader to Cairo as a diegetic space and because of its influential relation to *Metro,* a book entirely about and set in Cairo. Brian T. Edwards states that El Shafee himself was inspired by Sacco's formal use of space, and that Sacco's work "was a visual innovation within graphic fiction [*sic*] representing Egypt specifically" (*American Century* 59). For El Shafee, it was the way that Sacco used the space of the page in order to represent the crowdedness of Cairo that was revelatory, and influential on his own work. Shafee's acknowledgment of Sacco's influence leads to a preliminary examination of how Sacco, as a foreign journalist, mobilizes space within the constraints of the comics

2. "The terms 'domestication' and 'foreignization' indicate fundamentally *ethical* attitudes towards a foreign text and culture, ethical effects produced by the choice of a text for translation and by the strategy devised to translate it" (Venuti, *Translator's Invisibility* 19).

page and the graphic narrative. Thereafter, I examine El Shafee's own mobilization of paginal design and the translational differences that ensued upon *Metro*'s global distribution.

Sacco's *Palestine* was originally published as a serial comic and then collected into two book-size versions—*Palestine: A Nation Occupied* (1993) and *Palestine: In the Gaza Strip* (1996)—by publisher Fantagraphics, before finally being published as a single volume in 2001. *Palestine,* in book form, has been translated into at least thirteen languages, including Arabic, the official language of Egypt.[3] The work chronicles Sacco's journalistic travels through Israel and Palestine in 1991 and 1992 and offers a counterpoint to *Metro* due to the location of Cairo in terms of both the work's narrative and the book's material construction.

On the first page of the work (see figure 2.1), "Cairo" appears in large block letters only slightly occluded by small narrative boxes. The place-name is represented as itself obstructing great amounts of city "traffic," while a policeman is drawn giving a "stop" signal toward the top left corner of the page. The narrative boxes function as a curving road for the reader to follow from the policeman's signal, across Cairo and down to the bottom of the page. Simultaneously, these boxes indicate that readers' (linguistic) journeys through Cairo and their ability to locate it as such come at the expense of the city's inhabitants, who are shown struggling behind words. The large block letters interrupt the space of composition in the panels of the first page, and the regimes of toponymic location, pictorial representation, and textual expression are assembled to suggest hierarchical relations among them. Sacco's work maps Cairo as a space of dense urban traffic (traffic of bodies and vehicles in space as well as traffic of words, images, and locative tools) *and* as a point of transit to other destinations. Cairo's appearance in a work called *Palestine* draws attention to Sacco's position as an outsider to these places and orients the reader similarly, as one who is not immediately *in* Palestine but who must move through other spaces in order to arrive there.

Sacco's use of the page as a compositional framework evokes the tension between linear and tabular reading models—as described by

---

3. Allen Douglas and Fedwa Malti-Douglas stipulate that while Arabic dialects are closest to the Western style of comic book writing, these dialects are normally not written and are mutually incomprehensible: "only one dialect is sufficiently well known in the region to have any pretensions to wider accessibility, and that is the dialect of Cairo, Egypt" (4).

FIGURE 2.1. Joe Sacco, *Palestine*, page 1

Pierre Fresnault-Deruelle in the seminal text "Du linéaire au tabu-laire"—whereby a reader of comics reconciles the composition of the page as a unified surface with that of the fragmented and perspectiv-ally dissonant story space ("surface et espace" 17). Edwards quotes El Shafee as stating that Sacco's use of layout was the first time that he saw the comics page used effectively to represent *zahma,* or the traf-fic jam, of Cairo (*American Century* 57). Edwards riffs on this claim to further argue that Sacco's layout offers a "new way to represent the *hisa* [noise] of Cairo" (57) and to assert that the visual innovation of Sacco's layout was directly tied to its representation of "Egypt spe-cifically" (58). For Edwards, then, Sacco's layout and its particularly jammed or noisy composition links foreign forms with the represen-tation of Cairo in terms of the unique balance of surface tension.

El Shafee's appreciation of Sacco's layout as a way to rhetori-cally represent Cairo led to similar compositions in *Metro.* Sacco and El Shafee tend toward page compositions that theorist Benoît Peeters has categorized as "rhetorical layout." In his work on differ-ent "conceptions of the page," Peeters describes how the layout or the mise-en-page will work in tandem with (or against) the break-down of the story or the *découpage.* Peeters categorizes four types of mise-en-page: (1) conventional—in which the layout is standardized, (2) decorative—in which the layout is guided by aesthetic effect, (3) rhetorical—in which the layout reflects the narrative, and (4) produc-tive—in which the layout of the page directs the narrative (*Lire* 49). Challenging and expanding Peeters's schema, Thierry Groensteen in his *System of Comics* stipulates that the relative conventionality or decorativity of a layout will depend on the context of the page and whether it is consistent across the work itself or whether the work features heterogeneous layouts (98–99). Both Sacco and El Shafee use what one might call consistently inconsistent mise-en-page. That is, their layouts change every page along with the narrative content. This dynamic use of the space of the page poses an interpretive chal-lenge for translators who must determine how to change aspects of the découpage or the relationships between panels without irrevoca-bly shifting the compositional unity of each page.

Further, the effect of the format on how a reader encounters the site of Cairo in the narrative of Sacco's *Palestine* reminds us that com-ics is "an art of tensions"—in the words of Charles Hatfield. As Hat-field describes, readers negotiate multiple tensions in reading comics: (1) the basic tension of code versus code or word versus image, (2) the single image versus the image in series, (3) sequence versus surface (a nearly identical formulation of linear vs. tabular), and, finally, (4) text as object versus text as experience (36). These tensions work together in complex ways, and we may see in the situation of Cairo in *Palestine* the work of all of Hatfield's tensions—how the word *Cairo* works against and with the images it tops, how the images on the page simultaneously form a unitary collage as well as individual moments in space and time, and how the distinctions between print formats delineate different reading experiences. Hatfield proposes a somewhat static conception of "comics' materiality, includ[ing] not only the design or layout of the page but also the physical makeup of the text, including its size, shape, binding, paper, and printing" (58); however, his description of the tension is capacious enough to account for the significance of changes made to the comic as object that both *Palestine* and *Metro* demonstrate. That is, rather than a stable design, layout, or physical makeup, *Palestine* materially exists as single-issue editions, two-volume collections, and a single graphic novel, all multiply translated (not to mention the special edition); and *Metro* exists as multiply translated, excerpted, digitized, and reformatted volumes. Hatfield's focus on how, for example, the reader's awareness of the page weight will shift the experience of the narrative is readily complemented by recognizing that different readers are presented with different objects under the guise of a similar "text as experience." Just as the visual and narrative role of Cairo changes depending on which format of *Palestine* one is reading, the entirety of the visual cohesion of *Metro* is changed according to the physical ramifications of its translations.

Locating *Metro*

By beginning this chapter on Magdy El Shafee's *Metro* with a section about Joe Sacco, I hope to achieve a number of comparative aims, much like the scene of Cairo in Sacco's *Palestine*. Like *Palestine*, *Metro*'s publication as a graphic novel was an essential component of its transnational circulation—as well as a key element in its marketing. The Italian edition of *Metro* even features a circle with the words— in English—"Graphic Novel" on the cover. Similarly, the relationship between space and place in both works is noteworthy. As noted, *Metro* is a fictional story, yet it uses the real Cairo subway system, incorporated into the book as subway maps, as a way to visually situate the narrative and the reader. Temporal shifts are demarcated by sections of the Metro map with circles around the stations at which subsequent narrative events occur. And as *Palestine* uses the word *Cairo* in a toponymic and visually affective way, so *Metro*'s subway maps are both locative and visually counterposed with the action of the narrative, which concerns a robbery, political corruption, and growing popular unrest. The maps weave these elements together and work in contrast to El Shafee's impressionistic drawing style. Finally, and most importantly, both works are instantiated as world comics only through acts of translation.

As a journalist, Sacco describes a place for those who are not there. Hence, he writes *Palestine* in English and uses a translator to interview subjects in the work. El Shafee's book is instead written in Arabic, with a readership slightly more ambiguous than Sacco's. While Egyptian professor Iman Hanafy argues that the translation of *Metro* into German, English, and Italian confirms that *Metro* gained "a world-wide acceptance after it [was] banned in Egypt" (422), Edwards argues for the untranslatability of *Metro* outside of Egypt, and James Hodapp and Deema Nasser contend that the book can be qualified as a work of African literature, reflecting broad concerns and cultural traditions from the continent. Considering how each of these scholars interprets *Metro,* its translations, and its translatability, I seek to push argumentation about *Metro* beyond the literary consideration of the graphic novel's translation as a matter of language and themes. As I demonstrate, *Metro*'s singular status as "the first" Egyptian graphic novel and the unique graphic tensions that it embodies as such—its nonstandard layout, its onomatopoeias, its verbal-visual semantics, its interpolation of cartography—create the conditions for disorientation among the readers of the book's multiple translations. Although read as a theoretically consistent narrative across translations, the differing global versions of *Metro* register the struggle and dissensus that occurred in the process of carrying *Metro* across languages and geographic regions.

Following Venuti, I concur that every text is translatable, because every text can be interpreted (*Scandals* x), and yet—as *Metro* makes clear—a graphic narrative is a composite of translatable and untranslatable elements, owing to the commingling of word and image. That is not to say that the images are not themselves interpreted, and I will both adumbrate and consider how these interpretations have been undertaken by critics and translators alike. However, the images and layout of *Metro* create a translational paradox that the existing criticism on El Shafee's work has largely overlooked. Hanafy, Edwards, and Hodapp and Nasser focus on the interpretation of the *words* of *Metro* as a way to gauge its translatability, but as any comics theorist will attest, words and images are not easily sundered in this medium. Although Chip Rossetti and Dominic Davies both consider the spatial composition of *Metro* in terms of mise-en-page and narrative, neither examines how his own theses compare with the other's given that Rossetti is working from a copy of the Egyptian book, and Davies from Rossetti's 2012 English translation.

Indeed, *Metro* foregrounds the instability of domestication and foreignization in translations of graphic narrative. Fragmentary English and Spanish digital translations; book-length Italian, German, and English translations; and the book's Arabic reprinting all constitute unique editions and unique attempts to manage the diversity of semiotic forms—dialogue, onomatopoeias, images, panels, maps— alongside vernacular cultural practices. Each edition constitutes a reinterpretation of the hierarchical organization of these elements in the construction of narrative and the situation of the edition vis-à- vis Cairo as an imagined and historically real location. The comparison of these editions illustrates that this negotiation between textual, visual, cartographic, and historic Cairos produces dissensus within and among editions, disallowing a neat categorization of foreign and domestic in the work.

Metro: A Story of Cairo (2008/2010/2011/2012/2013/2015)

Metro's realist depiction of Cairo as a place contributed to the book's material *dis*placement from Egypt. *Metro* was initially released by Egyptian publisher Malamih in 2008, and banned on its first printing. Officials cited the book for offensive language and sexual content, and El Shafee and his publishers were arrested and fined. *Metro* was specifically condemned for "offending public morals." While there is a brief scene of nudity, many people, including translator Rossetti, believe that the rationale behind *Metro*'s ban was "its bleak view of late-Mubarak-era Egypt" ("Translating" 306). Or, as translator Humphrey Davies suggests, some of the visual details were too recognizable, such as a corrupt politician character who "bears an unfortunately close resemblance to a known public figure . . . This almost guaranteed that it would be confiscated" ("Davies").[4] Because the book balanced a tension between the "fictional" narrative and the realist depictions of location and context, the combination of image and text presented the risk of a certain interpretation by political figures in Cairo. "All copies" (C. Davies; Hanafy 421) of the book were seized by authorities, who "forbade the publisher to print *Metro* again. The police also ordered booksellers to deny all knowledge of the book and delete any relevant data from their computers" (S. Harris). These stipulations resulted in the book's unavailability in Egypt for five years (Holland; Evans-Bush). Thus, the work that would be touted as Egypt's first graphic novel spent little time in circulation in Egypt.

Outside of Egypt, however, *Metro* circulated and proliferated. In 2008 an excerpt was translated into English by Humphrey Davies and published on the website of the organization *Words Without Borders*. In 2010 Ernesto Pagano produced an Italian translation of the work that was published by il Sirente. In 2011 a second edition in Arabic was released in Lebanon through the Comic Shop, an Arabic-language comic book publisher. And in 2012 the Henry Holt and Company imprint Metropolitan Books published the first book-length English edition, translated by Chip Rossetti, while Swiss publisher Edition Moderne produced a German edition from translators Iskandar Abdalla and Stefan Winkler. It was not until 2013 that Arabic-language editions of *Metro* were again sold in Egypt (Qualey; Jaquette).[5] Later, in 2015, the Spanish organization Fundación al

---

4. El Shafee himself confirms this point: "'The political and business figures in this book, they are easily recognisable to the Egyptian public,' said Shafee, who cannot name them publicly for fear of arrest.

'These are very corrupt and disgusting people who rule Egypt, who are in the pockets of the regime, and it is the ordinary people who love Cairo who are suffering'" (Koutsoukis).

5. Cf. Kirk, who states that the book reappeared in Egyptian bookstores in August 2012: "While it's possible that the Morsi regime allowed the return of the book, being all too happy to support negative depictions of its former opponent, it's more likely that the chaotic, less regulated atmosphere of publishing post-Mubarak had more to do with it."

Fanar published a fragmentary translation by Mona Galal, Mónica Carrión, and Pedro Rojo on its website.[6]

Hodapp and Nasser imply that *Metro*'s peregrinations are noteworthy given the Egyptian government's desire to suppress the work and its author: "*Metro*'s ability to travel, given its specific cultural milieu, has been the subject of considerable attention, particularly in the light of the internationally publicized and protracted court proceedings against el-Shafee that threatened him with several years in prison" (26). *Metro* not only represents spatial transit in its form and content; it became a work in transit, spending more time in print and digital circulation throughout countries and linguistic regions other than Egypt.

Frequently cited as lacking a precedent or a national tradition in Egypt, *Metro* is alternately referred to as "Egypt's first graphic novel" (Jaggi)[7] or as the "first adult Arabic graphic novel" (H. Davies, "from *Metro*"). As M. Lynx Qualey notes in *Egypt Independent,* more than *Metro*'s content, it is perhaps *Metro*'s graphic novelty and thus transnational generic comprehensibility that made it rotten for Egyptian censors and ripe for cultural translatability:

> Many far racier books remain on the local market. Yet few paint as vivid a picture of corruption at the opening of the 21st century. And perhaps none are as accessible as "Metro," which is written in a colloquial language that is spicy at times, and illustrated in Shafee's hyper-kinetic, multi-layered, sometimes chaotic style.

---

6. Denominations for editions are difficult owing to the linguistically ambiguous yet politically inflexible borders through which *Metro* passes. Both editions from Dar al-Malāmih and the Comic Shop are in Arabic, yet I use the 2008 edition (which I refer to as the Arabic edition), as it also provides the basis for most of the other editions. Meanwhile, although I frequently call Abdalla and Winkler's version "the German translation," this is a heuristic, as the publisher is Swiss. Although both Abdalla and Winkler frequently reside in Germany, Abdalla emigrated from Egypt, making it not entirely incorrect, if unbearably wordy, to refer to this book as an Egyptian-German-Swiss text. Moreover, because both Davies and Rossetti write their translations in English—with the distinction of British vs. US provenances—I frequently refer to their translations by the translator's name, or specify Rossetti's as the US edition. Yet I do so fully aware that, especially in the case of a large corporate publisher like Henry Holt, many others contribute to the editorial process and the production of the text. Further, because Holt is a multinational company, calling Rossetti's the US edition ignores its circulation in Canada and other anglophone nations.

7. It is worth noting that the "Godfather of Egyptian Graphic Novelists," as Jaggi terms him, was born in Libya.

Therefore, its seeming incongruity or originality makes *Metro* susceptible to both national sanction and transnational imagination. El Shafee notes that it is forbidden to mock politicians in cartoons in Egypt (Jaggi), and yet the book's taboo determination to expose prerevolutionary corruption is often cited by critics as its most important reflection of Egypt. *Metro*'s literal and material translatability is brokered by its untranslatability as a singular national object received by extranational consumers as an authentic, generic representation of the revolutionary zeitgeist.

The narrative follows engineer Shehab and his friend Mustafa as they rob a bank in order to escape from a loan shark and inadvertently become caught up in a murder conspiracy. Shehab's love interest, Dina, is a reporter who frequents protests, and much of the book explores class hierarchies, political and economic corruption, and police violence. As the US translation's book jacket notes: "Magdy El Shafee has delivered a prescient portrait of a crumbling society and Egypt's coming eruption . . . *Metro* sounds the cry for a better, freer, future" (Rossetti n. pag.). This perception of the work, shared by many US reviewers, reveals how a so-called Western reader, reading in English, might orient themselves to the work in light of recent geopolitical events in Egypt.

The same incongruity that led to its banning in Egypt thus appeals to a Western imaginary. Indeed, much of the press coverage and marketing of *Metro*'s translations reflect only slightly subtler versions of Swiss publisher Edition Moderne's announcement "In Ägypten verboten!"[8] The specific terms of the ban—immoral images and similarities to living political figures—are used as a marketing device on the back cover of the Italian translation. El Shafee's US literary agent actually states that he "was working with Magdy before the revolution but I waited until Mubarak resigned to sell it" (qtd. in C. Davies), making explicit the investment in a retroactive reading of the book as a Western-oriented explainer of recent events. How can one understand the so-called Arab Spring and its source? Just read *Metro*.

Metro's literal and material translatability is facilitated by its untranslatability as a singular object—the first Arabic graphic novel. It orients Western consumers as an authentically Oriental, yet recognizable object—the graphic novel, that, because of its condemnation by governmental forces, appears to be oriented toward the revolu-

8. This selling point is listed on the publisher's website, https://www.edition-moderne.ch/buch/metro-kairo-im-untergrund/.

tionary zeitgeist. Hanafy goes so far as to call the graphic novel "a revolutionary genre" (422) and to claim of *Metro* that "in light of what occurred in 2011, El Shafee's novel almost looks as if it ushered in that critically important Egyptian event: the Egyptian Revolution" (430). Indeed, Humphrey Davies refers to the book as "uncannily prescient" ("Davies") in its ability to depict a historically accurate Cairo on the verge of upheaval.

From this account, it would seem that *Metro* presents the Western reader with a proximity to danger in the trope of a backward regime incapable of understanding literary forms (specifically, the graphic novel) that have already been embraced in Europe and the US. As marketed through its association with risk, the book affirms the superiority of the Western reader in collusion with the burgeoning democratic spirit of the Arab Spring. Consequently, the Western reading subject, intellectually prepared for novelty to enter the world, understands the value of *Metro* as an object of world literature. The book that was impossible in its originary location finds a new home in exile thanks to translational appeal.

Whence and Whither *Metro?*

Although *Metro* has been heralded as a ready-made export for Western consumption, not all scholars are in consensus about its translatability; nor are all readers engaging with the same *Metro.* Even Hanafy, writing from Benha University in Egypt, uses Rossetti's translation as the basis for her critical reading of *Metro.* She characterizes the book in a didactic framework that presumes a readership outside the immediate context of the book's setting: "El Shafee's graphic novel helps the readers to understand partially what caused the riots that led to overthrow of Egyptian President Mubarak" (432). By contrast, other scholars have challenged such an assessment of the graphic novel's intended audience or exigence.

In his book *After the American Century: The Ends of US Culture in the Middle East,* Edwards constructs a provocative thesis regarding commerce between the US and the Middle East. Edwards argues that digital pathways of cultural transfer as well as shifting attitudes toward the US in the twenty-first century have, contrary to popular opinion, *not* extended the hegemony of American culture so much as fragmented the meanings of "American cultural objects and forms"

(1) in North Africa and the Middle East. Edwards investigates a number of case studies of what might otherwise be referred to as glocalization—the local revision of globally circulated cultural products (films, poems, books, literary forms, etc.). The chapter "Jumping Publics: Egyptian Fictions of the Digital Age" examines transnational exchanges that take place in literary forms and genres between Egypt and the US in order to see how some objects or concepts "jump publics." For Edwards, while it is assumed that US cultural forms and products circulate widely throughout global networks of neoliberal transactions, in actuality, some cultural products represent end points of circulation. Edwards thus explores the "limits of American models of democracy as they are imagined in the West as exportable products" (35). He focuses on Cairo and shows how the "Arab Spring" in 2011 led to a revisitation of the "narratives by which Orientalist tradition had previously translated a storied city" (35). As Edwards contends, the narratives around the #Jan25 uprising in America reflected more about US ideologies and imaginations than it did about Egypt (42).

Mutatis mutandis, Edwards tracks how US forms were reimagined in Cairo, devoting the majority of his chapter to *Metro.* He cites both Sacco's page from *Palestine* and American superhero comics as sources from which El Shafee formally and culturally borrows in *Metro* (59). Yet Edwards critiques the assumption that the reception of comics in Cairo is part of a process "in which US cultural forms contribute to making a new Egypt, a new Arab world, crafted in an image with which the West can . . . feel comfortable" (55). Instead, he considers how these American forms were excavated of translatable meaning and how *Metro,* in particular, "leav[es] behind the register familiar to Western readers. It is an example of the end of circulation from which an outside form cannot return to legibility. *Metro* cherishes its very locality" (56). Although he offers few specific examples, Edwards contends that the references in *Metro* are not intelligible to a reader who is unfamiliar with the locations and situations depicted in the work. *Metro,* in Edwards's view, does not intrinsically speak to the West but instead takes a "Western form"—comics—and creates a work that is explicitly addressed to a Cairene reading public. However much Edwards credits *Metro* with "foreshadowing the #Jan25 movement of 2011" (61), he also stipulates that the work does not "jump publics" to the US as a "translatable value." Edwards further describes his own struggles in translating a different El Shafee comic, given that the "Egyptian Arabic used is especially colloquial" (68). As Edwards contends, El Shafee's comics ultimately prove impossible to translate because the intended reading public for his work must be conversant in the transnational references and form of comics as well as the local Egyptian references and dialect.

Edwards's argument that *Metro* contains a number of references that only an Egyptian readership would grasp is countered by James Hodapp and Deema Nasser in their chapter "The Complications of Reading Egypt as Africa: Translation and Magdy el-Shafee's المترو (Metro)." For Hodapp and Nasser, Edwards and similarly inclined theorists have done a disservice to the study of *Metro* by positioning it always as "World literature and Arabic literature rather than African literature" (22). They consider *Metro* against Rebecca Walkowitz's category of literature that is "born translated" or "written for translation from the start" (Walkowitz 3). Although one might assume that *Metro,* a worldly text from its first publication and subsequent circulation, is the type of book Walkowitz describes when considering those works that "start as world literature" (2), Hodapp and Nasser demur by examining the original Arabic work and its US translation to argue that "*Metro* is a graphic novel with an inherent African reading public" (25). As Africanists, the authors claim that Edwards fails to acknowledge *Metro* as an African work by concentrating solely on the relationship between Cairo and the US.

One basic problem they find in his analysis is the myopia with which Edwards considers the "West" and the "Middle East" as the only nodes in a circuit of translation and transnational exchange for *Metro.* As Hodapp and Nasser stipulate, both English and Arabic are primary or national languages in a number of African nations, which share other cultural and political points of comparison with Cairo. The authors stress that reading *Metro* as an African text is not easy but is important for the recognition and establishment of African literary studies. Such a unified field is undermined by the "rift" instantiated through readings like Edwards's as well as by the specifics of *Metro*'s translation.

Hodapp and Nasser also take issue with Rossetti's translation and the way in which it changes or Westernizes *Metro.* They analyze how Rossetti's translation both "flatten[s] experiences in the narrative that would resonate with African publics" and "reorients political elements to support the claim by *Metro*'s American publisher that it presages the 2011 Tahrir Square demonstrations often characterized as part of the 'Arab Spring'" (32). They do not lodge the same critiques against Humphrey Davies's partial English translation, which they contrast with Rossetti's in terms of accuracy and intent. They object further to specific translations of lines within the text as well as the US version's attribution of a line in the book to Hosni Mubarak. For Hodapp and Nasser, these translational particulars are further evidence of the intent to demonize Mubarak and depict protagonists like Shehab and Dina as liberal proto-revolutionaries. This particular interpretation, they argue, goes against the narrative itself, in which no revolution actually occurs:

> *Metro* is not about revolution though and ends bleakly with one character betraying another to escape and two others finding no solution to their predicament . . . It is this sense of being overwhelmed, rather than optimistic, that imbues the novel, gesturing away from Western, particularly American narratives of meritocracy towards more historically prevalent African ways of living in the corrupted ruins of empire. (34)

Admittedly, Hodapp and Nasser offer a broad-brushstrokes conceptualization of divergent reading publics. Nevertheless, their analysis serves as a valuable reminder that translation is necessarily interpretive. Their central point of critique turns on the way that Rossetti's translation interprets *Metro* for Western readers, and they use counterinterpretations to justify their thesis.

On the other hand, Edwards questions the translatability of El Shafee's comics—not only *Metro* but also "The Parkour War"—by looking specifically at ways in which his comics "defy translation" (83) or fail to reproduce the specific relation of the work to "the public it addresses" (69). The view on translation that Edwards proposes is what Venuti would call instrumentalist, suggesting the possibility of a direct transfer of meaning from source to target, one that is, in this case, defied. But, and this is essential, insofar as Edwards is correct that certain formal elements—what Venuti calls *interpretants* (*Contra* 2)—may serve as direct or indirect impediments to an instrumental translation, El Shafee's works *are* translated. In fact, Edwards himself translated "The Parkour War," a short collaboration work by El Shafee and Ahmed Alaidy. In Edwards's own translation, the question of trying to make the *meaning* legible to a new audience is the central focus, rather than the question of how to translate form.

Given that Edwards describes *Metro* as "about the cage of Cairo and the impossibility of escaping it" (61), the role of spatiality in the composition of the book is an intrinsic component of its central thematic and one that creates an issue for translators. While Edwards's examination of the translatability of El Shafee's comics extends beyond the linguistic translation, his claim that "the graphics advance its meaning more surely than do plot or text" (63) demonstrates a misrecognition—perhaps founded on his reliance on McCloud for formal analysis—of the imbricated way that images and text correlate to narrative in comics. Instead of imagining comics as composed of separable or even quantitatively comparable meaning-making forms, the project of reading for difference must attend to the inseparable combination of "graphics" with text in space and diegetic time. Among the diverging views of Hanafy, Edwards, and Hodapp and Nasser, translatability is assessed according to how *Metro* is interpreted by readerships in spaces outside of Cairo, but for the sake of comics studies, it is just as important to consider how different readerships—translators—have interpreted spaces *inside* of Cairo as they are graphically composed in *Metro*.

Translating Sound

Already well established in French-language comics scholarship, theories of page layout such as those noted above by Fresnault-Deruelle, Peeters, and Groensteen[9] have been much slower to infiltrate scholarship in the US, perhaps owing to McCloud's focus on sequence over page surface as the central model for understanding comics. Although sequence—as in the sequential succession of panels, images, and words—is a central component of the technicity of comics, a singular focus on sequence often obscures the ways that comics, as Hatfield states, "exploit *format* as a signifier in itself; more specifically, that comics involve a tension between the experience of reading in sequence and the format or shape of the object being read" (52). Hanafy, Edwards, and Hodapp and Nasser focus most of their interpretation of *Metro* on its translatability as a story pictorially and verbally developed in sequence.

---

9. Also belonging on this list: Baetens, Lefèvre, Smolderen, and Chavanne, among others.

Focusing instead on the translations of form, or formal elements, gives a very different picture of *Metro*'s translatability. *Metro*'s page layouts require concerted attention to the shifts enacted through translation. That is not to say that layout is separable from other page elements, as Groensteen explains:

> The page layout does not operate on empty panels, but must take into account their contents. It is an instrument in the service of a global artistic project, frequently subordinated to a narrative, or, at least, discursive, aim; if it submits a priori to some formal rule that constrains the contents and, in a certain way, creates them, the page layout is generally elaborated from a semantically determined content, where the breakdown has already assured discretization in successive enunciations known as panels. (92)

Among the varying *Metros* in existence, a number of idiosyncrasies are notable in the relationship Groensteen articulates between the contents, panels, and formal constraints. Similarly, in the translations, different prioritizations of sequence or surface cohesion create entirely different texts.

The different texts meaningfully demonstrate how comics provide new vantages onto translation theory. Rather than staid concepts of foreignization and domestication, translations of comics feature multiple points of translatability that are sometimes at odds with each other or with the compositional themes of a work. In order to orient an English reader to the text, the Rossetti translation flips the direction of the pages from the right-to-left orientation of the Arabic. None of the other translations follow in the flipping of pages, but they feature other translational markers to alert readers to the "difference" of the text.

Some of these differences multiply through the tension of code versus code, or "image and written text" (36), as articulated by Hatfield. As Hatfield notes, in comics this distinction is not a stable dialectic:

> Comics, like other hybrid texts, collapse the word/image dichotomy: visible language has the potential to be quite elaborate in appearance, forcing recognition of pictorial and material qualities that can be freighted with meaning . . . conversely, images can be simplified and codified to function as a language. (36–37)

Translation scholar José Yuste Frías elaborates further to contend that in a translation the text will "guide the interpretation of the image" while the "image provides an orientation for the reading of the text," yet images are not universal, complicating further this complementarity (255). *Metro*'s use of language is frequently inextricable from or extricable only at the expense of the images it accompanies. Thus in the English, German, and Italian versions, the translator and/or editors interpret panels and image-text combinations variably.

Among many categorizations of text types in comics, Nadine Celotti identifies "four loci of translation": balloons, captions, titles, and the whole group of "verbal signs inside the drawing: inscriptions, road signs, newspapers, onomatopoeia, sometimes dialogues, and so on" (38–39). While the first three text types will generally undergo a translation (Celotti says "always"), the fourth provides the most variability, as some translators will treat "sound words" and inscriptions as part of the picture rather than as a linguistic element (39). For Celotti—as for other comics translation scholars—the relative shape and containment, or lack thereof, will play a large role in determining how much and whether texts within and outside the panels will be translated. Federico Zanettin describes the assumptions underlying this "constrained approach" to comics translation, which treats only words enclosed in boxes or balloons as translatables and assumes the universal meaning of images (21). Instead, as Yuste Frías, Celotti, and Zanettin all argue, visual elements, including verbal signs within a drawing, are culturally interpretable as well, entailing that a translation will determine whether and how to translate these verbal elements in ways that prioritize one interpretation at the expense of others.

The German translation of *Metro* includes a note on the "sound-words" which were left in Arabic in order to produce a story that was "faithful to the original." But given the state of the work as a banned text, the ability to discern the significatory import of all the markings on the page was not always easy; nor was concretization of "the original" *Metro* necessarily possible for its translators. In conversation, Rossetti explained the difficulties that he had with obtaining a full text for his own translation:

> It was hard to get a copy that was not a copy of a copy . . . I would go to book fairs in the Arab world and would desperately look to see if anyone has a copy of El Shafee's *Metro*. It was a Borgesian

book that didn't exist. I really had to ask Magdy himself: "I can't read what's here because it's greyed out." I knew there were things where I could see that it wasn't right, and I could only see when I finally got the proofs at the end. Magdy was being very careful about what he would send out online. He may not have had the file from Egypt, it might have been stored elsewhere. I had to keep asking: "Do you have a better resolution of this? I can't see what's on this page." (Telephone interview with the author)

In Rossetti's description of *Metro*'s Borgesian existence, the concept of the "original" is thrown into doubt. Karen Emmerich has argued that it is in fact translations and later editions that create "originals." Rather than derivative "copies" or lesser versions, Emmerich asserts that translations are interpretive forms (26) that simultaneously indicate the instability of literary originals and create the concept of an original text which they interpret.[10]

Every version of *Metro* evinces different choices that in turn gesture toward differing interpretations. Owing to the proliferation of sound words throughout the book, there are countless sites of translational deliberation, from a panel with a subway train rushing into the station to a phone ringing. The subway train appears on the second page and is overwritten with a series of ﺟs (*wāw*s). In the short Spanish excerpt, the Arabic letters appear without any translation. In Davies's translation of the same page, the original Arabic letters accompanying the train are overlaid with a series of "w"s; the German similarly preserves the Arabic while adding "RATTATTAT" below. Pagano's and Rossetti's translations both erase the Arabic letters, but in the Italian version, the Arabic is replaced by "w"s, while the US translation adds the word "WHOOSH." Each version of the same panel (see figure 2.2) demonstrates a distinct interpretation of the relation between the onomatopoetic letters and the image.

Based solely on these differences in the interpretation of a single panel, one can acknowledge, as W. J. T. Mitchell states, how "the relationship between words and images reflects, within the realm of representation, signification, and communication, the relations we posit between symbols and the world, signs and their meaning" (43). Floating letters indicating the sound of an approaching train relate

---

10. And as Thomas A. Bredehoft notes, comics are "always implicated in an economy of reproduction" (134).

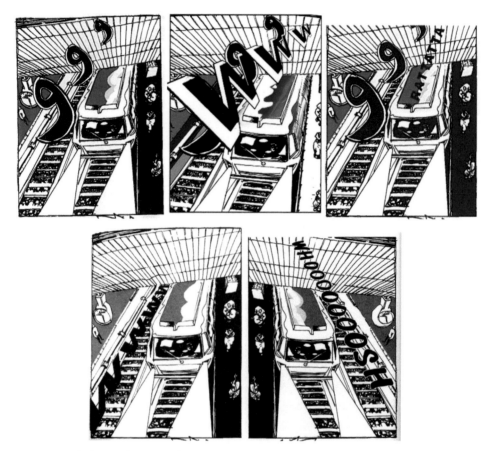

FIGURE 2.2. Left to right, top to bottom: Comparison of panel from Arabic, English, German, Italian, and US *Metros*

to the space of the page as well as to the relative correlation between image, letter, sound, and context, and result in consistently inconsistent interpretations of how a "sound word" functions within a pictorial plane. The rendering of the "word" itself, at an angle parallel to the train, suggests that a reader see it as a pictorial element, taking part in the two-dimensional representation of three-dimensional space. An orientation to the sound word as a pictorial, as opposed to linguistic, element, corresponds to the Spanish translation's decision to leave the letters in Arabic. On the other hand, Davies, Abdalla, and Winkler treat the letters as verbal enough to need a translation mounted atop or below them, yet pictorial enough to demand their inclusion alongside the "translations." As suggested by Pagano's and Rossetti's texts, these translations all vary in terms of whether they treat the و as representative of a sound requiring an aural correlate ("RATTATTAT" or "WHOOSH") or as a letter that may be transferred into a Latinate script as "w" with no further modification.

These differing interpretations of how the image and text unify in the service of the narrative present a limited example of what amounts to a profusion of differing ideas about signs and their meaning within the contexts of comics composition writ large and *Metro* in particular. *Metro* is chock-full of sounds emanating from people, electronic devices, various forms of transportation, and weapons. The translations' approaches to these letters indicate differing orientations within linguistic and cultural systems of recognizing sound as image or text. Each translation encodes implicit readerly and viewerly assumptions about how to render an image-text that complicate the distinction in meaning between the terms "image" and "text."

Translating Space

Metro offers another form of code-based tension through its employment of maps and map fragments. A Cairo subway map—a digitally produced, abstract representation of space—begins every narrative section, showing where the characters are, based on the nearest subway stop. Throughout the book, *Metro* juxtaposes one specific cartographic orienting technique with others. The maps in panels, as background, or as full splash page, share representational space with images of landmarks, characters moving through space and time, and words announcing location as well as transit between locations (see figure 2.3). The multiplication of these techniques destabilizes the sovereignty of any one and creates multiperspectival tabular compositions, where the map of the subway station is interwoven with the surrounding cityscape (as drawn images) and the narrator's commentary (as text). Accordingly, the translations' varying methods of dealing with the maps as spaces of representation or representations of space produce epistemologically diverse grasps of the spatiotemporal situation of maps within the book.

Scholars have interpreted *Metro*'s repeated use of maps in different ways. For Dominic Davies, the map is used in such a way to

FIGURE 2.3. Magdy El Shafee, *Metro*, pages 32–33

evoke[ ] the flattening, telescopic perspective of the neoliberal urban planner. The gridded infrastructure of the metro, which transforms the heterogeneity and density of Cairo's urban fabric into a series of regimented lines and clearly labelled locations, functions metaphorically as both a cartographic and material embodiment of oppressive urban governance. (*Urban Comics* 62)

Davies largely supports his interpretation through the final scene of the narrative in which Shehab and love interest Dina realize the hopelessness of their predicament and decide to "get out of this tunnel" (Rossetti, *Metro* 91). Yet Davies also allows that at times Shehab is able to use the subway tunnels as a way to avoid capture amid the omnipresent surveillance state aboveground.

Rossetti instead describes the metro system as the book's organizing metaphor, one which "symbolizes the hidden lines that connect a city of vast socioeconomic differences" ("Translating" 307). Rossetti contrasts the visual composition of panels that tend to represent the vertical hierarchy of the city through angles viewing subjects either from above or below with the hidden, unseen, horizontal network of connections shown through the "neat lines" of the metro map (318). For Rossetti, there is a direct tension between what Hatfield would describe as single image versus image in sequence in that the maps and the panels create different perspectival orientations—evoking a sense of socioeconomic difference.

Although their readings differ, both Davies and Rossetti conceptualize the maps metaphorically, even using the term *metaphor* in their analyses. However, from a comics studies vantage, it is important to think beyond the hermeneutic, in order to analyze how the maps work in variegated semiotic and material registers. As Zanettin asserts: "From a semiotic point of view, the translation of comics is thus concerned with different layers of interpretative activities, which can be variously conceptualized as inter- or intra-semiotic or systemic, depending on one's definition of system" (12). To return to Hatfield's conception, maps create a triplicate dilemma of encoding and decoding in that they are positioned in the same picture plane as the pictorial images, and yet they function as a distinct way of representing three-dimensional space through text and image. Whether a translation treats the map as a linguistic or a pictorial signifying space differs in each edition's approach.

The Pagano translation replaces all the subway maps from the Arabic edition with other maps of the Cairo subway but makes no change in the book's singular use of a street map. Thus, for the Italian text, there is a meaningful difference between what a subway map says and what a street map shows. The subway maps are interchangeable in their content and composition—they give information. The street map must then—by dint of the difference in treatment—visually or aesthetically signify in meaningful ways.[11]

Alternately, the Rossetti translation replaces all maps, using the subway map in place of the street map (figure 2.4), as if to edit the Arabic edition through visual coherence. This translation marks a categorical difference between map and image, ultimately determining that a map is not an image insofar as it can be replaced with no effect

---

11. I was unable, in my research, to locate the distinct map objects used in the different versions of *Metro*. However, a simple Google search reveals images that resemble the network maps, including one attributed to R. Shwandl at UrbanRail. net, and updated 2006, 2012, and 2014, and one located at Wikimedia commons, authored by Jpatokal and dated 2008.

FIGURE 2.4. Chip Rossetti, translator, *Metro*, pages 36–37

on the visual composition. Hodapp and Nasser object to this inter-pretation and explicitly critique the decision to replace the maps as more evidence of the "cultural manipulation" of the US translation. They argue that the replacement maps efface the Egyptian history expressed in the originals and do not even "depict the same geo-graphic spaces that are in the original" (34). To be sure, as Hodapp and Nasser point out, this change in the map itself constitutes an interpretive rewriting of the graphic work. By determining that the graphic appearance of the map was not integral to the visual narra-tive, the US translation devalues the map's function in the visual nar-rative to merely locating the characters.

Here Hatfield's tension between image and text must be reimag-ined in order to account for the tensions between different spaces of representation and representations of space. That is, maps, text, and images have their own culturally situated, epistemological models by which a reader orients herself to the marking system. Fascinat-ingly, between the Italian and US translations, two distinct views of the map as—in Tom Conley's terms—a cartographic idiolect in the context of the comics idiom emerge. As Conley specifies of a similar encounter—the appearance of a map in the field of a film—the appearance of maps in the *planche* or compositional plane of comics introduces issues of "perspective, visual style, narrative economy, scale, [comics] and history, the stakes of mimesis, and reception" (2). The Italian edition treats the subway map as an informatic image-text. Its appearance is contained by the representational plane of the page in a way that does not interact with the picture plane but is instead ancillary to it. For the US translation, all maps are given merely an informatic, positioning function. These systems only articulate location as opposed to representationally or aesthetically signifying within the composition.

The Italian and US translations also leave untranslated the contents but not the headlines of a newspaper depicted on page 45, while the German translation also renders the contents of the articles in German, again drawing attention to how each translation or edition treats the relationship between representational regimes and the world. Do maps or even newspapers function as representations of space, or are they merely units within spaces of representation? The varying interpretations evince radically different approaches to cultural techniques such as cartography, typography, and drawing within the space of the same page.

Nodes and Networks

By Hatfield's schema, the use of maps engenders a crisis in the tension of code versus code. The maps (and newspaper contents) seem to form differential readings between the imagistic and the verbal, yet the maps also create different readings in terms of the other tensions described by Hatfield—specifically those of single image versus image in sequence, and sequence versus surface. The imbrication of cartographic, textual, and pictorial marking systems locates both reader and characters in the city through multiple transitions between places and times. It also creates translational dilemmas between space and sequence.

Metro's narrative temporality is mapped, literally, in that the narrator, Shehab, begins at Mohamed Naguib Station in the narrative present, until four pages later the subway map showing the station

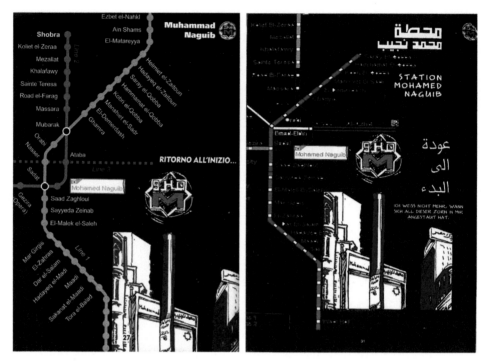

FIGURE 2.5. Ernesto Pagano, translator, *Metro,* page 27 (left); and Iskandar Ahmad Abdalla and Stefan Winkler, translators, *Metro,* page 31 (right).

precedes a flashback sequence keeping the characters in the same spatial proximity while delineating the temporal lapse. The return to "the present" is later indicated with a full-page spread of the metro map, with Mohamed Naguib Station outlined and, in the Arabic, Italian, and German editions, also highlighted in white (figures 2.3 and 2.5). This splash-page map recalls the earlier fragment of the map with a difference: as Groensteen notes, narration in comics is "pluri-vectoral," meaning that a reader makes sense of a given panel based on preceding panels as well as on panels that are within the same page or picture plane as the panel itself. Thus, the reader understands the second map of Mohamed Naguib Station as being larger than, as well as a black-white color-inverse of, the earlier map.

How the map then relates to narrative sequence or overall thematic and aesthetic import depends on what Groensteen calls *tressage,* or *braiding.* Groensteen's schema differs from Hatfield's in that it describes the system of comics in terms of mise-en-page (or layout), sequence, and braiding. Groensteen describes iconic solidarity as the definitional tenet of comics: "interdependent images that, participating in a series, present the double characteristic of being separated . . . and which are plastically and semantically over-determined by the fact of their coexistence in praesentia" (*System* 18). As he notes, these images, in the form of panels, may be apprehended at once, enter into dialogue across a page, or even across the work itself, "establishing relationships among non-adjacent pages" ("Braiding" 89). The maps of Mohamed Naguib Station thus shift their meaning in the narrative based on their repetition. The text spurs a reader to visually recognize the map the second time it is shown and to interpret this repetition.

In this particular instance, the second map is overlaid with text that, in Arabic, states as a direction to the reader, "عودة العو لبدء," or, "return to the start." The Pagano and Davies translations both render the text similarly: "Ritorno all'inizio" and "Return to the present. Shihab and Mustafa set off to rob a bank," respectively. Pagano translates literally, as if secure in the ability of the reader to recognize that the Mohamed Naguib Station is also where the story began and that the reader will understand the return to the narrative present from the map and the verbal directive. On the other hand, Davies gives the reader slightly more of a narrative synopsis as a way to further explain what "return to the present" means in the context of the narrative. Alternately, both the German and the US translations reprint the opening line of narration from the first page ("Ich Weiss Nicht Mehr, Wann Sich All Dieser Zorn in Mir Angestaut Hat" and "I don't remember when I became so angry") on top of the map, as a means of verbally signaling how the map and the text work together (see figure 2.5 and figure 2.7). The German edition also keeps the Arabic text, creating a profusion of signs in which the German line from the start of the book fulfills—literally—the Arabic injunction above it, changing the meaning of the map from a spatiotemporal signifier to a background image.

Further, because the US edition standardizes all the maps—even the street map—into subway maps, the appearance of the street map on page 37 at Anwar Sadat Station is deprived of its particular significance in the network of map images (see figure 2.4). Hodapp and Nasser decry the substitution's focus on train stations at the expense of roads labeled with English and French place names (34) as well as the complete erasure of the accompanying quotation from Sadat. As they write:

[The excised quote] translates into: "This isn't a popular uprising . . . This is a thieves' uprising" . . . The statement is significant in light of the original context as it detaches itself from inciting sentiments of popular revolt and instead insinuates that those demonstrating are not innocent but rather those who want to take as much power as they can for themselves. (34)[12]

From a visual perspective, the street map is unique in its mimetic and representational capacity, especially as an incongruity in a series of other maps. Its appearance forces greater attention to the page and the context. As in Groensteen's formation, its presence is overdetermined by the co-existence of other maps in near identical composition but with entirely different symbolic idioms. The US version instead creates a continuity of maps throughout the book, making a visually consistent, yet distinct interpretation of how and why the maps are included.

Sequence versus Surface

For Rossetti, *Metro* "depicts the character of the city through the spatial organization of images" ("Translating" 314). Rossetti points to the necessarily spatialized narrativity of all comics, and specifically examines how the "anti-human nature of space in Cairo" (315) is enacted through El Shafee's use of "spatial organization of the illustrations" (320). Yet, this organization is changed in the very translation Rossetti worked on. Considering how the maps and the page layouts play into Hatfield's tension of sequence versus surface reveals further differences in interpretations and readerly orientations.

In Rossetti's translation, pages with more than one panel are flipped so that a reader follows the narrative from left to right. The subway maps are separately reproduced for the English version, thus operating as an indicator of the reorientation of the work, in that they are not flipped along with the page but are reproduced in order to keep the same schematic as the original. This decision is indicative of a particular set of culturally and ideologically inflected judgments about reading and visual interpretation. From the perspective of page layout, the unique simultaneity of the page "as sequence and as

12. In our interview, Rossetti attested that he had translated the quotation and could not explain why it was not included in Metropolitan's published version of *Metro* (telephone interview with author).

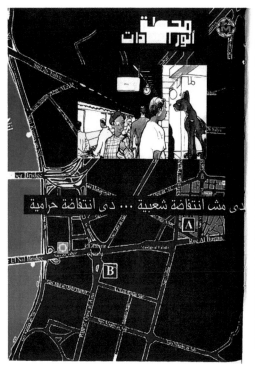

FIGURE 2.6. Magdy El Shafee, *Metro,* pages 42–43

object, to be seen and read in both linear and nonlinear holistic fashion" (Hatfield 48) is changed entirely through the US recomposition of map space.

One telling example demonstrates how the flipping of pages and maps intervenes in the relations between surface and sequence. Pages 33 and 43 in the Arabic version resemble each other in terms of composition (see figures 2.3 and 2.6). Both feature splash-page maps with a black background and toponymic information rendered in white. Both pages occur at pivotal moments in the story and work as a counterbalance to pages 32 and 42 in terms of narrative and composition. These two maps bring a reader "forward" visually and narratively, with curving lines that draw focus to the end of the two-page spread and toward the next page. The first map—as mentioned above—is the subway map at Mohamed Naguib Station that brings the reader "back to the start." The panels on the preceding page stand in contrast based on their all-white composition as well as their narrative position in the past, at the moment that Shehab decided to rob a bank. The full two-page planche, or composition, thus brings together present and

past, and narratively leads a reader "forward" from the panels depicting Shehab's decision directly to the "Back to the start" text, which is
positioned adjacent to Shehab's speech balloon and leads the reader
visually from balloon *cum* bank-robbery decision to narrative exhortation to symbol of the station on the subway map, positioned at the
leftmost edge of page 33. The composition provides narrative momentum as the reader visually moves from past to present and to the edge
of the page, which, when turned, begins the bank-robbery sequence.

Page 42 depicts the end of the robbery sequence and shows Shehab and his accomplice, Mustafa, departing into the subway in the
final panel of the page, which directly leads to the large street map
on page 43. The page again draws the reader from the event forward
into a new space, one limned on the leftmost edge by the Nile. These
two compositions create a narrative counterpoint: the two moments
provide the exigence for the narrative arc. Although it is not known at
the moment, page 42 also provides a key panel that is later repeated
as a way to explain the corruption that Shehab and Mustafa unwittingly enter into through their robbery. Pages 33 and 43, by their juxtaposition, are "predisposed to speak" (Groensteen, *System* 35) to the
preceding pages and, by means of what Groensteen calls tressage, or
braiding, they will also speak to each other through their compositional similarities such that these pages become "isomorphs" and resonate with each other across multiple pages.

Yet, in the US version, the specificities of the mise-en-page on
pages 33 and 43 (or 27 and 37 in the US version)—the way the maps
work as organizational units within a contiguous composition—are
fundamentally changed. The subway map on 27 no longer curves
toward the edge of the page; it now curves inward toward the book
spine and precedes the accompanying text, shifting the narrative
sequence within the composition (figure 2.7). Because the subway
map is used on both pages 27 and 37, the text no longer draws attention to the important difference between the subway and the street
and to what this difference might visually imply for the composition
(see figure 2.7 and figure 2.4). A judgment is made about the relative
importance of the map as it references a space external to the page
and the map as an internal unit of spatial design.

The judgment that the US edition evinces in terms of linguistic
versus compositional orientation has a radical transformative effect
for the panel contents. Because the direction of panels—but not
maps—is made to follow the direction of English, the majority of panels have images and texts that are backwards. The drivers of cars and

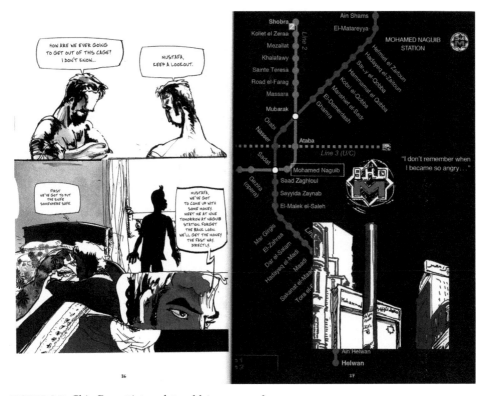

FIGURE 2.7. Chip Rossetti, translator, *Metro,* pages 26–27

trains suddenly appear on the right side of their vehicles, the opposite of where drivers are situated in Cairo. Arabic-language inscriptions on buildings, or in other "background" spaces of panels, are
printed backwards, and buildings and statues are reversed, such as
the statue of Ibrahim Basha, who now points with his left hand rather
than his right. Because a couple of panels are not flipped, the main
character, Shehab, suddenly becomes ambidextrous. From Rossetti's
view, the changes were made for an intended audience of US readers, who would be unlikely to notice the incongruities; as Rossetti
notes, "even a real Cairene might not remember which way the Pasha
statue is pointing" (telephone interview with the author). However,
the flipped images and unflipped maps posit a certain theory of realism and signs: the map is understood as a visual object from outside
the narrative, one whose visual reality must be preserved even at the
risk of the composition.

What's more, while the US edition is generally the most egregious
in its revision of sequence and surface relations, the German edition

is likewise noteworthy in its curious vertical flipping of the fourth-to-last page. In the Arabic edition, this page appears upside down as a kind of hidden response to Shehab's question at the end of the preceding page as to why the bank robbery was never reported. The upside-down page features a small narrative box next to an image of Shehab and explains "What Shehab didn't know . . ." The upside-down panels—which a reader must flip to read—begin with a panel from page 42, in which the bank director is ordered by a corrupt politician to disavow the politician's involvement. In the subsequent panels, the director orders his subordinates to destroy all evidence of the money ever having existed at the bank. As Rossetti describes the layout of this page:

> In flipping the book upside down to view the otherwise "hidden" panels and illegible words, the reader participates as both protagonist and author: like the protagonist, he finds a truth that exists below, one that must be brought to the surface to be understood—in this case, the corrupt means by which the bank will keep the loss of the stolen money off their books. The reader also becomes his own graphic novelist, as he manipulates the visual space of the page in order to construct the narrative. ("Translating" 320)

In both the US and the German editions, this page is (despite Rossetti's interpretation) not printed upside down.[13] Of the three full translations, only the Italian retains the vertical flipping. The US edition does not even include the narrative box with small Shehab icon at the top of the page; the German edition keeps this box but places it at the top of a page in which the box is no longer set in opposition to the direction of the panels below, and therefore no longer indicates the "hidden" truth Rossetti describes.

Text as Object versus Text as Experience

The specificities of print cultures are also evident in the tension—Hatfield's fourth—between *Metro* as a reading experience and *Metro* as a physical object. The Humphrey Davies translation of *Metro*, as

13. Rossetti expressed dismay at this decision by editors: "I think it was a missed opportunity to retain some of those themes that I say obviously the artist wanted in there and would not have hurt the book much or made it incomprehensible to readers" (telephone interview with the author).

an online fragment, presents a distinct reading experience in that all pages are displayed in a vertical scroll, allowing a reader to apprehend all of them at the same time. Pages are not flipped; they are presented with Arabic text in word balloons replaced by type in English. At the top of the page the reader is exhorted with an arrow and printed directions to "please read right to left." This disjuncture is in and of itself remarkable in that the reader still reads the English text left to right, but the instructions emphasize the reading of the *panels,* positioning the text as a mere subunit, or creating a mildly paradoxical instruction (should one also attempt to read the English text right to left?).

The digital versions—both Humphries's and the Spanish excerpt—comport with what Aaron Kashtan claims about digitization practices in *Between Pen and Pixel: Comics, Materiality, and the Book of the Future.* Kashtan considers digitization of print comics "in terms of translation or adaptation rather than simple copying" (182). When the pages of *Metro* are produced in a digital scroll composition, the tabular reading of the work irrevocably shifts as a result of the co-presence of so many pages within the same viewing surface. Every translation of *Metro* into a Romance or Germanic language must grapple with how to orient a reader accustomed to left-to-right linguistic progression when faced with a book with right-to-left progression; yet the online versions add a vertical reading vector that encompasses multiple pages at once.

Even print translations feature a number of material modifications that reflect cultural standards. The Italian translation of *Metro* uses a different trim size from the other editions, following the shape and size of the common Italian format of the *bonelliano* (Rota, "Aspects" 82). Despite the overall change in shape, the translation retains the Arabic right-to-left reading system, which is disclaimed with a curious announcement to the reader: "Questo libro comincia dalla fine e si legge come un manga giapponese." Paradoxically, the reader of Italian is informed that this book begins at the end and is exhorted to read this Egyptian graphic novel as if it were a Japanese manga. In much the same way, *Metro* in German features a warning page to announce the reading direction. The instructions note that the story begins on the last page of the book, and a "graphic" (Grafik) is included to demonstrate, through numbers and arrows, how to proceed through each page.

Both the Edition Moderne and il Sirente editions still print the cover in a left-to-right orientation, meaning that a reader "opens" the book at the end. Yet the Edition Moderne *Metro* bemusingly reprints the cover as endpapers at the beginning and end of the print body, creating an internal mirror limning the contents. The physical formatting of both these versions creates an idiosyncratic book in which the cover(s) work at odds with the contents, and—in the Edition Moderne edition—the covers multiply to the point where one can no longer be sure what a cover is even supposed to signify.

Thus, each formatting element that is meant to orient a reader to the text also reminds a reader of textual difference. The graphic novel as an international form does not only—as Edwards argues—work as a homogenizing export of American values and form. It also leads to a fragmenting and fascinatingly diverse series of formal and material interpretations and transformations among the editions of the "first Egyptian graphic novel." To track these interpretive changes as a reading practice is an essential way to produce counternarratives to the bugbear of Edwards's book—the hegemony of US culture in the era of globalization.

Siting Translation

Whether we hold with Venuti's hermeneutic view of translation or not, we can observe among the Rossetti, Davies, Pagano, and Abdalla and Winkler translations vastly different interpretations not only of the plot and its relevance but also of the book as a whole. As shown, while the Rossetti translation interprets *Metro* as a precursor to the #Jan25 uprisings, it does so at the expense of the work's realism. In the flipping of pages and the creating of a sort of "backwards" world visually, elements of realism from the original are lost, thus producing a paradox between the "real" precedent and an inverted fantasy.

Alternately, the Abdalla and Winkler text, in its stated desire to produce an "unverfälscht," or authentic story, creates a compositional palimpsest, replete with layers of multilingual strands of words and phrases that transform the compositional unity of the work as well as its aesthetics. Panels where German words and letters now underline their Arabic counterparts appear more cluttered and busy than El Shafee's regular kinetic and spare drawings. By keeping the Arabic sound words, the translators and editors privilege one view of fidelity to the original, preserving the appearance of linguistic signifiers rather than the pictorial composition.

The translation of *Metro* is a remarkable indication of how cultural techniques of inscribing and marking location can orient, reorient, and disorient a reader in space and time through multiform literacy. The specificity of print cultures and reading practices brushes up against linguistic and cartographic spatial organization. All translations, rather than extending the Western reader's mastery, engage a reader's awareness of herself as a reading subject in an encounter with another reading subjectivity. The reader's disorientation toward *Metro* additionally reorients the process of translation itself. The translations take space as work that travels, while the representations of space within the work force the reader to physically travel the reading space in disorienting ways. The works thus call attention to literacy as a spatialized and physical labor, one that is often taken for granted. As readers, we repeat movements with our eyes, hands, and fingers that orient us to our labor. These repeated movements structure our approach to our work. They physically overdetermine how we engage our reading texts.

The term *read* is often used in a decidedly figurative way: to describe "reading globally" is to describe knowledge work that entails a certain ethical, cultural, moral but not physical disposition. Comics such as *Metro* reassert the physicality of reading and even the politics of where we are reading from. The Italian instructions to the reader of the translated *Metro* reveal the act of reading and translating to be a physical as well as mental endeavor. A reader of Italian physically shifts her relation to the book; one "begins at the end"— not in terms of narrative. One begins at the end of the standard publication format for Western books. The reader moves eyes right to left along the page and left to right along the text within panels. These movements produce friction within the disciplined reader's body. The disorienting reading motions also reorient the reader to the frictions spatialized in the place from which she is reading against the place where she is not.

CHAPTER 3

PERSEPOLIS AND THE CULTURAL CURRENCY OF THE GRAPHIC NOVEL

How Newness Enters the Discourse about *Persepolis*

In the years since Marjane Satrapi's *Persepolis* became an international phenomenon, selling millions of copies, adapted into an award-winning film, and added to a number of school curricula, the text has inspired a cottage industry of critical responses considering the work in terms of culture. Yet the focus of the extant discourse on *Persepolis* rests almost entirely on the cultural negotiations between Iran, a major setting in the works and the birthplace of the author, and the West, imagined alternately as a homogeneous site of freedom and prejudice, or in terms of specific locations such as France (when authors need to make a point about the hijab ban) or the US (when authors need to make claims about 9/11). Providing a shorthand for this conventional analysis of *Persepolis*, Hillary Chute calls Satrapi "a translator of East to West" (*Graphic* 137). Inspired by Chute's claim, this chapter reorients such analysis onto the other translation at work—the one Chute is reading, which is a US adaptation of a French book.

Situating *Persepolis* as a work that brings Iran to the "West" provides an obvious reward as well as a scholarly risk: as Satrapi herself states in the foreword to the US version of the first volume of *Persepolis*, the books intervene at a particularly fraught historical moment in which stereotypical views of Iran prevail amid the ongoing myth of the clash of civilizations.[1] It is therefore a boon to cross-cultural exchange that comics and literary scholars have used Satrapi's text as a platform for research and discussion of Persian miniature aesthetics and the tropes of the *Shahnameh*.[2] Conversely, casting the text as an Iranian work displaces *Persepolis,* as a cultural object, from its original site of publication and the networks of translation and distribution that attended its success. Such inattention to the material history of the work risks complicity in a mode of Orientalism whereby knowledge of the "East" is extended through Western products and consumer tendencies.[3]

This chapter insists on the specificity of geographic territory, and the need to analyze *Persepolis* according to a far more materially situated East-to-West—or West-to-West—transit: France-to-the-US. It is Satrapi, not *Persepolis,* who moves from Iran to France, or "the West." And while a biographical approach to reading may seem suitable for an autobiography, such a framework obscures the real relations of power, access, and comics production that attend *Persepolis*'s transatlantic publication. A critical examination of the publication of *Persepolis* first in France and then in the US furnishes a mode of analysis that intervenes in the monolithic imagining of the West as a homogeneous site of reader expectations and values. The commercial trajectory of *Persepolis* highlights the need for an analysis of comics translation— both literal and cultural—*within* regions of the so-called West. I focus on how the rise of the comics *auteur* triangulated graphic memoirists Art Spiegelman, David B., and Satrapi in a transnational US–France circuit of influence such that each author's success provided a framework for familiarizing readers with the other authors. In its function

1. Edward Said debunked the myth of Samuel Huntington's texts ("Clash?"; *Clash*)—in a number of lectures and publications including the article "The Clash of Ignorance."

2. See, for example, Chute ("Texture" 99; *Graphic* 144–45), Ostby (560), Leservot (118–19), A. Miller ("Marjane" 43). for examples of such analyses.

3. See, for example, Spivak, "Three Women's Texts" 243; Mufti 19–20. Clearly the urtext for this discussion is Said's *Orientalism.*

as a matrix of domestication, this circuit also reflected cultural differences conditioned by the transnational marketplace; these differences become visible through a detailed material history of the changes made in the translation of *Persepolis* for a US readership.

Ultimately, these two poles of analysis—the rise of a certain type of author figure in international graphic narratives and the material transformations of books according to diverse reader expectations—dovetail in a complex of familiarity and difference. While Satrapi is continually cast as a "foreign" author and *Persepolis* as a "foreign" work, these categorizations work in conjunction with associations made among her and white male authors in France and the US. The book as a commodity object and the author as a correlate figure are made legible through specific types of comparisons; this is how the readers of the *New Yorker* come to understand and appreciate graphic novels as objects like *Maus* and *Persepolis.* At the same time, as Homi Bhabha writes of cultural translation, *Persepolis* in its "foreignness" exposes the "performativity of translation as the staging of cultural difference" (*Location,* 325). As a graphic novelist, Satrapi is familiarized according to standards set by David B. in France and Art Spiegelman in the US, yet as a cultural figure and object, Satrapi and *Persepolis* are exoticized as foreign. To some extent this is merely a condition of the frisson of the new or the foreign as a condition for productivity in capital-driven markets. Yet, in the case of Satrapi, this fetishization of difference takes on a neo-Orientalist cast that directs all consideration of her work away from the milieux of production in France and the US and toward an exotic "Middle East."

This continuing exoticization becomes more visible in the reception of Zeina Abirached's Angoulême award-winning book, *Mourir, partir, revenir: Le jeu des hirondelles* (2007; *A Game for Swallows: To Die, To Leave, To Return,* 2012). Upon release of Abirached's book, in French and in translation, reviewer after reviewer, in a number of disparate publications, staged a *praeteritio* in which they compared Abirached to Marjane Satrapi through the disavowal of the value of such a comparison. This strange noncomparison comparison of two women working in bande dessinée or francophone comics was so glaring as to demand further inquiry. By examining the translations of *Persepolis,* its comparison to earlier precedents, *Maus* and *L'Ascension du haut mal,* and its comparison to subsequent work like Abirached's, I seek to reconstruct ex post facto the Orientalist implications that condition the recognition, marketing, and reception of

Persepolis. I argue that these implications are concomitant with, rather than separate from, contradictory marketing strategies used to broker the publication of *Persepolis* between France and the US. To return to Bhabha's formulation—Satrapi and her work lie at interstices of foreignness and familiarity even within a seemingly unified field of Western print cultures.

A number of commenters explicitly highlight the cultural translation that *Persepolis* enacts, focusing on its author, its genre, its style, its medium, or some combination of all these criteria. Rocío G. Davis credits *Persepolis* with no less than a "reconstruction of the memoir" which she claims is "necessarily inflected by the relationship between creative writing and immigrant or ethnic configurations of subjectivity and national affiliation" (265). For Davis, *Persepolis*'s revision of the genre of memoir "destabilize[s] ideology and conventional strategies of meaning in order to enact distinct sociocultural situations" (265). Much as Bhabha describes cultural translation as the mode by which "newness enters the world," according to Davis, Satrapi revises the memoir genre, and provides a new way of writing the self.

Patricia Storace, writing for the *New York Review of Books,* instead places the preponderance of cultural translation on the formal properties of the medium:

> Like a pair of dancing partners, Satrapi's text and images comment on each other, enhance each other, challenge, question, and reveal each other. It is not too fanciful to say that Satrapi, reading from right to left in her native Farsi, and from left to right in French, the language of her education, in which she wrote *Persepolis,* has found the precise medium to explore her double cultural heritage.

Storace's account is somewhat ambiguous as to the seemingly figurative way in which these linguistic and visual registers combine under the calculus of cultural heritage. Is comics the precise medium only because of Satrapi's bilingual (later multilingual) upbringing? Or is it the precise medium because Satrapi depicts growing up in two different countries?

Among others, Davis and Storace demonstrate how readers have approached *Persepolis* as a particular kind of border-crossing work, producing a number of sometimes contradictory analyses. To be sure, the resounding success of *Persepolis* prompted a tremendous amount of scholarship considering the cultural heritage or situation of Satrapi's work, but little consensus. Readers have called *Persepolis* "feminist" (Chute, "Retracing" 94), "humanizing" (Whitlock, *Soft Weapons* 189), "self-aggrandizing" (Singer 154), "didactic" (Place-Verghnes 258), "Iranian exilic" (Malek 354), "the first Iranian comic book" (N. Miller 15), "full of traces of the globalism of the Persian miniature aesthetic" (Ostby 568), "very Western" (Bahrampour), "avant garde" (Chute "Retracing" 99), "draw[ing] on an ancient and transnational precedent" (Ostby 560), "nation-centered . . . yet thoroughly global" (Ostby 562), "democratic" (Mazhari 290), "postcolonial" (Naghibi and O'Malley 235), "a mosaic of Middle Eastern and Western" (Hajdu), "complicat[ing] the simplistic scripts Westerners have assigned to the region labeled 'the Middle East'" (Tensuan 952), "neoliberal" (Singer 154), and "beyond a global, neoliberal agenda" (Gilmore 157). These disparate claims leave a reader wondering just how to locate Satrapi and her work.

Many have even located contradictory meanings or messages within the work itself. Nima Naghibi and Andrew O'Malley claim that *Persepolis* "upsets the easy categories and distinctions that it appears to endorse," a claim they extend both to questions of culture and identity and to the comics medium (243). For Naghibi and O'Malley, Clifford Marks, Shadi Mazhari, Amy Malek, and Marie Ostby, *Persepolis* draws from Western traditions and audience expectations while subverting these expectations.[4] Marks praises *Persepolis* for the way it "introduces a relatively underdiscussed and misunderstood culture . . . to a Western audience that has mostly been persuaded to identify Iranian culture inaccurately with Arab culture" (164). Mazhari stipulates that *Persepolis* simultaneously confirms reader expectations—"Western readers have heard numerous testimonies of human rights violations in Iran, a fact that disposes them to trust Satrapi's life story with its litany of lost, exiled, tortured or executed friends and relatives"—while using this trust to subvert stereotypes (297). Furthermore, Malek argues that Satrapi appropriates Western cultural forms (specifically comics and autobiography) in order to "express and preserve Iranian culture and historical identity" (359).

---

4. See also Mostafa Abedinifard: "By choosing to present her story through the medium of comics, Satrapi further establishes a dialogue with the Other, in the form of her engagement with the established Western attitudes and aesthetic values that surround the production and reception of comics" (84).

The complicated discursive tangles about the rhetorical situation of *Persepolis* have even been schematized by Alex Link as breaking down into four categories: (1) *Persepolis* promotes cross-cultural
understanding, (2) *Persepolis* contributes to Orientalist projections, (3)
Persepolis is an example of "indigenous Orientalism," and (4) *Persepolis* frustrates attempts to essentialize "Persian cultural identity, by
opposing attempts to foreclose upon it by both the Iranian regime
and the Western media" (241). In between the third and fourth categories, one might add Typhaine Leservot's contention that *Persepolis* actually depicts Iranian Occidentalism (116), intervening in Iran's
construction of the West.

I argue that ultimately these positions reveal more about the critics occupying them than about the actual relationship that *Persepolis*
engenders between Iran and "the West." The one point of similarity that disparate critical stances all seem to share is the stability of
the "West" as a unified area of consumption and reception. Rather
than revisit the thoughtful and provocative questions raised by
many scholars about Satrapi's use of Persian miniature aesthetics
or her repurposing of such an aesthetic framework for a defamiliar-
izing effect, this chapter considers the ways in which *Persepolis* was
simultaneously foreignized and domesticated as a graphic narrative. Previous scholarship has located *Persepolis* as a book in transit between Iran (where it was never officially published) and "the
West." As I analyze in what follows, the West is a heterogeneous site
for comics publication and reception, marking areas of difference and
disjuncture.

Authors like Bart Beaty have diligently inscribed *Persepolis* within
a particular moment of Franco-Belgian comics production, and I
contend that it is imperative to note the changes made to *Persepolis*
as it became a successful book in the US as well. It does not detract
from Satrapi's accomplishments to materially study her texts, not as
"culturally and aesthetically global" (Ostby 573) but as works that
undergo cultural translation even between seemingly similar markets in the West. *Persepolis* is an example of the burgeoning trend of
autobiographic graphic novels in both anglophone and francophone
comics production, which means that many readers, even literary
scholars, tend to conflate the information offered in the narrative of
Persepolis with the historical biography of its author, Marjane Satrapi.
The text, as an autobiography, invites certain readings of the narrative based on the influence of Persian art or Iranian ideology, yet this

type of reading frequently conflates the story of Marji the protagonist of *Persepolis* with the material history of *Persepolis* the graphic narrative. Similarly, as Beaty notes, Satrapi's work highlights "the difficulty that many literary critics have when evaluating a narrative form that is primarily visual" (248). The relevant question is not how did *Persepolis* come from Iran to the West but, instead, how did this text reach particular readers in France and the US at particular moments in time? What were the transcultural negotiations and translations that accompanied its material production? And how did readers learn to place this work?

Marjane Satrapi: A Girl David B. or a Childlike Art Spiegelman?

At the initial appearances of *Persepolis* in France (2000) and the US (2003), critics and readers positioned its author as a certain kind of inheritor of certain kinds of comics traditions. When her work was first released in France, Satrapi was predominantly compared to artist David B. (the pseudonym of bande dessinée artist David Beauchard), while in the US she was mainly compared to Art Spiegelman. As central figures of the rise of the graphic memoir genre, these artists constellate transnational networks of comics, genres, and forms, while often overdetermining market conditions, publishing concerns, as well as the fraught politics of identity, otherness, and authenticity. Further, these three authors—Satrapi, David B., and Spiegelman—are inextricably bound up in a transnational historical moment tracked throughout this book—the production of the *literary* graphic novel. The comparisons made between these authors reveal the underlying commercial development of the world economy of graphic novels and show that this development required some transatlantic negotiation.

Writing for the French alternative comics site, *du9*,[5] in 2001, Appollo (the pseudonym of Tunisian-born novelist and bande dessinée writer Olivier Appollodorus) begins his review of Marjane Satrapi's first book of *Persepolis* with the following line:

---

5. The name *du9* is a play on the dual meanings of *neuf*—"nine" and "new"—which in this case refers both to the ninth art (*le neuvieme art*), as comics are known in France, and the newness of the material that the site covers compared with more mainstream comics.

> The first thing that you think opening *Persepolis* is "Look, it's a girl
> David B.," and it is true that Satrapi's art exudes influences from the
> central figure of l'Association.

Appollo's assessment is far from the only instance in which these two authors are directly compared. The working relationship between David B. and Satrapi, their superficial stylistic similarities, and the diegetic corollaries between their works make the comparison seem *almost* self-evident. Both David B. and Satrapi's most recognized works—*L'Ascension du haut mal* and *Persepolis,* respectively—are autobiographical, interweaving elements of fantasy or imagination in narratives spanning many years of the authors' childhood, adolescence, and adulthood. Both works were published by French avant-garde bande dessinée publisher L'Association during overlapping time periods, and David B. even wrote the preface for tome 1^6 of *Persepolis*. Given that *Persepolis* and *L'Ascension du haut mal* were published in black and white by the same Parisian publishing collective after their authors met while working at l'Atélier des Vosges—David B.'s work appearing in six volumes between 1996 and 2003 and Satrapi's in four between 2000 and 2003—"a girl David B." may well have been the first thought for a number of readers opening *Persepolis*.

However, the *New York Times* review of Satrapi's first book of *Persepolis* invokes a different figure for comparison. As Fernanda Eberstadt writes in 2003, "Like [Art] Spiegelman's 'Maus,' Satrapi's book combines political history and memoir, portraying a country's 20th-century upheavals through the story of one family. Her protagonist is Marji, a tough, sassy little Iranian girl." The period in between Eberstadt's sentences acts as a contrapuntal bridge and a subtler version of Appollo's exclamation: it links Spiegelman and Satrapi while presenting her "girl"-ness as a (sassy) marker of distinction. In the same newspaper's review of the second volume of *Persepolis,* a year later, Luc Sante invokes Spiegelman's *Maus* in the second sentence, and then proceeds to contrast the works not on the basis of gender (at least not explicitly) but on the relative maturity of the styles: "Like Art Spiegelman's 'Maus,' it is a 'graphic memoir' . . . but unlike 'Maus' it is executed in an apparently simple, childlike draw-

---

6. I use *tome* consistently in this chapter to refer to the European versions of the serialized installments of *Persepolis* and *L'Ascension du haut mal*. Each tome number is italicized as a way to indicate the title of the French volumes.

ing style" ("She Can't Go Home Again"). The plot thickens. Marjane Satrapi: a girl David B. or a childlike Art Spiegelman?

To complicate matters further, reviewing *Epileptic,* the US translation of *L'Ascension du haut mal,* for *New York* magazine in 2005, Douglas Wolk writes that David B.'s book "is being marketed as a comics memoir in the vein of Art Spiegelman's perennial *Maus* and Marjane Satrapi's recent two-volume hit *Persepolis.* (B. was Satrapi's mentor and teacher.)" ("Sweet"). Wolk goes on to disservice all three authors by contrasting B.'s work with that of the other two memoirists on two points—Wolk stresses that David B.'s artwork is superior to Spiegelman's and Satrapi's, and that his book lacks any engagement with history.[7] Furthermore, Wolk's parenthetical again positions Satrapi as the acolyte of David B. despite his book's relative position in Wolk's schema. Her work may be the hit that his emulates, but she is still a student to his teacher.[8]

Marjane Satrapi, girl David B.? Marjane Satrapi, David B.'s student? Marjane Satrapi, childlike Art Spiegelman? Every apposition is also an act of comparison (even enacted through apostrophe, period, or parentheses). I draw attention to the specificity of these comparisons here as a way of explaining how Satrapi, who was only deemed the "Persian star of French comics" (*Libération*) after the success of her first three tomes, was familiarized—differently—to readerships in francophone and anglophone areas as a mode of marketing and domestication. Amy Malek explains how David B. and Spiegelman functioned in the reception of Satrapi's text: "The success of these forebears readied a readership for *Persepolis,* whose embrace led to its translated publication throughout Europe, the United States, and Canada, where it has enjoyed enormous popular and critical success" (370).

Persepolis reveals the ways that certain discursive forms of sameness or difference are foregrounded by critics, scholars, and publishers alike, while others are implicitly or explicitly overlooked for the sake of the cohesion of aesthetic or commodity registers. There are many similarities between *Persepolis, L'Ascension du haut mal,* and

---

7. Cf. Ostby, who describes *L'Ascension* as "a personal and national reckoning with the specter of the Algerian War" (571).

8. Even Marc Singer, whose chapter on Satrapi otherwise assiduously—and vitriolically—argues for her debt to David B., allows that Wolk's characterization of Satrapi as David B.'s student is unsubstantiated (156). On similar "patronizing evaluations" of Satrapi, see Tensuan 957.

Maus, yet too frequently, unacknowledged assumptions about the West and the rest determine how Marjane Satrapi is recognized as a subject—albeit sometimes a slightly lesser, girl, student, subject— in the same vein as the authors to whom she is compared. These assumptions also overlook *different* precedents by which *Persepolis* may be read in France and the US. How a US reader recognizes a graphic novel published by literary imprint Pantheon differs significantly from how a French reader recognizes what Beaty refers to as avant-garde, "legitimate art" (54), bandes dessinées, published by L'Association.

The Symbolic Life of Marjane Satrapi

Within national, linguistic, and transnational frameworks, Spiegelman, David B., and Satrapi are all indicative of a specific break in comics grounded in modes of autobiography and *auteur*ism that lead to the development of specific types of author figures and author functions. Spiegelman's, David B.'s, and Satrapi's birthdates are separated by a decade each—1948, 1959, and 1969, respectively. *Maus* begins in the pages of *RAW* magazine in the US in 1980, while *L'Ascension*'s first tome is published in France in 1996, and *Persepolis*'s in 2000. Each of these points in time marks a materially distinct historical and epistemic moment. Each also establishes the possibility for lines of influence between preceding and subsequent authors and works. All three are symbolic, in interrelated yet distinct ways, of the rise of the *author* of comics, in terms of an *auteur,* an autobiographical figure known through artistic, antimainstream production.

In his book *Breaking the Frames,* Marc Singer claims that scholarship on *Persepolis* has erroneously sought to "authenticate Satrapi's work by locating it outside the tradition of comics" (153).[9] Singer goes on to state within one paragraph that "David B. is routinely cited by comics critics as a profound influence on Satrapi's style" (155) and that "much of the academic scholarship on Satrapi downplays or

---

9. Cf. Tensuan, who, writing a decade before Singer, stipulates that "only a handful of critics situate Satrapi's work in an artistic and cultural matrix that takes account of the influences stemming from her participation in the French collective of comic artists known as L'Association, thus attending to the ways in which one might read *Persepolis* in a heterogeneous and transnational cultural context" (956–57).

minimizes this influence when it doesn't ignore David B. outright" (156). Although Singer lists a number of scholars who mention David B. in their research on Satrapi, these mentions do not seem to meet his quota and are explained away in a variety of increasingly creative dismissals. Yet there are at least two fundamental issues with Singer's premise: the first is the concept that there is a single homogeneous "tradition of comics" to which both Satrapi and David B. belong. The second is the assumption that Satrapi's and David B.'s works travel unchanged between France and the US. Because Singer focuses entirely on anglophone, and mostly US, scholarship in his critique of the "minimization" of David B., he ignores the wealth of francophone scholarship devoted to this comparison as well as the anachronism of such a comparison in the US, where the publication of Satrapi's books preceded that of David B's.

Singer's contention that Satrapi's work has been overly compared to the tradition of Persian miniature painting to the detriment of the tradition of comics raises evocative questions regarding authors, national cultures, artistic traditions, and the transnational boundaries of comics production. Although Singer never explores the Orientalist implications of situating Satrapi's work in a Persian lineage[10]—he is far more interested in faulting her for being a neoliberal hero—the scholarly labor of locating Satrapi as an author working in a Middle Eastern tradition is inextricable from a host of related projects, from Michel Foucault's author function to Spivak's worlding of the Third World to the continuing development of "world comics." Interrogating the precepts that allow one to "locate" Satrapi as an author-subject according to certain aesthetic values and expectations is a way of treating world comics as a meaningful yet problematic canon.

However, Singer instead seeks to return Satrapi to a "tradition of comics" by stressing her debt to David B. There are neocolonial implications in this effort—Satrapi has qualified early statements she made regarding her indebtedness to David B.[11]—but even more

---

10. This structure of comparison also implies a denial of co-evalness. Because Persian miniature painting is viewed as an ancient form, by linking one of the most avant-garde comics artists to this tradition, her currency is tempered with a backwards-facing view of her cultural production; cf. Gikandi 641–42.

11. In a telling exchange in the *Independent*, Satrapi is asked: "You once said that David B drew like a god, whereas you were less gifted." "'Yeah,' she says, with only the hint of a smile. 'Well I've changed a bit since then. I have my own style. I've learnt to communicate emotion using very little detail'" (qtd. in Chalmers).

vexing is the misrecognition of *Persepolis, L'Ascension* (*Epileptic*), and *Maus* as traditional, given that each of these texts originates in decidedly alternative modes of comics or bande dessinée production. Indeed, the triangulations between David B., Satrapi, and Spiegelman are indicative of nationally differentiated and yet transnationally brokered kinds of comics or bande dessinée production directly opposed to "tradition."

In the definitive English-language treatment of the subject, Charles Hatfield describes the rise of *Alternative Comics* in the US as being especially indebted to "iconoclastic" publications like Spiegelman's *Maus* (x). As Hatfield recounts, Spiegelman and other artists contributed to a "reenvisioning of comics" through the "rejection of mainstream formulas" (x). Furthermore, "Spiegelman's achievement, unprecedented in English-language comics, served to ratify comic art as a literary form; the reception of *Maus* suddenly made serious comics culturally legible, recognizable, in a way they had not been before." Hatfield concludes that *Maus* in fact represented a "revolution in [comics] reception and practice . . . Spiegelman's success only crystallized a larger trend of which he had been a part: the development of a new breed of cartoonists and comics writers, for whom comics were first and above all an acutely personal means of literary expression" (xi). Far from traditional, *Maus* challenged the US comics tradition so decisively that its influence would ripple across the Atlantic.

In the definitive English-language treatment of the subject, Bart Beaty describes the rise of avant-garde comics in France as being especially indebted to the "revolutionary" nature of publisher L'Association and to publications like *L'Ascension du haut mal* and *Persepolis*. Beaty demonstrates how these works and others like them were intrinsic components of the rise of *Unpopular Culture,* or, as the subtitle of Beaty's book would have it, they were responsible for "transforming the European comic book in the 1990s." Beaty charts how these books, through their aesthetics, material components, autobiographical focus, and alternative market practices, forced a reconsideration of "what is meant by the term 'comic book' in the contemporary cultural landscape" (3). The "innovative and avant-garde cultural practices" (6) enacted through publications from L'Association and other small-press, bande dessinée producers "fundamentally altered over the course of the past fifteen years of comics production in Europe" (7). Far from locating Satrapi within a European comics tradition, Beaty places her alongside David B. and other artists engaged in remaking francophone comics production entirely.

It would be irresponsible to claim that these authors have *no* relation to preceding models and products of comics publishing. It is, however, more revealing to recognize the cultural position these authors share with each other in producing comics that did not replicate existing traditions but instead broke in visibly consequential ways from the forms, styles, subject matter, and publishing models established in Europe and the US. Instead of claiming Satrapi as belonging to a "tradition of comics," *pace* Singer, one must recognize her reception and role in both France and the US as belonging to a recent alternative, revolutionary development of a new kind of comics that necessitates an *auteur,* and of which Satrapi is both a practitioner and a leading figure. As Foucault notes, the proper name of the author is not simply an "element in a discourse" because it "performs a certain role with regard to narrative discourse, assuring a classificatory function" ("Author" 210):

> Such a name permits one to group together a certain number of texts, define them, differentiate them from and contrast them to others. (210)

> The author's name manifests the appearance of a certain discursive set and indicates the status of this discourse within a society and a culture. (211)

Thus, as an *auteur,* Satrapi, alongside Spiegelman and David B., has become inextricable from the alternative comics category of autobiographic graphic novels because she figures so prominently in the historic construction of this internationally recognized genre. As autobiographies, books such as *Maus,*[12] *L'Ascension du haut mal,* and *Persepolis* moved comics away from the "tradition of comics" into a recognizable literary tradition that could be categorized according to authors, who could in turn be grouped according to categories of national and transnational culture.

---

12. *Maus* is not an autobiography per se as much as it is a "collaborative autobiography" (Iadonisi).

The Material History of *Persepolis*

The discursive appearance of comparable author subjects operates in conjunction with the coalescence of an internationally recognized category of narrative discourse. Yet, at the protean stage that I have been tracing in reverse, the aesthetic and commercial domination of the literary graphic novel was in no way predetermined; nor was its genealogy identical from a national framework. While *Maus, Persepolis,* and *L'Ascension* map out distinct territories within the broader scope of bandes dessinées and comics, I argue against critics like Singer who conflate the four-tome French *Persepolis* (2000, 2001, 2002, 2003) with the two-volume *Persepolis* (2003, 2004) in English translation. The dominant publishing trends that *Maus, Persepolis,* and *L'Ascension* responded to differed significantly according to location and time. As Valerio Rota stipulates, "Each culture produces different kinds of comics: the size and contents of publications, for historical and practical reasons, vary from nation to nation, accommodating to the tastes and expectations of the different reading public" ("Translation's Visibility"). To give an overgeneral description: US comics production prior to and even following the rise of the graphic novel was characterized by the studio system of collaborative production, serial issues in color, with issues measuring about 16.8 × 26 centimeters (6.625 × 10.125 inches). As described in chapter 1, Franco-Belgian bandes dessinées were sold as albums, bound color books, with usually forty-eight A4 (22.5 × 30 centimeters or 8.85 × 11.8 inches) pages.

Maus, as an irregular, small trim-size text, represented a challenge for publishers when Spiegelman first attempted to sell his account of his parents' survival during the Holocaust. As Spiegelman recounts, after *Maus*'s publication in *RAW,* he unsuccessfully attempted to publish the series with "every reputable publisher" (*MetaMaus* 78). The idea of publishing a small, black-and-white graphic narrative with a US literary bookseller in the 1980s was unthinkable, as borne out by the rejection rate. It was only through the intervention of Louise Fili, the art director at Pantheon, who showed the work to the publisher, André Schiffrin, that *Maus* became the book that would so influence the success of the black-and-white graphic novel.

The form and genre of *Maus* are co-determinate and reflect the zeitgeist of the graphic novel. In their book *The Graphic Novel: An Introduction,* Jan Baetens and Hugo Frey explain that *Maus*'s intervention "to tell a serious life story in a serious mode through texts and images—set up a model repeated in significant future productions, including, of course, autobiography" (99). Baetens and Frey, among other comics scholars, have gestured to the rise of nonfiction and autobiographical comics as a correlate of the literariness of the graphic novel format. Although the rise of autobiographical comics was variegated across the US and Europe, where publishers like Ego comme X in France began anthologizing autobiographical comics in 1994, the autobiographical content of *Maus* proved a transnational influence, in much the same way that the formal aspects of the book contributed to a profusion of the graphic novel.

Spiegelman's innovation influenced the founding of L'Association by a collective of artists, including Jean-Christophe Menu, Stanislas, Mattt Konture, Killoffer, Lewis Trondheim, Mokeït, and David B. in 1990 (L'Association). According to Dan Mazur and Alexander Danner, L'Association's focus on autobiographical comics as a way to distinguish their products from "the escapist mainstream . . . reflected the influence of Art Spiegelman's *Maus*" (254). Pursuantly, *L'Ascension* was a similarly consequential work in the development of autobiographical comics. The volumes detail the struggles of David B.'s family as they grapple with his older brother's epilepsy. The story interweaves the minute details of Beauchard family life— for instance, attempting holistic and macrobiotic lifestyle changes to combat Jean-Christophe's condition—with fantasy, dreams, and an underlying story of the author's own development as an artist.

Trondheim and David B. met Satrapi after she moved to Paris (Spurgeon) and encouraged her to write her own comics, which were first published in installments in L'Association's anthology series *Lapin*. *Persepolis* was published in the Ciboulette collection, and tome 1 won the Coup de Coeur award for an author's first book at the Angoulême International Comics Festival. With the publication of the three following tomes, *Persepolis* became a best seller, by some accounts saving L'Association.[13]

However, the unprecedented commercial success of *Persepolis* acted almost in tension with the antimainstream aesthetics of the publishing collective. The guiding aesthetic ethos of L'Association was a reaction to the standardized, color, glossy album that pervaded

13. "Their first major and defining hit was Marjane Satrapi's *Persepolis* (1999–2004), which made L'Association a robust commercial actor in European comics and helped secure its positioning in bookstores" (qtd. in Wivel).

bande dessinée production (Beaty 29–30). L'Association publications favor heavier paper, black-and-white artwork, smaller formats, and genres more closely aligned with literature, such as autobiography. Menu describes the different collections of L'Association publications in a discourse that bridges the print cultures of bande dessinée and *littérature*: "Ciboulette is graphic-novel like, Eperluette gets the classic 'album' size (even if we don't use this word) . . . Mimolette is a brand of 30-page comix, Côtelette has a more 'literary' orientation" (Menu and Harkham). Among these varied series, *Persepolis*'s publication in the Ciboulette collection was especially influential in its reception. As Beaty states of this collection:

> The resemblance to novels has helped L'Association to position themselves as significantly different from other comic book publishers, and the conception of the comic book as novel has resulted in the books being regarded as akin to literature. Certainly Marjane Satrapi's four-volume autobiography *Persepolis* (2000–2003) benefits from the perception that it is simply a novel with pictures. (38–39)

Thus, although David B.'s preface in the premier tome of *Persepolis* refers to it as "the first Iranian bande dessinée album" ("le premier album de bandes dessinées iranien"), formally, the original publication of *Persepolis* is indicative of a shift in *Franco-Belgian* comics production, enacted by L'Association, that positioned works like *Persepolis* as literature according to European readers' expectations. Within this context, while *Maus* serves as a precursor to David B.'s work, *Persepolis*'s comparison to *L'Ascension* has added geographic, temporal, and commercial relevance. On the other hand, both *Maus* and *Persepolis* shared the distinction of originating in an antimainstream comics or bande dessinée model aligned with literature over glossy escapism, yet both achieved unprecedented—or unexpected—commercial success.

Menu states that "when they found out what the print run of *Persepolis* was, booksellers were shocked to realize that *Maus* was not an isolated case, and that the same coup could be brought off again. It would be naive to think that *Persepolis* has had no influence on this renewed infatuation for the black and white small-format comic book" ("Patch" 328). Menu here sketches a reciprocal dynamic between the publishing conventions of L'Association, which shaped the format of *Persepolis,* and the success of *Persepolis,* which increased the popularity of L'Association's aesthetic. He also triangulates this system of aesthetic influence and extends it across the Atlantic by invoking *Maus,* which was the key to *Persepolis*'s US publication.

Satrapi herself is more than cognizant of the *Maus* comparison, having stated in an interview that she apologized to Art Spiegelman for the fact that every graphic novel is now compared to *Maus.* She added:

> It's not a problem for me. *Maus* is a masterpiece. To be compared to *Maus* is nothing but a compliment. But for him that should be extremely tiring. If I was him I would have hated all these younger graphic novelists being compared to myself. So that is why I called him once, to tell him that none of this propaganda is being made by me, that it is other people who say this. (Qtd. in Tully)

Satrapi's humility notwithstanding, the comparison of *Persepolis* and *Maus* was a central component of the transatlantic constellation of *auteurs* working within the new discursive parameters of the literary graphic novel. This comparison is also a functional instrument in the France-to-US cultural translation of *Persepolis.*

To understand the anglophone[14] *Persepolis* that *is,* one must consider the *Persepolis* that *almost was.* Seattle-based Fantagraphics Books is a publishing company with a genealogy more comparable to L'Association's than to that of Pantheon. Like L'Association, and unlike Pantheon,[15] Fantagraphics mostly publishes comics, and its catalog is devoted to what is called either indie or alternative comics, by artists like Joe Sacco, Charles Burns, and the Hernandez Brothers. Given certain parallels between L'Association and Fantagraphics, *Persepolis* seems like a fitting addition to the Fantagraphics list, and it was actually included in a listing of upcoming publications as a result of owner Kim Thompson's negotiations with L'Association editors.

But the Fantagraphics version of *Persepolis* exists only as a line in a spec sheet. In the words of owner Gary Groth, "Kim was not very proprietary," and before Fantagraphics could publish its translation of *Persepolis,* the US rights were acquired by Pantheon. Groth's

---

14. The UK publisher, Jonathan Cape, is a subsidiary of the same corporation that holds Pantheon.

15. Douglas Wolk's article for *Publishers Weekly* refers to Pantheon as "the GN [Graphic Novel] Imprint That Isn't."

description of his own reaction is illuminating: "At the time, I remember thinking it was annoying, but I didn't realize how well it was going to sell. It was just another foreign book and those things never sold very well" (telephone interview with the author). Although Fantagraphics and L'Association shared similar roles in the development of alternative comics traditions in both the US and France, Groth intimates a disjuncture even between these print cultures and hints at the importance of recognition and reception.

As noted in the introduction and in chapter 2, to domesticate a foreign comic is not a simple question of changing the words in the speech balloons. Because comics are a visual medium, but also a medium with strong literary parallels, a number of elements such as how the work *looks,* its form, and its author and language must be accounted for in the translation of a graphic narrative from one location to another. Groth's partner Thompson was a champion of "foreign" comics in the US, having grown up in a number of countries and being fluent in at least four languages. But, as Groth notes, Thompson's desire to publish *Persepolis* did not correspond to a successful market precedent. Beaty stipulates that among the "significant differences between the comics communities of the United States and Europe" is that "the American comic book market has been more resistant to the idea of comics as books." Furthermore, the US market is far less welcoming to comics in translation, with one exception: "Aside from Marjane Satrapi, few European cartoonists of the small-press movement have fared as well in the United States" (114). The US market for European comics was thus a tenuous prospect without pre-existing success stories. But another editor, Anjali Singh, saw in *Persepolis* a work that could be not only artistically unique but also commercially successful in the US. It was Singh's recognition of *Persepolis* as not just another "foreign" work that instigated its translation and publishing at Pantheon.

The role of Pantheon in the publication of both *Maus* and *Persepolis* is noteworthy given its history as a literary publishing company originally founded by European immigrants to the US, who were especially invested in English translations of European texts. As the son of one of the founders and a former editor-in-chief, André Schiffrin, describes, Pantheon was the project of European exiles deeply concerned with cross-cultural literary exchange. Schiffrin was infamously forced out of the company, but not before he published the first volume of Art Spiegelman's *Maus* in 1986.[16] Despite Schiffrin's support for *Maus*, Spiegelman stayed with Pantheon for his second volume rather than moving to Schiffrin's nonprofit New Press, stating: "I loved publishing with Andre, but I need more money for the time it takes to finish a book" (qtd. in Italie). Thus, a complex condition of possibility preceded *Persepolis*'s translation: Pantheon had a history of publishing literary works in translation and had achieved financial success with its publication of the graphic novels *Maus I* and *II*, but Schiffrin's expulsion demonstrated the company's prioritization of financial success, making a risky acquisition of *Persepolis* improbable.

As Singh describes it, the decision by Pantheon to publish *Persepolis* was a contingent—and in no way inevitable—event. Despite the commercial and critical success the publisher had achieved with *Maus*, as a primarily prose-based publisher, Pantheon did not have a specific process for developing graphic narratives. In 2003 Dan Frank, Pantheon's editor-in-chief, characterized the publisher's graphic novel selection process as predicated on "mutual enthusiasms." Speaking to Dan Nadel at *Publishers Weekly*, Frank stipulated, "We publish what we like—*we* meaning myself, Chip Kidd, and now Anjali Singh." Nadel editorializes on this trio: "Kidd and Frank are well known for their enthusiasms; Singh, however, is less familiar." In Nadel's usage, one supposes that "less familiar" refers to Singh's newness to the profession (Vintage was her first editorial position), but it also carries a racial and gendered charge when used to describe the only woman of color in a group otherwise composed of white men.

By her own account, Singh fought hard to get *Persepolis* published because of the scarcity of works authored by and representing the experience of women of color. The "less familiar" aspects of Singh initially extended to her most successful acquisition, and at least one colleague "told [Singh] she just didn't see an audience for it" (qtd. in Gagliano). Kidd himself responded to an interview by admitting, "I mean, I'll be totally honest, I thought 'Persepolis' was a great, worthy project, but I never ever thought that it would become as huge as it was" (qtd. in Dueben, "Kidd"). Singh had to actively counter these doubts, and what she describes as the subjective bias of editorial acquisitions, or "who gets to decide that there's an audience"

---

16. Schiffrin addresses his ouster from *Pantheon* in both *The Business of Books: How the International Conglomerates Took Over Publishing and Changed the Way We Read* (2001) and *Words and Money* (2010).

(qtd. in Gagliano). Singh highlights the role of identity politics in the publishing world as well as the importance of transcultural or translinguistic interest. For Singh, the publication of *Persepolis* was at least aided if not made possible by the specific group of gatekeepers at work in the Knopf Publishing Group at the time: Singh credits Knopf editor-in-chief (Knopf acquired Pantheon in 1961) Sonny Mehta, himself internationally raised[17] and educated, for giving the go-ahead to *Persepolis*.[18] Singh also notes Frank's ability to read French as a contributing factor for the situation of *Persepolis* at Pantheon.[19] Of course, Singh's own ability to read and translate French was a prerequisite for the project, and she has subsequently credited Satrapi's command of English for 90 percent of the book's success.[20]

Certain proclivities toward foreign or unfamiliar projects influenced the acquisition, but it was also Singh's recourse to a domestic precedent that convinced Pantheon to acquire *Persepolis*. While *Persepolis* was already an unprecedented financial success for L'Association, Singh pitched it as "the next *Maus*," discursively situating *Persepolis* in the same network as Spiegelman's Pulitzer-winning project: "Now *Persepolis,* like *Maus,* reached a huge readership because it overlapped with so many other categories—memoir, history, Middle East studies, coming-of-age—but we still had a firm platform from which to launch it" (telephone interview with the author). Alternately, she cautions, "You could also have looked at it as a comic book about the Islamic Revolution by an unknown Iranian author based in France" (qtd. in Gagliano). In this comparison, Singh outlines the tension between the points of domestication and foreignization in *Persepolis*'s cultural translation.

The local specificities of avant-garde comics production in Paris and corporate American publishing houses must be brokered or

---

17. He "grew up all over the world" (Eggers).

18. A veteran of transatlantic literary acquisition at Paladin, before making the transatlantic move to Knopf, Mehta was known for publishing books by US authors that were otherwise unknown in the UK.

19. "I was lucky enough that the first person who could give me the go ahead, Pantheon's wonderful editor-in-chief, Dan Frank, could read French and supported that acquisition" (qtd. in Gagliano).

20. "I feel like 90% of Persepolis' success was due to the fact that we had an incredibly charismatic author that went on the road tirelessly. Otherwise that could have been just this graphic novel that was going around that a few people had heard of. The question of the editors speaking another language, but also having connections with other editors in other countries[,] is a really big one" (qtd. in Valenti).

translated so that *Maus* and *Persepolis* come to circulate in, determine, and even overdetermine the commodification of the international graphic novel. Plying *Maus* as a precursor helped Singh convince Pantheon to acquire *Persepolis*. Conversely, the comparison between the two comics was essential for convincing L'Association to sell the rights. As Singh declares, "The French publisher was initially reluctant to work with a big American corporate house and said no. But . . . I wrote them an impassioned letter about why we should publish it, and it really helped that I could say we had published *Maus*" (qtd. in Lee). Understanding *Maus* as a historical and local precedent for the US acquisition and publication of *Persepolis* counteracts Singer's confusion about why US scholars tend to compare Satrapi to Spiegelman but not to David B.; so, too, does an examination of the ways that *Persepolis* was *Maus*-ified for US audiences.

The Translations of *Persepolis*

Contra the authors of the blog *Marjane Satrapi: Persepolis,* who claim that "the English translation of Persepolis first appeared in 2003: the art was unaltered," the Pantheon production of *Persepolis* diverged in ways both artistic and cultural from the French version. Discrepancies between *Persepolis,* tomes 1 through 4, and the US volumes worked subtly but consequentially to make the books appear more familiar to a US audience that might know *Maus* but wouldn't be familiar with titles from L'Association. The US volumes were physically smaller in terms of page size but longer in terms of page count. They shifted from the original four tomes, which were 16 × 24.5 centimeters and between 71 and 95 pages, to two volumes, which were 14.75 × 22.5 centimeters and 153 and 187 pages.

In France, the trim size of *Persepolis* corresponded with an aesthetic tendency toward books rather than bande dessinée albums. Beaty notes of the books in L'Association's *Ciboulette* collection that "the resemblance to novels has helped L'Association to position themselves as significantly different from other comic book publishers, and the conception of the comic book as novel has resulted in the books being regarded as akin to literature" (39). However, the page size in the US *Persepolis* volumes is noticeably smaller than the originals. Singh attributes the difference in size to two reasons—a standard trim size cuts production costs, and it also tells readers "this

FIGURE 3.1. Marjane Satrapi, *Persepolis 1*, n. pag. (left); and Satrapi, *Persepolis: The Story of a Childhood*, page 26 (right)

book is like other books. This book is not out of the box. This isn't like an oversize book" (Skype interview with the author). These two considerations—publishing costs and familiarity on the part of readers—coincide in a number of the changes made to the US translation, but here we see the familiarity of US readers diverging from that of Franco-Belgian readers. What makes a graphic narrative look "like other books" varies across the two print cultures. Furthermore, altering the page size necessitates a complete rearrangement of the pages, where opening banners announcing each section are resized in the US version so that they no longer fill the width of the page (see figure 3.1). In the French tomes, these introductory panels extend across the entirety of the page; in the US edition, they are truncated, changing the visual cohesion of the page.

Reader familiarity and the ability to market a book in a new context affected not only the physical size of the pages but also the page count of the US works. *Persepolis* was published in two volumes in the US, just like *Maus*,[21] but also because—as Singh notes, "from an American perspective or you know corporate, commercial publishing, an eighty-page book isn't going to fly" (Skype interview). In France, the page count of each tome already signaled an increase from the standard forty-eight pages for albums. But in the US, page-count expectations for a literary publisher like Pantheon led to an entirely different set of products.[22]

For comics studies, the changes between formats are artistically and narratively meaningful. As Pascal Lefèvre describes in his chapter "The Importance of Being 'Published': A Comparative Study of Different Comics Forms": "Format will always be decisive. Even the dimensions of the publication are important" (92) because of the role of materiality in the visual and narrative aspects of comics production. Lefèvre stipulates that formats are defined not only by materiality but also "by [their] temporal aspects" (98). Thus, *Persepolis*'s shift from four to two volumes for the US market fundamentally changed its visual storytelling. In the age of "binge watching," the distinctions between serial and contained narratives might be more difficult to parse, but as Lefèvre reminds his readers, "each analysis of comics has to start with a study of the form in which it is being published" (99). Neither the French nor the American version of *Persepolis* quite comports with any of the standard formats that Lefèvre lists, for the most part because neither L'Association nor Pantheon have any history of "mainstream" bande dessinée and comics production. Yet even if both houses represent a similar aversion to the formats of the mainstream, each *Persepolis* aesthetically and temporally reflects a standardization in its site of publication through divergent covers, narrative sequence, and titles, as well as paratexts such as introductions.

As a component of the shift in format, the reduction and change of cover art in the US version further denotes the temporal-aesthetic

---

21. *Maus* was itself only published in two volumes because of Spiegelman's desire to get the book out before the film premiere of *An American Tale*, which he felt was a sanitized rip-off of *Maus* (*MetaMaus* 78–79).

22. Jennifer Worth specifically claims: "By choosing to present her story through the graphic novel, Satrapi is clearly placing herself outside the mainstream. The American editions of the books try to downplay this aspect by publishing Persepolis on thick, creamy paper in two hardback volumes as a way of marking its cultural cachet and seriousness as a piece of literature" (153).

change between works. The covers of each of the L'Association tomes of *Persepolis* reference the contents figuratively, much like the albums of *L'Ascension du haut mal*. Each tome of *L'Ascension* is only additionally titled with a number *1* through *6* and features, on the cover, the main characters, brothers Pierre-François and Jean-Christophe, as they age from five and seven years, respectively, into adulthood. Behind the characters appears a mass of black, monstrous figures that "ascend" or grow from tome to tome against the yellow background until the sixth volume, where this figurative "haut mal"—"high evil," representing Jean-Christophe's epilepsy—has become a black background against which the adult characters stand. The covers reflect the progression of Jean-Christophe's illness as well as the ages of the characters in the central narrative. The four covers of *Persepolis* likewise have a locative and narrative function: Tomes *1*, *2*, and *4* each feature mounted riders on horses facing right (or East, according to post-Ptolemaic cartographic convention) (see figure 3.2). Ostby analyzes the first two riders as representative of Persian heroic figures from the *Shahnameh*, and the narrative is likewise oriented East, as the majority of both books is set in Iran. The figure's increased pugilism on the cover of tome *2* (galloping forward with sword in hand) corresponds to the diegetic onset of the Iran–Iraq War in tome *2*. Tome *3* features a rider in European attire and a Napoleonic pose[23] riding in the opposite direction, and the book describes the main character Marji's exile from Iran to Austria (going East to West, or cartographically leftward). The fourth cover shows an adult Marji on a horse facing right again and signifying her return to Iran. Thus, as preceded by the covers for *L'Ascension*, the covers for *Persepolis* demonstrate narrative progress and correspond spatially to the settings of each volume and the protagonist's emigration from Iran to Europe and back again.

The US volumes of *Persepolis* instead feature portraits of Marji surrounded by decorative ornamentation (see figure 3.3). The first-edition hardcovers were die-cut to form a window framing the portrait. As Singh states, "The idea with Pantheon books in that graphic novel line is that the package should be really beautiful" (Skype interview). These covers were designed by Satrapi and Menu working together and represented a major shift in the narrative correspon-

---

23. Insofar as the image bears a visual similarity to Jacques-Louis David's *Napoleon Crossing the Alps*.

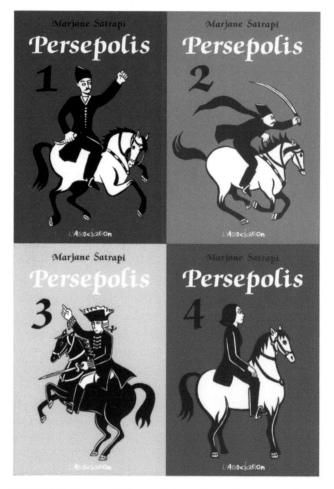

FIGURE 3.2. Covers of Marjane Satrapi, *Persepolis 1, 2, 3,* and *4*

dence between the cover and the text. Among anglophone scholars, Naghibi and O'Malley read these covers as indicative of a clash of familiarity and difference. The veiled child on the cover of *Persepolis: The Story of a Childhood* represents the "radical other," but "at the same time, the image is familiar because it is of a perceived universal figure: the child" (229). Simultaneously, because the image is "framed by stylized Persian art," this framing "evokes difference" (230), in their view.

Covers may seem paratextual, but examining the visual differences of the initial print runs demonstrates how the books were

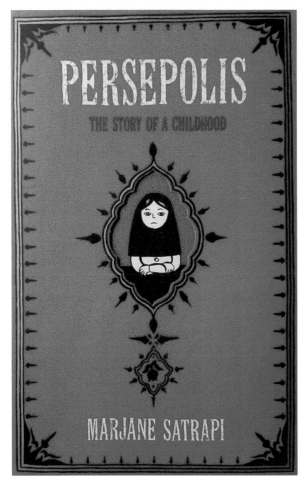

FIGURE 3.3. Cover of Marjane Satrapi, *Persepolis: The Story of a Childhood*

packaged for and presented to distinct audiences in France and the US.[24] Because paratextual elements represent a category of creative production that is not always under the author's control, these differences reveal distinctions between readers and markets in both areas. Singh notes that the L'Association covers "would never fly in our market" (Skype interview). Elements taken for granted in the materiality of translation attest to cultural differences between

24. The collected volumes of *Persepolis* in French and English, both released in 2007, also have entirely different covers from each other and from the initial print runs in France and the US.

reading publics and print cultures. In the case of *Persepolis,* the covers required "domestication" in ways that significantly changed the appearance of the books. The different covers also metonymically link the books to their narrative resegmentation as a progression from childhood to adulthood.

The titles of the books also reflected the changes in narrative structure. The four volumes in France each had only a number for subdesignation within the series, while the two US volumes—again, like *Maus*—acquired subtitles. Writing of the original title, Leservot argues that through her use of the Greek name for the ancient capital of Persia, "Satrapi symbolically identifies her work as western in name only, but deeply, truly Persian, a political gesture aimed at an Islamic regime which refuses Iran's diversity of opinions and identities" (128). Although Satrapi felt that this nuance would be well understood by an English-language readership, Singh insisted to Satrapi that Americans would not be as familiar with the connotation of *Persepolis* as readers in Europe, and that a generic reading line was necessary. Singh went with something "that anyone could read and understand" (Skype interview). Thus, the first Pantheon volume of *Persepolis* collected tomes 1 and 2 under the subtitle *The Story of a Childhood.*

The title ascribed to the first volume led a number of anglophone critics and scholars to read the entirety of *Persepolis*—which extends to Marji's mid-twenties—in the context of childhood. Such an inflection is obvious in the distinction that both Eberstadt and Sante make between Spiegelman as adult and Satrapi as child. A number of scholars also use the titling to make claims such as "Satrapi's autobiography is the 'story of a childhood,' and *Persepolis*'s style reflects this perspective" (Chute, *Graphic* 146). Chute is hardly alone in basing an entire aesthetic analysis on the title of the US translation of the first volume. However, this line of analysis indicates a broader trend in the impact that seemingly small differences in publication between two "Western" sites have on the global interpretation of the work.

More egregious is the titling of *Persepolis II,* which would have riled up devotees of spoiler alerts. *Persepolis II* collected tomes 3 and 4 under the subtitle *The Story of a Return.*[25] The entirety of tome 3 is, in fact, the opposite of "The Story of a Return"; it is instead the story of Marji's exile in Austria. Only on the final pages of tome 3 does the

---

25. An indication of how Singh's titling has influenced interpretation is also evident in Mostafa Abedinifard's claims that "Satrapi's use of the word story in the subtitles of both *Persepolis* and *Persepolis 2* is noteworthy" (104).

character prepare to return to Iran. Tome 4 does depict Marji's return to Iran but then concludes with another departure, as Marji leaves for France. By collecting tomes 3 and 4 together under a title that only describes the latter, the Austrian section is minimized in importance, as is Marji's conclusive leaving of Iran.

As a sequential medium, comics and bande dessinée are formally shaped by progression and cessation. Each issue, volume, album, or tome will end, but it will also gesture toward the next installation. Thus, tome 1 of *Persepolis* ends with a death—Marji's uncle—but also with the verbal intrusion of a beginning "It was the beginning of the war . . ." ("C'était le début de la guerre . . ."). The ellipsis on the final page verbally draws a reader onward, while its composition is in direct tension with the facing verso page, which begins with Marji's "last meeting" ("dernière rencontre") with her uncle and an unframed panel announcing his execution in the newspaper. From a tabular reading perspective, this two-page spread artistically mobilizes a tension between an end, which the reader can sense by virtue of the last page itself, and which is also metaphorically rendered through Anouche's death, and a beginning, announced through the literal "début" and ellipsis.

The shift in narrative progression is marked by *Persepolis*'s further division of each tome into sections, the rhythm and relations of which are changed in the transition to volumes. In the first US volume—*The Story of a Childhood*—the ultimate section of the original tome 1, "The Sheep" ("Les Moutons"), leads directly into "The Trip" ("Le Voyage"). Yet, in the original tome 2, the use of "Le Voyage" as the opening section establishes symmetry with the final section "The Dowry" ("La Dot"). Both sections involve voyages away from Iran, but "The Trip" is a family vacation escape to Italy and Spain that lasts only one splash page and six panels, while "The Dowry" concludes with Marji's separation from her family as she prepares to travel to Austria alone. From a narrative standpoint, the symmetry between "The Trip" as the opening words to the start of tome 2 and Marji's anguished face from the airport window at the end of the tome is lost in the US *Persepolis*, where there is no longer any indication of the original division of sections. The narrative relationship between "The Sheep" and "The Trip" is made slightly confusing since the Iran–Iraq war—which "begins" at the end of "The Sheep"—begins again at the end of "The Trip" in the antepenultimate panel, where Marji's grandmother announces the news to the family. Thus, in *Persepolis:*

The Story of a Childhood, the Iran–Iraq war "begins" twice, while in *Persepolis,* it is foretold at the end of tome 1 and announced in the first section of tome 2, allowing readers new to the series or in need of a reminder to pick up where the last tome ended. Therefore, from an artistic and narrative perspective, *Persepolis: The Story of a Childhood* and *Persepolis,* tomes 1 and 2, differ in the symmetry and redundancy of their composition.

Other changes between the L'Association and Pantheon publications highlight how the former aligns *Persepolis* implicitly and explicitly with the work of David B., while the latter appears intended as the "next *Maus.*" These changes also reflect divergent geopolitical climates of each publication. Tome 1 from L'Association features an introduction by David B., which details the history of Iran up until the American involvement in and exploitation of the Iranian governmental structure for the sake of acquiring oil. Written before 9/11, this introduction provides a trenchant critique of US incursion in sovereign nations and goes so far as to lay responsibility for the political and religious turmoil described in *Persepolis* on US interference. The Pantheon version, published almost concurrently with the US invasion of Iraq in 2003—making the bundling of tomes 1 and 2, in which Iraq and Saddam Hussein are repeatedly denounced by the protagonists, quite auspicious—instead features an introduction by Satrapi where the American influence is shifted to a mostly supporting role for British interference. The CIA-instigated coup is mitigated as being performed by "the CIA, with the help of British intelligence" following a British retaliatory embargo on oil exports.

In her introduction for Pantheon, Satrapi describes the exigence of *Persepolis* not in the nationalist terms of David B.—"the first Iranian bande dessinée album"—but rather as a work of cultural translation.[26] In the wake of so many negative stereotypes, Satrapi knows that the image of Iran is "far from the truth" and wants to correct it. Writing in 2002, when a number of media outlets had already begun discussions of US military action in Iraq, Satrapi concludes her introduction with a penultimate line mentioning those "Iranians who died in the war against Iraq," aligning Iran and the US substitutively through a common enemy.

Introductions are also paratextual, and while their composition is generally retroactive to the manuscript, they can tell us about the

---

26. See also Malek 380.

context and the audience expectations that were imagined at the time of publication. In the case of publication histories, David B.'s and Satrapi's separate prefaces indicate different rhetorical situations for the L'Association and Pantheon publications. Given Satrapi's denunciation of the popular image of Iranians as terrorists and fanatics in her introduction, the excision of David B.'s drawings accompanying his introduction—one of which poses a young Marji on a horse with a large gun—seems a logical adaptation in light of US Islamophobia. As subtle as it is, the shift between introductions refigures Satrapi from a victim of US and British intervention in Iran who became a comic artist under the aegis of famous French artists into a cultural ambassador hailing from a country that suffered a common enemy in the form of Saddam Hussein's Iraq.

While the scholarship on Satrapi tends to conflate France and the US under the umbrella of "the West," radically variegated histories and geopolitical relations map the transits among Iran and these Western nations. As Leservot argues, "Over the course of the twentieth century, the discourse of Iranian intellectuals about the West became increasingly divided between the long-standing, rather positive view of France and an increasingly negative view of Anglo-Americans" (119). Books are not published in geopolitical vacuums, and recognizing how factors like the Franco-German alliance against the US invasion of Iraq—and the ensuing Freedom Fries movement—affect how and why a book is received as a French or an Iranian work is essential to breaking away from problematic reading practices whereby responders evaluate a work based on its universal appeal while ignoring the material and cultural translations that accompany its international reception.

Years of translation scholarship have insisted on the acknowledgment that a translation and an original are fundamentally different texts. This universal difference—every word is different—between translated texts in some ways works to obscure the actual work of translation. Lawrence Venuti's *Contra Instrumentalism* insists on the radical difference between a text and its translation:

> For a text is a complex artifact that sustains meanings, values, and functions specific to its originary language and culture, and when translated this complexity is displaced by the creation of another text that comes to sustain meanings, values, and functions specific to a different language and culture. Any correspondence or

approximation thus coincides with a radical transformation. As a result, no translation can be understood as providing direct or unmediated access to its source text. (2)

Yet Venuti's hermeneutic model of translation does not fully account for what happens in a work like *Persepolis,* where some aspects *do* provide direct or unmediated access to unchanged drawings, layouts, paneling, and tabular composition.

Rather than a universality of difference as in linguistic translations, comics represent heterogeneity of difference. Materially, the translations between the French and English *Persepoleis* reveal the complexity of the type that Venuti mentions between the originary culture and the translating culture, but they do so *because* other aspects remain unchanged. It is through this variegated field of difference and sameness that one must address the translation of *Persepolis* as, in Venuti's terms, "an interpretive act that necessarily entails ethical responsibilities and political commitments" (6). Without laying the entirety of a complex of decisions and deliberations on her shoulders, I have highlighted the necessity of Singh's interpretation, seeing *Persepolis* as the next *Maus* and modifying the work in ways that might allow "everyone" to "read and understand."

Alternately, as Singh asserts, one might attribute to the work a type of ungovernable or unsaleable position due to its "unknown Iranian" author, or, in Groth's words, its status as "a foreign book." In highlighting the material and formal translations of *Persepolis* from France to the US, I want to trace how a foreign work is domesticated and made familiar, at the same time attending to the aspects that—as a graphic narrative—escape translation. We have seen how Satrapi was first compared to two successful, white male predecessors as a way to broker her unique and unprecedented role as author of "the first Iranian comic book." Yet, once the domestic success of *Persepolis* was assured in both Europe and the US, Satrapi's cultural capital as well as her cultural role shifted again. Her success made her into a brokering figure of a different order.

Satrapi as Precedent

Persepolis's transatlantic border crossing made familiar—and also marketable—certain kinds of texts. We have already noted a number of occasions where reviewers cite *Persepolis*'s success as the precedent for any number of possibilities in publishing—graphic novels, autobiographies, commercial successes, translations. Yet the author function of Satrapi took on other folds of connotation and translatability. In some ways this is a problem of genre, or even gender—Satrapi's text is a woman's memoir of boundary crossing. From this unique categorization, the comparisons to David B. and Spiegelman seem facile. However much Satrapi, Spiegelman, and David B. constellate a transnational economy of comics, it is Satrapi, above all, who comes to metonymize the global in what Arjun Appadurai terms "the global cultural economy" (295).

For Menu, Satrapi's East-to-West, France-to-the-US success created an new condition of possibility for global economies of comics:

> I also think that a lot of so-called "independent" French or European comics can find a US readership. I was always surprised in the years before that so few of them had been translated, and I've noticed a change in the last few years in the States. Maybe the success of Pantheon's English version of *Persepolis* helped; it had kind of paved the way in France for big publishers to include the (so-called again) "graphic novel" approach, mainly only reached before by the small independent publishers. (Menu and Harkham)

Thompson similarly told the *Comics Reporter,* "'Art comics' have achieved enough big successes now, *Persepolis* in particular, that we may be stuck with the image of book-sized graphic novels as being serious literary work" (Thompson and Spurgeon). Certainly, it was not until after the second volume of *Persepolis* was published by Pantheon that the company also acquired David B.'s *L'Ascension du haut mal* from Fantagraphics, translated and collected in one volume as *Epileptic.* Hence the inversion of publication order, whereby David B.'s *L'Ascension* preceded *Persepolis* in France, but *Epileptic* was published after *Persepolis* in the US.

Furthermore, despite Spiegelman's own immigrant history, or the setting of *Maus* in Poland, it is *Persepolis,* not *Maus,* that is read again and again as a text of cultural translation. This reception is especially legible in the comparisons made between Satrapi and other women-of-color graphic artists. While being compared to Spiegelman or David B., in Singer's terms, embeds an artist in the comics tradition, being compared to Satrapi seems to entail a different comparative apparatus. Drawing from Gayatri Spivak's 1985 article "Three Women's Texts and a Critique of Imperialism," I question how Satrapi's author function shifts from that of inheritor of white male authors' precedent to Middle Eastern cultural translator. Spivak asserts that the lack of attention to the role of imperialism in the reading of nineteenth-century British literature demonstrates the "continuing success of the imperialist project, displaced and dispersed into more modern forms" (243). In the case of global comics, the *displacement* suggested in her formulation is especially appropriate. How are "foreign" products sold in European and US markets, and how is this commodification elided or amplified by the discourse attending these products?

I begin by analyzing the welter of critical receptions that compare Satrapi and Zeina Abirached. The same could be done for a number of authors, as everyone from Palestinian American author Leila Abdelrazaq[27] to Franco-Syrian author Riad Sattouf[28] to Magdy El Shafee has been compared to Satrapi. Yet the pairing of Satrapi and Abirached, as two women originally born outside Paris who published their work there, serves a specific analytic function. This analysis is guided by questions regarding global comics as an emergent textual form that complicates world literature as a system of cultural recognition: What role does the emphasis on these two women authors as Middle Easterners play in the reception of their books in Europe and the US? How do transnational literatures capitulate to Orientalist projections? How do comics, by introducing new criteria for literary assessment, compel us to radically remap the location of culture?

Black and White and Brown All Over

Upon the publication and translation of Zeina Abirached's *Mourir, partir, revenir: Le jeu des hirondelles* in France in 2007, translated as *A*

27. Among others, Alex Mangles, in reviewing Abdelrazaq's book *Baddawi* for the *LA Review of Books*, notes, "It's hard not to think of Marjane Satrapi's *Persepolis* when reading Abdelrazaq's *Baddawi*."

28. To cite two of the most parallel among hundreds of examples, Adam Shatz, writing for the *New Yorker*, notes, "Not since 'Persepolis,' Marjane Satrapi's memoir of her childhood in Khomeini's Iran, has a comic book achieved such crossover appeal in France," while Rachel Cooke, for the *Guardian* notes, "Not since *Persepolis*, Marjane Satrapi's graphic memoir of revolutionary Iran, has a comic book seemed so important, or been so acclaimed."

Game for Swallows in the US in 2012, a curious trend developed. In a range of popular, academic, French, US, and UK online, print, and in-person reviews, blog posts, interviews, and introductions, Abirached and Satrapi were explicitly denied comparison through an implicit comparison. The comparisons indicate a homogenizing "Western" conceptualization of graphic novels. Unlike *Persepolis,* which was alternately compared to *Maus* or *L'Ascension* (or even Persian min-iatures), *A Game for Swallows,* or *Le jeu des hirondelles,* is consistently compared to *Persepolis* in an array of national and cultural platforms and settings. We might read this as Satrapi and her work outstripping her predecessors to become the predecessor nonpareil. Or we might examine these points of reception more closely. As Caren Kaplan states of reception: "Too often, Western feminists have ignored the politics of reception in the interpretation of texts from the so-called peripheries, calling for inclusion of 'difference' by 'making room' or 'creating space' without historicizing the relations of exchange that govern literacy, the production and marketing of texts, the politics of editing and distribution, and so on" (138–39). Following Kaplan, it is not enough to recognize or even celebrate the inclusion of two "Mid-dle Eastern" women's books in the publishing circuits of graphic novels between France and the US. We must work to understand what the inclusion of these texts indicates about access, marketing, and consumer expectations. Without diminishing the artistry of each woman, we must consider what their conflation says about the cul-tural positioning of the reviewers, as well as the editors, translators, and publishers involved in the process.

Pamela Paul's *New York Times* review of Zeina Abirached's *A Game for Swallows* begins with the line "It is hard not to think of Marjane Satrapi's groundbreaking graphic memoir, 'Persepolis,' while read-ing Zeina Abirached's moving account of her childhood in Lebanon in the 1980s." As described at length above, Satrapi's *Persepolis* is a multivolume autobiographical account of her life in Iran before and after the 1979 revolution and her subsequent emigration to Vienna and later return to Iran. Abirached's book recalls a single night of her family's life in Beirut in 1984, during intense shelling in the Leba-nese Civil War. Thus, the scope and location of the books is quite distinct, and Abirached is slightly more than a decade younger than Satrapi. However, these differences have not stanched the outpour-ing of comparisons. Paul's review is hardly the first or last space in which the graphic narratives of Abirached and Satrapi have been compared.[29] Some media outlets, like the French culture and lifestyle magazines *Télérama* and *L'Express,* attempt to qualify the comparison by specifically enumerating the similarities between Abirached and Satrapi: their mutual use of black and white, their similar characters, their Eastern and/or wartime settings, and autobiographical and/or childhood-memory narration styles:

> Same use of black and white, similarity of characters, Oriental context, autobiographical inspiration: the style of Zeina Abirached immediately makes one think of Marjane Satrapi's style. For all that, to reduce *The Game for Swallows* to a sub-*Persepolis* is purely bad faith. (Jarno)

> From the graphic perspective, the style of the album [*The Game for Swallows*] is reminiscent of Marjane Satrapi's *Persepolis*: same fullness of the black-and-white drawing, same false naïveté of the narration, same setting of a wartime city, same childhood memories. But the comparison stops there. (Bisson)

These two lists provide a rubric for how one might compare Abirached to Satrapi while implying that the limits of the list indicate the insignificance of that comparison. In both reviews the lists take subjunctive form: one *could* compare them—here are the criteria by which to do so—but why would one?

In fact, the comparison has become its own trope to the extent that Cameron Hatheway of *Bleeding Cool,* a UK-based comics blog, avows that his review of *A Game for Swallows* will *not* function solely to compare the two works—unlike other, unnamed and uncited reviews— a claim that seems rather discredited by the review's opening and closing paragraphs, which both mention Satrapi. Hatheway, via paraleipsis, structures an entire review of *A Game for Swallows* from start to finish—literally—in comparison with Satrapi, while simultaneously claiming a unique exemption from this specific comparison.

---

29. Previously, the French Embassy in the US offered a game on its website, https://frenchculture.org, that allowed users to play "Marjane Satrapi vs. Zeina Abirached." Players were shown a series of ten black-and-white images and offered only two options: "Marjane Satrapi" or "Zeina Abirached." The user scored points for correctly identifying which images—taken from a range of works by both authors—are by which artist.

Other cultural critics go further in stressing the error of the comparison. *du9* begins its review of Abirached's *Le jeu des hirondelles* by highlighting the fundamental difference in the two artists' approaches: "Her approach is fundamentally different from another Middle Eastern author with whom she is too frequently compared, Marjane Satrapi . . . and with whom she has but one ultimate point of comparison, that of being a female graphic artist recounting in black and white the difficult moments in the recent history of her country" (Voitachewski). While *du9*'s Voitachewski insists on the fundamental difference between the two authors, he too offers criteria for comparison.

By way of introducing Abirached at Duke University, Professor Claire Tufts critiqued reviews such as Paul's (whom she refers to as "one critic . . . in the *New York Times*") for comparing the two authors. In this critique, Tufts echoes both the caveat and the criteria listed by *Télérama* and *L'Express* and contends that "the similarities between [Abirached] and Satrapi don't go much beyond the fact that both writers are women from the Middle East, both work in black and white, and both have written graphic novels about war as seen through the eyes of a child narrator" ("Beirut Partita"). She supports her claim by noting that Satrapi's work is frenetic and more taken with representing war, while Abirached's is more "warm" and concerned with familial relations. In *A Game for Swallows,* she explains, war is often figured as a "white panel or blank page" ("Beirut Partita"). Herein, although the comparison has already been disavowed, Tufts, a professor in the Romance Studies division, continues to compare the two works. She uses a close reading to demonstrate the divergences that most other reviews allude to only through the disavowal of comparison.

As a comparatist myself, I am compelled to argue for the exigency of recovering the material and aesthetic histories that are *mystified* in these preceding comparisons. Despite the heterogeneity of the receptions, culled from a number of different cultural spheres and spanning rarefied, comics-specific criticism as well as broader cultural or lifestyle interests, they share a rhetorical approach that requires further examination. Why do these readers feel the need to stage a *praeteritio* of comparison? What forms of cultural capital are enabled through the trope of a denial of comparison which itself enacts a comparison?

The rhetorical situation of Abirached's reception in French, US, and UK publications reveals a particular unease on the part of these

"Western" readers. They evince a recalcitrance to use Satrapi as a met-onym for otherness or a token of difference in their efforts to discur-sively "domesticate" Abirached's work. These critics do not want to reproduce an Orientalist cultural imaginary whereby female graphic memoirists from Iran and Lebanon are understood to be similar, regardless of their divergent sociopolitical lifeworlds and cultural products. And yet the very invocation of Satrapi demonstrates that the same readers find themselves unable to *not use* her as a figure by which to read Abirached and the complex circuits of commodities, artists, and aesthetics at work in marketing the graphic Middle East to a Western audience. Speculating about the mentality informing this contradiction, it stems from the lack of a legible array of successful, transnationally circulated comics by women alone, and by women of color in particular. Each comparison also acts as an effort by a reader in "the West" to place Abirached without resorting to Orientalism. Thus, readers disavow the connection to Satrapi as a way to disavow Orientalism, implicitly revealing its presence through negation.

The Global Graphic Novel

Just as I considered how the translations of Satrapi indicated more about the lack of coherence of the "West" than any reader seemed to acknowledge, I hold that the comparisons of Abirached and Satrapi reveal more about the establishment of a transnational graphic novel market than these readings manifest. With all due respect to Tufts, there *are* more similarities between *A Game for Swallows* and *Perse-polis,* and they are more materially fundamental than those that she and many other readers list. Both texts were originally published in Paris—a fact that goes unmentioned in every one of the reviews cited above. Rather than situating the comparison of these women in their birthplaces nearly fifteen hundred kilometers and a decade apart, let us acknowledge the role of the location in which their works were bought, published, and marketed just over six kilometers and less than five years apart.

Without flattening the unique and heterogeneous histories that preceded the publication of *Persepolis* and *A Game for Swallows* and that express themselves in the author functions of Abirached and Satrapi, I maintain that the bande dessinée and graphic novel pub-lishing industries must be foregrounded in questioning the similarities and differences between these books. Following Spivak, I want to draw attention to how the study and consumption of literatures in an age of globalization runs the risk of complicity in the continued "worlding" that began under imperialism to produce the "Third World." Spivak writes, "To consider the Third World as distant cultures, exploited but with rich intact literary heritages waiting to be recovered, interpreted, and curricularized in English translation fosters the emergence of 'the Third World' as a signifier that allows us to forget that 'worlding,' even as it expands the empire of the literary discipline" (243). In figuring Abirached and Satrapi as Middle Eastern artists, telling similar stories, with a similar black-and-white aesthetic, a discrete and consumable "style" is artificially identified and attributed to works from a heterogeneous area.

Our alternative is to attend to the market forces and histories that brought *Persepolis* and *A Game for Swallows* to us and to the aforementioned reviewers at specific points in time. By discursively placing Abirached and Satrapi in mystified relation to the spheres of production where their labor takes place—and to their own emigration and/or exile—these reviewers become unwitting participants in continued cultural imperialism. By ambiguously referencing aesthetic similarities without attending to the medial conditions of the work, they obfuscate the relation of industry to the networks of cultural production and critical valuation that inscribe these women and their graphic narratives in networks between Beirut, Rasht, Paris, London, New York, and even Minneapolis.

Persepolis and *A Game for Swallows* are texts by women born in Iran and Lebanon, but their existence as media objects is owed to a coincidental rise of French independent comics publishing and the graphic novel in anglophone discursive regimes. The uncritical comparison of a woman who left Iran as a self-described political exile and a woman who explains her emigration to Paris in terms of a lack of comic book publishing opportunities in Lebanon creates a false equivalence. At the same time, this comparison estranges these women from their own unique orientations and transnational biographies in order to domesticate the products of their labor within an imaginary of the Middle East as an area othered from the West. Instead, a critical comparison recognizes that the commonalities between *Persepolis* and *A Game for Swallows* implicate France and the US (as well as Lebanon and Iran) through print cultures, centers of productions, and geopolitics.

Abirached has stated that she moved to France to attend the École nationale supérieure des Arts Décoratifs and because, as she explains, "We do not have a comics tradition in Lebanon, and in all the Middle East" (qtd. in Dueben, "Beirut").[30] Abirached studied *graphisme* at Atelier de Recherche ALBA, a division of the Académie libanaise des Beaux-Arts, and cites among her influences David B., Jacques Tardi, Emmanuel Guibert, and a number of other bande dessinée artists. [She does not list Satrapi and has said—as she does in an interview with *L'Express*—that she does not really feel filiation with Satrapi: "Je ne me sens pas vraiment de filiation avec elle" (qtd. in Bisson).] Abirached's explanation for her relocation in Paris invites a critical retracing of the lines of comics production, circulation, and reception that fully accounts for her and Satrapi's awareness of the industry in relation to their own self-location. Such a retracing locates the artists as participants in a global media industry with a major node in Paris, which is informed by cultural and material histories of comics publishing.

The Graphic Novel and the Anxiety of Influence

Publisher Frédéric Cambourakis cites *Persepolis* as a turning point for introducing a new audience to comics, one that led to the appearance of many publishing houses, including his own, Éditions Cambourakis. In 2006 Cambourakis contracted Abirached's first book, *[Beyrouth] Catharsis*, written (and originally published) in 2002 when Abirached was a student at ALBA. His investment in Abirached paid off when her third book, *Le jeu des hirondelles*, was nominated at Angoulême, became a best seller, and was translated into English as *A Game for Swallows* five years later. Cambourakis insists that her success is based on the quality of her book and downplays the comparison of *Le jeu des hirondelles* to *Persepolis*. In Cambourakis's words, following such a *polémique* as the comparison between the two women's books, either popular success (*plébiscite*) or *boycottage* will follow. In Abirached's case, "the public overwhelmingly responded" (qtd. in Pasamonik, "Cambourakis").

---

30. Cf. di Ricco; Douglas and Malti-Douglas. Nadim Damluji, among many projects in his "improbable side career as 'Arab Comics Scholar,'" maintains the blog *Majalat: The Art of Arab Comics.*

It is telling that *A Game for Swallows* was the first of Abirached's books to become financially successful and be translated in the US, as its physical shape is much closer to that of other recognized and recognizable graphic novels than her first two works.

Abirached's oeuvre features a format progression that differs from Satrapi's, which was shaped by L'Association's influence.[31] Unlike a graphic novel or an album of bande dessinée, Abirached's first book, *Catharsis,* is a very small, single-panel-per-page book with a die-cut cover. As its name and subject suggests, her second book, *38, rue Youssef Semaani,* has a long, building-like rectangular shape; when opened, it unfolds to show the numerous denizens of the apartment complex at the titular address. Before this work's completion, Abirached "arrived in Paris with *[Beyrouth] Catharsis* and a proposal for a graphic novel, in search of a publisher" (Pasamonik, "Cambourakis"). Cambourakis published both of her more idiosyncratically shaped works in 2006 prior to the breakout success *Le jeu des hirondelles* in 2007. Just like *Persepolis, Le jeu des hirondelles* gained prominence once it was selected for the Angoulême Festival, but, unlike Abirached's previous texts, this book was recognizably—as she calls it—a "graphic novel."

Although Satrapi herself has rejected the term *graphic novel*— "Editors call me a graphic novelist and my work a graphic novel. However, this is a term I don't like because I'm a cartoonist and what I make are comics" ("State of Mind")—this formal designation gained in transnational appeal following Satrapi's success, such that David B. complains of its francophone adoption:

> The term *graphic novel* has been widely adopted in France by journalists who don't know anything about it, but who feel like they're selling something new with it. Same for editors, who before didn't want to use the term. (qtd. in Evenson)

---

31. As she describes, in order to develop her first book, Abirached began a casual form of fieldwork in order to research the street where she lived during the Lebanese Civil War before "the rebuilding of Beirut . . . when they were carefully erasing all the traces of the war" ("Artist's" 70–71). This research would eventually inform all three of her first publications. Using "words and images, to try to understand" ("Artist's" 71), she drew *Catharsis*. Having "explored the space of the street" in *Catharsis*, Abirached's next work, *38, rue Youssef Semaani,* describes "the life of [her] building" ("Artist's" 73).

Following Satrapi and others, *graphic novel,* as David B. alludes to, connotes not only a format but a transnational marketability, whereas the designation of graphic novel—following Foucault— involves a commercial calculus for standardizing the author-artist as a cultural figure. What Menu wrote of the influence of *Persepolis* on the size and aesthetic of a particular type of book, Beaty extends to Satrapi as well: "In terms of the industry, her success really cemented a desire to find the next great graphic novelist. The French industry is no different from the American: look and see what sells, try to find 100 more of those" (qtd. in Spurgeon). By these descriptions of the market forces, it is easier to understand Abirached's success less as a function of "Middle Eastern," "black and white" drawing and more as a sign of the graphic novel market as a normalizing field.

Abirached's work did not travel from France to the US materially unchanged. Just like *Persepolis* and *Epileptic,* its publisher, Graphic Universe, a Minneapolis-based imprint of Lerner Books, made a number of alterations to the size, page weight, and cover. And, again, anglophone readers did not attend to the comparisons between *Le jeu des hirondelles* and *A Game for Swallows*; instead, they focused on the similarities and differences between Abirached and Satrapi. Prior to the US publication of *A Game for Swallows,* Abirached's translator, Edward Gauvin, noted that

> at first glance, the parallels between Abirached's *Swallows* and Marjane Satrapi's *Persepolis* are obvious, and probably something many critics will remark on: memoirs of childhood by Middle Eastern girls drawn in a black and white, deliberately naïve style. To be slightly cynical, ever since *Persepolis,* American publishers have been looking for the next French graphic novel that would prove as big as Satrapi's hit. ("*Game*")

As cynical as such a description might sound, it goes a long way toward demystifying how *Persepolis* and *A Game for Swallows* have been linked according to industry expectations. Here Gauvin supplies precisely that point of comparison elided in the same lists provided by the reviewers cited above: commerce. Rather than reading the works as purely narrative or aesthetic objects, a feminist materialist approach recognizes the influence of economic factors in the production, consumption, translation, and valuation of graphic novels. In the geopolitical specificity of Satrapi's and Abirached's stories, we can discern the complex interplay between graphic novels, as local stories, and global markets with variegated readerships and reader expectations.

Graphic Aesthetics: Comics as a Problem for Literary Reception

The conflation of Abirached's and Satrapi's artwork is symptomatic of literary inattention to the aesthetics of comics, and of the privileging of story as text over graphic narrative, in which image and text are inextricably enunciative.[32] In form, as in other areas of reception, the critical discourse about Satrapi's and Abirached's art reflects more on the reviewer than on the work itself.

The issues that attend the reception of texts from West Asia are not new, but the ways in which the transnational circuits of the graphic novel affect and are affected by these issues are far more recent. As Beaty writes of the reception of *Persepolis,* while it was lauded for its topic, it was sometimes, especially in the US, criticized for its drawing style. For Beaty this criticism not only denotes an international division, wherein European appreciation for comics as art diverges from US attitudes toward the form, but also indicates the problems that *literary* scholars have in analyzing comics.

According to Beaty, rather than appreciate that comics art generally serves a narrative function, and thus operates in a different register from fine art, critics too frequently appraise the art style of comics according to the criteria they might a painting (249). Chute echoes this sentiment, dismissing criticism of Satrapi's drawing style by explaining that the technical efficiency of drawing in graphic narrative is in fact subservient to "the discursive presentation of time as space on the page" (*Graphic* 146). Additionally, the frequency with which critics use "black and white" as a point of comparison between Abirached and Satrapi reflects a misunderstanding of the role of colors in graphic narrative. In his article on the use of color in comics, Baetens explains that while it is frequently assumed that black and white is chosen for economic reasons, this is not true in all cases, and he cites Satrapi as the most notable exception. He goes on to claim

32. Although Tensuan specifically notes that these types of evaluations reflect a "gendered bias" and rarely see application in relation to male artists like Mark Beyer or Jeffrey Brown (957).

that black and white is viewed as having more of an "auteur" quality (just as in photography) that is associated with graphic novels as opposed to childish, brightly colored comic books ("Black and White" 112). Ann Miller further asserts that for francophone comics, black and white "has come to connote an album presented as a work of art rather than a commercial product" (*Reading* 95). Although Miller allows that there are exceptions in France, and Baetens notes exceptions in the US as well, their role *as exceptions* indicates the predominance of black and white in graphic novels.[33]

Other scholars view this predominance as another way in which the graphic novel capitulates to a literary format. A book-size, black-and-white object that features adult genres like nonfiction, war, and autobiography is much more likely to be found in a US bookstore, marketed to adult audiences, or reviewed in the *New York Times*. A reviewer accustomed to letters over images is less likely to attend to the unique parameters governing what Philippe Marion calls *graphiation,* or the whole account of markings and visual enunciation on the comics page. To compare Satrapi and Abirached on the basis of their mutual use of black and white is almost as meaningful as comparing prose writers who use the same font. While the color palette reflects an artistic and aesthetic choice, it also reflects industry standards; critique of its use can occlude deeper attention to artistic style.

Gauvin, who has translated works by both artists, states of *A Game for Swallows*: "I was taken by its strong design sense, complex motifs, and idiosyncratic use of sound effects in characterization; its use of B[lack]&W[hite] is, needless to say, very different from Satrapi's, and I tried when I could to help the book get out from under that shadow by emphasizing that" ("Re: Katherine Kelp"). As Gauvin notes, black and white alone is a thin point of comparison and one that, in the case of these two women artists, relegates one to the shadow of the other.

Framing Comparison

As transnational commodities, *Persepolis* and *A Game for Swallows* represent the migration of artists from Iran and Lebanon to Europe. They also represent aptitudes and proclivities within European and US markets for specific forms of cultural production. These aptitudes

---

33. See also El Hak 76.

are not uniform across the imagined "West"; nor are they ahistorical. *A Game for Swallows* is necessarily related to Lebanon, just as *Persepolis* is to Iran in ways irreducible to a Western categorization of "Middle Eastern" art. Similarly, the relations of both works to France and to the French language, and to English and the US, are neither ahistorical nor inevitable, but their erasure in discourses about Abirached and Satrapi demonstrates a reluctance to acknowledge the role of capital and geopolitics in literary reception.

In her discussion of orientations and Orientalism, Sara Ahmed stipulates that "we can see how making 'the strange' familiar, or the 'distant' proximate, is what allows 'the West' to extend its reach" (*Queer Phenomenology* 126). For Ahmed, Orientalism is a way of gathering objects and manufacturing differences among those objects. The West orients itself to the Orient as an object of desire, and then domesticates this Orientalism by differentiating between proximities, familiarities, and strangeness. The receptions of *Persepolis* and *A Game for Swallows* in the twenty-first century in Europe and the US denote an orientation toward the "Middle East" at specific moments in time, as well as a concomitant desire to orient the works of Satrapi and Abirached in the service of imaginative or affective economies. The rhetorical paraleipsis of the comparison of Abirached and Satrapi reveals the desire to align these women in the imaginative economy of "Middle Eastern" art while espousing a liberal reluctance to deny each product a unique market value. Regrettably absent from the discussions of identity and difference that attend the interpretation of the narratives and graphic aesthetics of the works is a consideration of the heterogeneous "Western" publishing industries that allow readers to subtly insist that they know more than one "Middle Eastern" woman who draws comics without ever asking *why.*

CHAPTER 4

BORDER THINKING AND DECOLONIAL MAPPING IN MICHAEL NICOLL YAHGULANAAS'S HAIDA MANGA

Decolonizing Comics

What would it mean to "decolonize comics"? This injunction has made its way through a number of comics studies conferences, email discussion lists, and publications (e.g. Howes; Dony).[1] Yet its general tenets seem diffuse and sometimes bound only to the linguistic—a call for comics in languages other than English, French, or Japanese—or the topical—a call for comics about areas other than the North Atlantic. In many iterations, the concept of "decolonizing" comics slides unmarked into the call for more attention to "international" comics. Without detracting from the worthwhile project of promoting scholarship on international comics—for which the present volume

---

1. This phrase has been employed innumerable times and claims its own Facebook discussion group ("Decolonizing Comics," https://www.facebook.com/Graphic Academia/), and talks at UC Davis ("Decolonizing Comics," https://culturalstudies. ucdavis.edu/events/decolonizing-comics-avy-jetter) and the Modern Language Association ("Decolonizing Comics and/as Activism," https://graphicnarratives. org/2020/02/19/mla-2021-special-session-cfp-decolonizing-comics-and-as-activism-deadline-03-15-20/), etc.

evidences my own dedication—I would like to counter the substitution of "international" for "decolonial" by focusing on the Haida manga of Michael Nicoll Yahgulanaas and their relationship to decolonization, transnationalism, and cultural syncretism.

As Eve Tuck (Unangax̂) and K. Wayne Yang assert, "decolonization is not a metaphor," and the employment of the term in inexact or figurative ways allows "the real and symbolic violences of settler colonialism to be overlooked" (2). Tuck and Yang warn that the "easy absorption, adoption, and transposing of decolonization is yet another form of settler appropriation" (3), one visible in the equivocation at work in the conflation of international comics with decolonial comics or the project of decolonizing comics. For Tuck and Yang, decolonization entails the "repatriation of Indigenous land and life" (21), a project that Yahgulanaas has pursued through his activism and art for decades.

Yahgulanaas is Raven[2] of the Haida First Nations Indigenous Peoples,[3] based in Haida Gwaii, off the coast of British Columbia. A descendant of acclaimed Haida artists Isabelle Edenshaw, Charles Edenshaw, and Delores Churchill, and a relative of artists Robert Davidson and James Hart, Yahgulanaas began creating politically motivated comics in the 1970s to draw attention to deforestation and the threat from resource-extraction industries to Haida Gwaii (Levell, *Seriousness* 16; Park 4). His first full-length comic, *No Tankers, Tanks,* was published in 1977 for the Coalition Against Supertankers and the Islands Protection Society,[4] as part of an ultimately successful campaign to block the transport of Exxon Valdez crude oil through the Hecate Strait. Yahgulanaas would go on to publish a number of comics critiquing environmental and political spoliation by the Canadian government and commercial interests, including work in most issues of Haida Gwaii–based *SpruceRoots Magazine* (1995–2005).[5] Yahgulanaas also served as the CEO of the Old Massett Village Council and on the Council of the Haida Nation. Organizing and participating in

---

2. Raven and Eagle are the two moieties of the Haida. See Nika Collison's explanation of the roles and interactions of the clans (Augaitis et al. 59–62).

3. Yahgulanaas himself discredits "First Nations" as a "politically convenient and legally soft term" that does not have the same protection of law afforded by "Indigenous Peoples" (qtd. in Park 5).

4. For the history of the Islands Protection Society (formerly the Islands Protection Committee), see May; Takeda.

5. See the interview in Park 34–46.

numerous antilogging actions and protests for Haida sovereignty, Yahgulanaas was arrested as part of the Lyell Island blockades in 1985. These efforts led to the establishment of the Gwaii Haanas Agreement and are depicted or referenced in many of Yahgulanaas's early comics.

Even in his later, larger narrative works, Yahgulanaas's art indicates the inextricability of art from land. While Tuck and Yang critique the value of epistemological decolonization without territorial repatriation, Seneca scholar Mishuana Goeman stresses the necessity of employing literature and imaginative responses to (re)map space. For Goeman, "(Re)mapping is about acknowledging the power of Native epistemologies in defining our moves toward spatial decolonization, a specific form of spatial justice" (4).[6] Thus, Goeman's writing considers imaginative repatriation as a meaningful form of decolonial work. The Native women writers Goeman studies use stories as tools for "reframing the project of decolonization and globality" (202), in much the same way that Yahgulanaas's stories remap both Haida land and the space of the comics page. Further, as a culturally syncretic work, Haida manga also corresponds to Goeman's insistence that (re)mapping is a reconceptualization of space as a product of encounters between different peoples (6). A form constructed in opposition to the North American settler colonial conceptualization of space, Yahgulanaas's Haida manga uses transpacific cultural and artistic affinities in order to reimagine, literally and figuratively, the terms and lines dividing space and place.

Yahgulanaas works in a variety of artistic mediums, and his art is frequently credited with either challenging or reinventing "traditional" Haida art.[7] Yahgulanaas has produced a number of sculpture exhibits and installations, in addition to his production in Haida manga, an art form demonstrated in a number of short works as well

---

6. As Goeman notes, she uses the term "'Native' when referring to those indigenous to North America and 'Indigenous' to refer to indigenous people on a global scale." I follow this custom here, and I follow her convention to use the terms "Native" and "Indigenous" in "the context of someone's work who utilizes the [respective] term[s]" (213n1).

7. Marie Mauzé asserts that "Yahgulanaas strives to go beyond traditional art practices with his hybrid visual art," while Louise Loik describes his work in slightly more violent terms: "Revolting against neatly packaged 'authentic Indian' art, he took cultural expectations and tossed them aside by mixing art genres and mixing mediums from unexpected components of modern and ancient, Japanese Manga, Chinese brushstrokes, North American Indigenous, serious, and comical influences."

as books, including *A Tale of Two Shamans* (2001), *The Last Voyage of the Black Ship* (2002), *War of the Blink* (2006), *Red* (2009), and *Carpe Fin* (2019). The author of *The Seriousness of Play,* a monograph on Yahgulanaas's practice, Nicola Levell, notes: "Through [his] creative mix or creolisation, Haida manga has emerged as a vibrant visual idiom for retelling Indigenous oral histories and other narratives and for offering different ways of seeing and knowing cultural complexes" (8). This particular formulation of how Haida manga engenders new optics aligns it with a comics studies application of what Walter Mignolo theorizes as "border thinking."

In his seminal work *Local Histories/Global Designs: Coloniality, Subaltern Knowledges, and Border Thinking,* Mignolo describes decolonization in concert with the "transformation of the rigidity of epistemic and territorial *frontiers* established and controlled by the coloniality of power in the process of building the modern/colonial world system" (12). Mignolo postulates a mode of thought that does not reinvest the epistemological difference between knower and known and between subject and object with epistemological privilege (17). Thus, his border thinking is a "machine for intellectual decolonization" (45), one which troubles dichotomies inherent in all forms of knowledge production, such as inside/outside (338) as a mode of distinguishing where knowledge is and is not. As Mignolo describes how border thinking might work in a place-based parameter, in order to get away from thinking of places as "an 'area' to be studied, we need a kind of thinking beyond the social sciences and positivistic philosophy, a kind of thinking that moves along the diversity of the historical process itself" (69). Mignolo's call converges with Goeman's in its incitement to "think beyond the ontologization of an area to be studied and move to a reflection on the historicity of differences" (69).

Goeman and Mignolo provide a framework through which to understand Yahgulanaas's work as it enacts a decolonizing form of "spatial justice." As I contend, from a decolonial standpoint, it is disingenuous to read Yahgulanaas's work as *sui generis* without reflecting on the encounters, contexts, and constraints that figure into the creation of Haida manga. But it is likewise unhelpful to conceptualize Yahgulanaas's work as merely reactionary. Instead, Haida manga mobilizes border thinking for the project of spatial decolonization, implicating in the process a wide swath of encounters between peoples, cultural techniques, nomenclatures, spatial demarcations, and commodity objects. I focus on his mural/book compositions as projects remapping the relations between the global and the local including the terminology used to describe the work, the space of the page, the linearity of narrative, and the commercial situation of the codex. Just as "epistemology implies and is embedded in a politics of location" (Mignolo, "I Am" 236), so Yahgulanaas's Haida manga must be understood in its situatedness.

The Time and Place of Indigenous Art

As a number of scholars of Indigenous art and literature have written, practitioners such as Yahgulanaas are frequently relegated to an imagined artistic undertaking in which Indigenous tradition constitutes a cloistered and unchanging system of production. Anthropologist Peter MacNair insists that "given the constraints of a centuries-old formalized art form, it is a great challenge to produce unique and ground-breaking variations" (Augaitis et al. 117). And while MacNair's might be read as a false binary between formalization and variation, curator Nicole Stanbridge notes that discussions of First Nations Indigenous art are always fraught with imposed categories of traditional versus contemporary. This problematic divide functions as a means by which Indigenous art is qualified in terms of its "authenticity" or "indigeneity," while ensuring that these qualifiers connote *past* or *nonmodern*.

Contemporary Indigenous artists, curators, and theorists have long grappled with how or whether to address the problematic of traditional versus contemporary. Art historian Charlotte Townsend-Gault asserts that the very word *tradition* is highly contested in Northwest Coast art, as "many stakeholders, including collectors and dealers, have vested interest in defining what tradition is and how it looks" (914). Representative curators in the *Decolonize Me* (Ottawa Art Gallery 2012) catalog from the influential exhibit of Canadian Indigenous artists vacillate between a complete denial of the relevance of such a structure (Loft 76) and the possibility of reworking these two terms in the service of a cyclical rather than linear view of artistic development (Candice Hopkins and Christine Lalonde qtd. in Stanbridge 16).[8] While there is no consensus among these curators as to whether or how to grapple with the oft-externally constructed

8. See also Ariella Azoulay's critique that "in most of the languages spoken outside of Africa, too, including European languages, there is no old word that effectively translates the word art as we know it today . . . The mastering of time is a key aspect of imperial violence that separates objects from people and places them

and evaluated legitimacy of tradition, Stanbridge stresses that such debates about identity and Indigenous art are a necessary counter to "the suppression of the Indigenous voice, not only in Canada's history but globally" (16). These contentions regarding the role of tradition as a problematic formulation illustrate the tension between a myopic approach to Indigenous art based on constraining imaginings of the time and place of authentic Indigeneity, and the realities of contemporary, globalized art.[9]

In rejoinder to such debates, Yahgulanaas speaks about the "tradition of innovation,"[10] asserting that these two words, while rarely combined, are actually co-constitutive (Sostar McClellan 38). Although Yahgulanaas allows that many conceptualize tradition as static and innovation as hybridity, he characterizes his great-great grandfather, master carver Charles Edenshaw, as demonstrating through his work the "tradition of innovation" ("Michael Nicoll"). The same can be said of Yahgulanaas's own work, which stages and formally depicts encounters and interrelations between Haida and other national configurations while at the same time acknowledging "colonial spatial process as ongoing but imbued with power struggles" (Goeman 11). Even in his early comics from the 1970s, Yahgulanaas's art has focused on how claims have been discursively or violently enacted over the Haida land by other First Nations peoples, by Canadian settlers, by the Canadian government, and by corporate interests — some Canadian and some multinational.

In *Old Growth*, editor Liz Park collects many of Yahgulanaas's early works, including editorial cartoons and longer works such as *No Tankers, T'anks*. In his early work, Yahgulanaas already grapples with questions of place and authenticity as they take shape in art. A note inside *No Tankers* qualifies the cover art by John Broadhead:[11]

---

in a progressive, linear timeline ('art history' is paradigmatic) in which colonized people and colonizers occupy different positions and roles" (60).

9. Cf. Reg Davidson: "There is a fashionable notion that 'traditional' art forms don't really exist anymore, that 'traditional' art is attached to a specific historical time period . . . this ideology has the unfortunate consequence of releasing us from the responsibility of caring for the sources of the traditional materials on which these art forms depend" (Augaitis et al. 38).

10. In his study *Northwest Coast Indian Art*, Bill Holm avers: "It seems that every Haida artist of any consequence was an innovator, and each developed his own distinctive handling of form and space within the prescribed system" (23).

11. Broadhead would go on to become co-director of the Gowgaia Institute, committed to producing planning maps for the Haida Nation (Takeda 8; Maher).

The graphic style of the Northwest Coast Indians used here cannot be considered accurate or authentic. It was produced by a member of the Canuck Tribe. The "formline" style was borrowed for its allegorical capabilities, and its use was inspired by the fact that, for whatever reasons, the Native Peoples at one time did a much cleaner job of caretaking the planet than we seem to be doing today. (Qtd. in Park 23)

This qualification locates the formline—which would become central to Yahgulanaas's later work—and the graphic narrative it covers in a particular site of encounter. While we might wonder at the dichotomy staged between "accurate and authentic" and "allegorical," the particular inscribing technique of the formline is claimed as a necessary practice despite the tribal affiliation (or lack thereof) of the artist. This note itself marks the publication of Broadhead's formline cover as a politically motivated prioritizing of aesthetic intent over authenticity. The note's ostensible purpose of justifying a non-Native appropriation of Native art serves the rhetorical purpose of alerting the reader to the appropriation of the style and justifying its usage based on a historical legacy of Native Peoples.[12] Rhetorically, the formline's use by a non-Native artist is necessary because of what it *represents* in the artwork itself. This justified appropriation presages Yahgulanaas's own shift to working in "manga" as well as his continued advocacy for attention to cross-cultural technicity.

Yahgulanaas's Haida manga has become almost synonymous with "cultural hybridity," but the majority of such descriptions rely on each noun—Haida and manga—in syntagmatic conjunction as the literal rationale for such an interpretation. Cultural hybridity, as theorized by Homi Bhabha among others, is a framework that both fulfills the urgent necessity to rethink cultural production in (post)colonial or global systems of exchange and problematically leads to a number of critics from privileged readerships making unqualified statements about so-called other cultures. The latter position is reflected in descriptions such as a *Vancouver Sun* article describing Yahgulanaas's work as a "distinctive hybrid of Northwest Coast formline and the visual language of Asian graphic novels" (Griffin), whereas Yahgulanaas has, in his own paratextual descriptions of his work, highlighted points of tension, contestation, or even what Jean-François Lyotard

---

12. Cf. Nika Collison's stipulation that the formline is intellectual property (Augaitis et al. 60).

would call *"le différend."* This unassimilable discursive situation, in which the claim to justice by one party cannot be articulated in the discourse of the rule of judgment, reverberates throughout Yahgulanaas's work as well as his paratextual explanations of the negotiations and conflicts inherent in cultural production.

Rather than approaching Haida manga as a seamless or even paratactically aligned hybrid, I argue that Yahgulanaas's work can and should be read for how it cultivates cultural difference as technical practice. No mere synthesis of two cultures, Yahgulanaas's art compels a reader to question and rethink ways of seeing, reading, and knowing, while simultaneously highlighting points of disjuncture or untranslatability in modes of discourse and inscription. Levell cites Yahgulanaas's 2001 book, *A Tale of Two Shamans,* as "the advent of Haida manga proper" (*Seriousness* 30), representing for her many of the elements that Yahgulanaas would go on to reproduce in other books. Less comic than picture book, the story features "bold asymmetrical calligraphic formlines" that Levell links to Haida design while noting that they structure the page and "[lend] a cadence and pace to the imagery, manga-style" (30). Aside from Levell's designation of the manga-style construction of images, the first edition of the book bears paratextual evidence of Yahgulanaas's approach to cultural specificity. The work begins with a note stipulating that the story is a "blend of accounts recorded at the turn of the nineteenth century in three of the once numerous dialects of the Haida language" (*Tale* n. pag.). A reader is likewise cautioned that the images throughout are "interpretations informed by [Yahgulanaas's] own cultural composition and life experiences," and the end matter features an interlinear translation of the text of the book. The paratext thus highlights the situatedness of Yahgulanaas's work—according to which the book's audience and constraints engender hybridity as a symptom of border thinking—while alluding to the incommensurability of different systems of discourse and inscription. Here, dialects, orality, and cultural composition and life experiences delimit how this "blend of accounts" can be translated into a verbal-visual composition. Constraints of form—the interpretive nature of the images, unassimilable differences in the interlinear translation—situate the work in the context of cultural encounters and a tradition of innovation.

Yahgulanaas's 2002 *The Last Voyage of the Black Ship*—which features the words *Haida Manga* on its cover—more overtly resembles later works like *Red* in that pages are all filled with images broken into panels by framelines, with small narrative and dialogue boxes.

In this work as well, the relative position of audience and work is accented through two footnotes explaining the trees in the cypress family and the location of Haida Gwaii. A large map on page 6 interrupts the visual coherence of the narrative in order to illustrate coastal logging of the Pacific Northwest with accompanying text asserting the necessity of cedar conservation efforts.

These earlier works establish a precedent by which Yahgulanaas asserts his right to bring together culturally distinct styles and dialects while attending to the rationale for doing so. This reasoning poses a challenge for "authenticity" while preserving its meaning as a signifier in Native cultural production. That is, Yahgulanaas gestures toward an "authentic" Native culture, one that he claims knowledge of enough to know what does and does not adhere to this formulation. Yet, in Yahgulanaas's works, this authenticity is pliable enough that it may be used in inaccurate, inexact, or even inauthentic ways because of rhetorical or aesthetic necessity. It is from this negotiation of "authentic" cultural production that one might analyze the border thinking inherent in Yahgulanaas's practice, and his development of Haida manga.

Comics versus Manga

TERMINOLOGY

Although Yahgulanaas has drawn comics, or what might at times be termed *editorial cartoons,* for over forty years, his critique of the term *comics* stems from its cultural situation. Yahgulanaas states that he chose manga specifically because of its association with Pacific culture and because "it is not part of the settler tradition of North America" (qtd. in Levell, *Seriousness* 10). Park suggests a rhetorical more than a formal connotation for the term, arguing that just as his work uses Haida tradition "flexibly," so too,

> "manga" itself is a term that the artist uses with a degree of elasticity. *Haida Manhwa* and *Manhua* are variant terms he has used, in Korean and Chinese contexts respectively.[13] This changing term suggests that Haida cultural productions can adapt and evolve in an ever-shifting world without compromising their basic cultural integrity. (Park 6)

13. See Chie Yamanaka, "Domesticating Manga?" and "*Manhwa* in Korea."

Park's characterization of Haida cultural production would seem to obscure the specificity of manga, manhwa, and manhua as cultural products with their own geographically inflected histories. Indeed, an article for *Canada's National Observer* stipulates that "identifying with the Manga graphic cartoon style was more of a political statement than stylistic" (Loik). While we may allow the political motive for selecting one term over another, such a claim problematically assumes the separation of politics and style.[14] Alternatively, one must grapple with both the politics *of* style and the historical location of manga within and without Yahgulanaas's employment of the term. To do so is to understand the complex of relations among manga, Japan, Haida, and Canada.

The question of whether Japan functions in Haida manga as a real site of production, or as an imagined other, is fraught. Brenna Clarke Gray has characterized the role of Japan in Yahgulanaas's discourse as "an imagined space of distance from Canada's colonial history," but one that "is anti-colonial only in relation to Haida experience" (183). Gray is ultimately critical of the way this usage attains cultural significance only through the evacuation of its Japanese cultural significance. It is not that Yahgulanaas does not recognize Japan and Japanese culture in his conceptualization of his work. Yahgulanaas has spoken of his own personal and ancestral connections to Japan, referencing stories told to him as a child of "Haida fishermen pursuing northern fur seals across the Pacific Ocean on hunts that would last months at a time and take them as far away as the shores of Japan" (Medley). In an interview with Kristine Sostar McLellan, Yahgulanaas stated that in his family "there were some ancestors who welcomed the opportunity to go to Japan and get away from Canada because it was so terrible to be an Indigenous person here. Haida men in Japan were treated like full people, like human beings" (39). Further, Yahgulanaas relocates his use of manga to Japan; while on a trip, Yahgulanaas attributes the adoption of the term to Japanese readers: "the use of the term *manga* to describe the kind of images he creates was

---

14. In response to a question as to "whether art is cheapened or made more potent when infused with politics," Yahgulanaas stipulates that "if you take a beautiful pole out of the village where it means these things and take it and place it way over there, does it mean the same thing? And I realized it doesn't mean the same thing . . . When art becomes in service of political and social contemporary issues, I think that's when it's really working well . . . And, now, when I have an exhibit or produce work, I see that as an opportunity to produce material culture in service of other issues and not simply to be a new type of wallpaper" (qtd. in Roberts-Farina).

suggested to him by students who saw him as a *mangaka,* or *manga* artist" (Mauzé). However, as Gray insists, Japan in this formulation becomes a "useful Other" only because Yahgulanaas "does not negotiate Japan's own colonial legacy" (184), leading to the problematic of whether Haida manga is really decolonial if it merely eschews one colonial nation for another.

Reading for difference necessitates attending precisely to the geopolitical and historical contexts that Yahgulanaas invokes. For him, as an Indigenous person, Japan's own history of colonialism does not resemble North American colonization and ongoing practices of incarceration, which he mentions when describing Japanese internment camps and the Japanese as a "demonized ethnicity" in North America. Yahgulanaas's position is a corrective to forms of postcolonial or even colonial theory that conflate drastically different settings and peoples. And yet, the construction that Haida manga takes throughout many of these conceptualizations is syntactically posed through negation rather than formal, historical, or material attribution. In many of these descriptions, Haida manga is described as manga because it is *not* North American. Thus, rather than a denotative term, *manga* is used to mean "not comics," as comics represents a specific genealogy of colonial occupation.

There are a number of Indigenous artists in North America who self-identify as *comics* artists, so Yahgulanaas's resistance to the term merits greater exploration. Lee Francis IV (Laguna Pueblo), founder of Indigenous Comic-Con (first held in 2016 in Albuquerque), CEO and publisher of Native Realities—an Indigenous comics press—and owner of Red Planet Books and Comics, has championed the use of comics and graphic novels as a way to reshape narratives about Indigenous Peoples. As Francis states, "Give me something exciting to read and we can foster a different understanding of native identity" (qtd. in Helou). For Francis and other producers and practitioners, Indigenous comics provides a valuable platform for reappropriating the means of representation and for promoting visions of Indigenous sovereignty and success.

Francis relates being tired of seeing only "tragic stereotypes" of Native people in mainstream media and wanting to present "stories of Native people as superheroes" as a way to unlock the "Indigenous Imagination" (Sorrell). Further, Canadian scholars Camille Callison and Candida Rifkind stage an analogous argument in their introduction to "Indigenous Comics and Graphic Novels: An Annotated

Bibliography." They begin by suggesting the problematic history of representations of Indigenous Peoples in comics, drawing from work by Michael A. Sheyahshe (Caddo) and C. Richard King, before championing the possibilities that comics can offer for Indigenous self-determination: "we have learned that Indigenous comics and graphic novels matter . . . that Indigenous characters can be just as brave, resilient, complex, messy, smart, and funny as any other comic book heroes" (147). This celebration of "comics" as a medium for Indigenous self-representation serves as a counterpoint to Yahgulanaas's characterization of his own graphic narrative work and leads to the question of what precisely distinguishes Haida manga from Indigenous comics.

In point of fact, King offers the opposite argument to Yahgulanaas's, asserting, "Native American artists have seized on the comic book not simply as a means to interrupt imperial idioms but also as a space in which to reimagine themselves and reclaim their cultures" (220). If, for King, the medium is the message as well as the technical a priori for Indigenous resistance and self-determination, how do we understand Yahgulanaas's insistence on the specificity of nomenclature as it extends to his work? Park notes the importance of "bestowing names," in that naming "powerfully evokes the relationships that bind the name-givers and the named" (4), especially in Yahgulanaas's colonially renamed and denamed Queen Charlotte Islands / Haida Gwaii. But given the role of naming in Indigenous sovereignty, the question remains, as Yahgulanaas himself asks in an early editorial cartoon, "What's a Name?," and in the case of his work, what is *manga?*

At a conference presentation on *Red,* a respondent queried the speaker about what makes Haida manga *manga.*[15] The question leads to an extensive problematic: because the term registers a relationship between nation/culture (Haida) and object (manga), while invoking the hybridity of two different linguistic systems, it must be considered in terms of location, or in the framework of Mignolo's local histories / global designs. This question can also be extended in a number of locationally significant registers: What makes Haida manga *Haida?* Or—as Richard Harrison asks—is there such a category as "the Canadian graphic novel," and how does Yahgulanaas's work

15. This question was posed by Margaret Galvan to Jeremy Carnes after his talk "The When and Where of Haida Art: Time and Place in Michael Yahgulanaas' Red: A Haida Manga" at the Modern Language Association conference in Seattle, 2020.

fit into such categorizations? These questions may all seem to revolve around similar claims of location and formal categories, yet the stakes involved in each should lead to increased caution against the erasure of cultural specificity or a complete resort to cultural relativism.

As Kwame Anthony Appiah reminds us, what is called *cultural syncretism* is often a vehicle for cultural imperialism or neocolonialism ("Is the Post- in Postmodernism" 348). The exigence inherent in any analysis of Yahgulanaas's work is the careful consideration of how to locate Haida manga in terms of at least three geographically and politically delineated categories. Is it representative of Japanese cultural production because of its formal categorization as manga? Is it, above all, a Haida work, as Yahgulanaas is Haida? Is it, as Harrison suggests, a Canadian work because

> politically, socially and artistically, Canada is a nation both Western and Indigenous, but not both at once. As such, a key element of Canadian identity lies in the way in which the term "Canadian" can apply (and often does) both to one thing and its opposite—among the qualities which, taken together, define the nation, there are contradictions that cannot be reconciled in the sense that they are dissolved, but must, in the end, sit side by uneasy side. (53)

Harrison's compelling case for the capaciousness of Canadian signification unfortunately replicates the imperial principle of allowing settler colonial terminology to absorb Indigenous sovereignty within the framework of the settler colonial nation. As Haida artist Reg Davidson asserts, "Haida live with the daily dichotomy of art and politics" (Augaitis et al. 38), whereby Haida art "is acclaimed as a Canadian symbol" but "the land question remains" (38). By this dint, while we might acknowledge that Yahgulanaas's work comports with Harrison's view of Canadian graphic narrative, Yahgulanaas's own naming project is a form of self-determination that stands in resistance to the national configurations of the North American continent.[16] Even more, as the official website of the Council of the Haida Nation notes, "Our traditional territory encompasses parts of southern Alaska, the archipelago of Haida Gwaii and its surrounding waters." This map

---

16. As Haida artist Robert Davidson stipulates, "One cannot overstate the importance of traditional Haida names . . . Names carry certain privileges and responsibilities, they carry prestige, and at one time carried ownership to lands" (qtd. in Augaitis et al. 50).

negates the relevance of the colonial Canadian–US borders, by connecting Haida Gwaii with the Kaigani Haida habitation in what is known as the US state of Alaska (according to settler colonial naming practice). Stipulating that "all people of Haida ancestry are citizens of the Haida Nation," the Council makes clear that Harrison's championing of the malleability of "Canadian identity" does not recognize Indigenous sovereignty on its own terms and in terms of its own self-determination.[17]

Pursuantly, to reprise both Goeman's and Mignolo's approaches to place and space, Haida manga is a way of "unsettling [the] colonial map" of Canada and "asserting sovereignty through language" (Goeman 11). It represents "border thinking" as "a dichotomous locus of enunciation . . . located at the borders (interior or exterior) of the modern/colonial world system" (Mignolo, *Local Histories* 85). The dichotomous coupling of two linguistically and geographically distinct nouns gestures toward their irreducible difference while positing their combinatory power as an epistemological intervention into naming, geography, art, and commerce. The significance of Yahgulanaas naming his work *manga* is not limited to the denotative import of this term. As I argue in what follows, Yahgulanaas's Haida manga forces a rethinking of the relationships between terminology, form, and sites of production. I contend that one must examine denotative and connotative facets of manga in order to analyze how this discursive construct is qualified or changed through Haida manga.

FORM

Writing about manga in North America, Frederik L. Schodt describes a comparative framework not dissimilar to Yahgulanaas's, noting the predilection for "true fans" to "discuss how they prefer the Japanese-style story lines and characters over American-style works" (23); thus, at least on the surface, a dichotomy between comics and manga is maintained. Yet Schodt goes on to complicate this division, explaining that for the majority of fans, manga merely refers to a certain visual style ("big eyes, big bosoms, very young-looking female characters, and a cute quality not native to America"; 23) that is easily repro-

17. Cf. Gill 18.

duced in Korean manhwa and Chinese manhua, leading to these forms also commonly receiving the nomination "manga."

Further, both the production of Original English Language (OEL) manga and the development of right-to-left printed books for readers in English has led to a convoluted range of products that fall under the classification of manga, especially as "the Americanized versions of [manga] are neither truly Japanese nor truly American, for they have text that is read left-to-right, horizontally, and images that are read right-to-left" (Schodt 23). Tellingly, when speaking at the Bill Reid Centre at Simon Fraser University, Yahgulanaas responded to a question from a student concerning his decision to make the reading direction left-to-right rather than right-to-left by asserting that "I had to think of my primary audience . . . as much as I wanted to position my community's relationship with Asia, which is longstanding, I had to realize that the audience I wanted to talk to is here." In this recognition of intended audience, Yahgulanaas situates his manga as belonging to the nebulous range of OEL manga that Schodt outlines, yet without the "visual style"—or at least without the big eyes and big bosoms.

Yahgulanaas is hardly the first artist to produce manga outside Japan or to use the term in a "flexible" way. Sociologist Casey Brienza has contributed invaluable scholarship on the ways in which manga travels outside of Japan. In her work on "global manga," Brienza looks at the phenomenon as "a medium which has incorporated requisite cultural meanings and practices from Japanese manga but does not otherwise require any Japanese individual or collective entity in a material, productive capacity" ("Introduction" 5). Brienza gives credit to Anne Allison's assertion that manga is "cool" in the US not because of any specific quality of Japaneseness but instead because in manga and other cultural products, "'Japan' operates more as a signifier for a particular brand and blend of fantasy-ware: goods that inspire an imaginary space at once foreign and familiar and a subjectivity of continual flux and global mobility" (Allison 277). Yet Brienza ultimately finds that the transnational domestication of *Manga in America* has led to a situation wherein the meaning of manga "has evolved to have less to do with visual style or content, or country of origin, and more about the presentation of the book as a mass-produced commercial object and the intended target audience" (*Manga* 12). For Brienza, who explains the origins and misuses of the word, a new contemporary moment in globalization entails that manga's cultural specificity has been irrevocably blurred by transnational commerce to the point where "whether or not it is from Japan is of secondary importance" (12).[18]

Both Schodt and Brienza direct a reader to understand manga as a category of commodity objects, the name of which bears cultural connotations that evoke but do not necessarily possess a direct connection to Japan.[19] This malleability of the term underscores Yahgulanaas's use but still does not fully describe whether Haida manga has an aesthetic or technical meaning *per se.* Is Haida manga a Haida practice *of* manga or a unique entity unto itself? Brienza describes "what the American manga industry does" as "domestication" (*Manga* 35): a means of naturalizing form while simultaneously distinguishing manga as a transnational—as opposed to global or national—cultural production. Yet Yahgulanaas's manga does not comport with all of the commercial and production-based aspects of domestication that Brienza outlines, again forcing the question of what makes Haida manga *manga.*

Critics have differed in whether they understand Yahgulanaas's manga as a kind of naming practice or a formal description. Both Park and Gray contend that Yahgulanaas uses manga connotatively rather than denotatively; Judith Ostrowitz instead argues that manga historically connotes a "nexus of Eastern and Western traditions" (81), thus asserting the value of Yahgulanaas's usage as a naming convention that is precisely used in this case. In a more formal approach, Miriam Brown Spiers relies on Scott McCloud's and Robin Brenner's work on manga to conduct a close reading of *Red* as manga, by using these comics theorists to explain how Yahgulanaas's work comports with the criteria distinguishing manga from comics. Of all critical responses, Spiers's is most earnestly and rigorously engaged in reading *Red* as formally manga. However, even this thoughtful attempt to firmly situate Yahgulanaas's work within the parameters of Japanese cultural production relies on tenuous distinctions between comics and manga. Spiers lists popular themes from *shonen* and *seinen* manga

18. Certainly, the production of the "first Arabic-language manga comic," *The Gold Ring,* in Dubai, demonstrates manga's global distribution (Good).

19. Japan may itself connote a broad range of meanings within scholarship on manga: "cherished or disdained premodern traditions, a desired Other or rejected colonizer, a language-wise closed realm or platform for transcultural interaction, a particular visual style or specific media format, and a business model" (Berndt and Kümmerling-Meibauer 2).

that *Red* uses, such as honor and heroism or sacrifice and obligation, only to assert that these themes are lacking in comics. In her reading, Spiers characterizes American comics as frequently "valoriz[ing] a quest for vengeance" as opposed to manga, which demonstrates "more formal and thematic experimentation" (49).

Because Spiers's reading rests on the idea that valorized "revenge" is an American trope, the reading appears both overgeneralized and limited. If this distinction is the main component that makes *Red* manga, rather than comics, what about all of Yahgulanaas's other Haida manga? A formal element that Spiers quotes from McCloud and attributes to *Red* as a marker of its "manga-ness" is the "subjective motion and dizzy POV framing" (49). Yet she goes on to assert that the subjective motion is especially evident in the reader's experience of *Red* not as a book but as a full wall mural. While it is true that if a reader accepts this perspectival criterion as a marker of manga, *Red* fulfills it, one must also assert that manga—as described by McCloud—are not presented as full wall murals, making the connection between Haida manga and manga further obfuscated rather than clarified.

Instead of focusing on the mural as a site of formal correlation, one might linger on the publication formats of both *Red* and "manga" as a point of comparison. The conflation of material substrates and experience belies the real significance of the preponderance of the book in both manga and Haida manga. Arguing that the situation of manga in the US is markedly different from other types of comics in terms of print conditions, Brienza notes that in the US, marketplace manga began "migrati[ing] away from comics" ("Books" 102) in the late 1990s. Unlike US comics' origins in newspaper and magazine fields of production and circulation, manga "is a subset of the book field" (109)—as are some, but not all, the objects termed *graphic novels* in the US. Similarly, while many of the Indigenous comics championed by Francis IV and King are originally published as comic books—or floppy, short narrative installments—Haida manga and manga are overwhelmingly circulated and sold as book-length objects. Brienza even goes so far as to provide evidence suggesting that manga, or the success of manga in US bookstores, engendered the affiliation of trade book and comic book publishing fields (*Manga* 67).

Before I highlight Haida manga's deconstruction of the book as object, I would like to underscore how Spiers's comparison might be revised to consider an important shared material substrate between Haida manga and manga. By looking at Haida manga and manga in terms of the book, one can question the endemic versus translational orientation of these forms: Are they published as books because this format is in some way traditional or amenable to the content? Are they published as books because, as discussed in chapter 2, they are "born translated" (Walkowitz), and books already have established circuits of transnational sales and exchange? Further, as Brienza notes:

> The habitus of the comics field makes it difficult terrain for new, aspiring actors of every sort, whether they be readers, sellers, or publishing companies: publishers who have not already been long situated in the field have trouble attracting extant readers; potential new readers, especially women and children, find extant material confusing and shops unwelcoming; shops not run by longtime insiders who know how to appeal to other longtime insiders cannot keep their customer base; and so forth. ("Books" 106)

Instead of relying on generalizations about revenge tropes and dizzying perspectives, one might consider how Haida manga and manga, as products excluded from the "long situated field" of comics that Brienza outlines, are marketed as book-length objects, shifting audience expectations as well as points of sale.

This critique is not meant to discredit Spiers's work, as Spiers is one of the only theorists who attempt an informed and sustained reading of *Red* according to scholarship on manga. Most readers are content to let mention of the "manga elements" (Haines) of Haida manga stand unexplored. Spiers's is a meticulous and forthright attempt to read Yahgulanaas's work through its own terms. However, I would like to suggest that another reading is possible.

Manga as a Toponymic Function

Insofar as Yahgulanaas's use of *manga* may well seem to stem either from negation of other terminology, and hence other artistic lineages, or from a "marketing ploy" (Brienza, "Introduction" 14), one must here reckon with a parallel slippage in the application of *comics* or *graphic novel* to a plethora of heterogeneous cultural products, many of which would otherwise be considered bande dessinée, *fumetti, komiks,* and so forth.[20] To return to both Goeman's and Mignolo's theoretical frameworks, *comics* is one way of mapping cultural production, and one that frequently serves as an imperializing nomenclature. As the previous chapter shows of the *graphic novel,* American English terminology often becomes the lingua franca of transnational comics production. In Mignolo's formulation, *comics* is taken as a global signifier to describe a number of "local" products, such as "manga." Yahgulanaas remaps both signifiers in meaningful ways.

Through *manga,* Yahgulanaas linguistically substitutes one settler colonial term of continued settler relevance for a term with a burgeoning and differently defined operational territory. This substitution represents an important intervention in what Mignolo describes as "cultural semiosis," or "the conflicts engendered by coloniality . . . in the sphere of signs" (*Local Histories* 14). To claim the power to name his practice according to his own affiliations and local/global situation, Yahgulanaas claims for himself the power that the colonizer has long held over social-semiotic relations and toponymic systems, just as his home of Haida Gwaii was long referred to by the Canadian government as the Queen Charlotte Islands, until Indigenous sovereignty and resistance movements forced the recognition both of the name for the place and the Haida Gwaii Reconciliation Act.[21]

The power to name is thus its own form of intervention and anticolonial endeavor, but I contend that Haida manga does not merely name a product; it names a place. Implicated in every aspect of Yahgulanaas's work is the destabilization of *land* as the sole form of ter-

---

20. In their introduction to *Manga's Cultural Crossroads,* editors Jaqueline Berndt and Bettina Kümmerling-Meibauer acknowledge both the cultural interconnectivity of all graphic narrative and the specificity of manga as a "cultural crossroads": "It goes without saying that all cultures are shaped by exchanges with others. Popular cultural practices in general and comics in particular have come to be built on appropriation and hybridization. Suffice it to mention the examples of the melting pot that gave rise to American comics, the impact of American comics—and later manga—on bande dessinée, the manga piracy rife in 1970s South Korea, and the recent transcultural success of the graphic novel. However, manga usually attracts the most attention when culture is at issue within comics studies, at least pertaining to culture defined in a geopolitical or national sense" (1).

21. Although Haida activist and leader Guujaaw acknowledges the "title and rights" as a compromise with Canada, "The compromise is that we accept that we will make accommodation with Canada rather than the USA, Russia, or Japan— which are still options . . . And there are other [options], like decolonization" (qtd. in Gill 18).

ritoriality and cultural production in favor of a transpacific concept of borders and belonging. As Yahgulanaas suggests through his own descriptions of transpacific exchange, the Haida partake of cultural and aesthetic practices that mobilize water as both medium and meaningful space. Schodt and Brienza conceptualize the Pacific as an uncultured space between two cultural sites of production. Through his terminology, his narratives, his page layouts, and his material practice, Yahgulanaas remaps cultural production, suggesting that while *comics* may be a settler colonial term that can fill all landed space, *manga* offers a new map, one that joins sites of artistic practice through the water that also fills his stories, structures his comics, and determines his objects.

Although Gray and Brienza rightly insist that Japan is transmuted or revised in North American manga practice, I argue that rather than a "useful other," Yahgulanaas remaps Japan as a place directly connected to Haida Gwaii, just as much as Haida Gwaii might be connected to Ottawa. Eschewing colonial borders of national demarcation, Yahgulanaas suggests alternate configurations that do not discount the role of the ocean in place-making. The executive director and curator of the Haida Gwaii Museum, Jisgang Nika Collison (Haida), has explained the interconnectivity of place and art. As a Haida artist and cultural docent, Collison maintains that "in our world, it is understood that you cannot separate the land and the water . . . In the same way, you cannot separate Haida art from our way of life" (qtd. in Augaitis et al. 57). The *Haida Land Use Vision* notes, "Our oral history traces the lineage of our families back to our ocean origins" (Council of the Haida Nation 4), and further explains the imbrication of land and water, noting how much of Haida Gwaii was once above water, while the past century has entailed that "the sea level has fluctuated by almost two hundred metres, while the fish, forest life and our people adapted to the changing times" (6). Yahgulanaas's books *Red* and *Carpe Fin* both document the habitation of the water, depicting vibrant human–sea filiations and transactions (figure 4.1); the terminology he uses to describe these works also remaps the limits and connections between and among seemingly disparate locations.

This new epistemological framing, whereby Haida manga operates as both a narrative and a toponymic practice, is made explicit in the introduction to *A Lousy Tale* (2004), one of Yahgulanaas's *Rocking Raven* episodes, published as a fifteen-page floppy book. The

FIGURE 4.1. Michael Nicoll Yahgulanaas, *Carpe Fin*, n. pag.

three paragraphs that introduce the work require a large amount of McCloud's "closure" in order to understand the associations being made from section to section: The first and second are both five lines long, the former narrating the story of "an Englishman who said he had named a Pacific island after a British Queen," the latter explaining how Haida manga, "assisted by Raven," "challenges fundamental cartoon elements" (n. pag.). The first paragraph begins, "Once upon a time," invoking a fairytale- or lore-based modality; the second paragraph uses only present-tense verbs to describe the formal capacity of an artistic practice. Yet it is the direct, if otherwise unconnected, juxtaposition of the final term of the first paragraph, *Queen Charlotte,* with the first term of the second, *Haida Manga,* that stages both the colonial encounter and its remapping.

The first paragraph is linguistically tinged with fantasy, so that the reader can grasp the irony of the idea that a colonial toponym "filled the emptiness of the Haida inhabitants with the fullness of George's wife Queen Charlotte." The subsequent section, by never referring explicitly to the content of the first in its colonial terminology, provides a decolonial counterpoint, asserting, "Where a typical comic represents time and space as an empty white gutter, Haida manga, assisted by Raven reveals that time/space is an active, twisting and expanding vitality where no island needs renaming." Although *Haida Manga* may not seem to be semantically paradigmatic to *Queen Charlotte,* their juxtaposition visually creates a direct correlation between the colonial toponym and the artistic practice, as well as between land and sea. *Queen Charlotte* is positioned as a prosthetic form filling that which need not be filled, while *Haida manga* arises from this redundant naming, as a medium for land and sea and art and design. Yahgulanaas likens Haida design to "the study of water," as there is a tension "where space is either obviously filled or seemingly empty, compression seeking expansion" (qtd. in Augaitis et al. 156). Haida manga is, then, a radical approach to remapping, one that supplants the primacy of land as the determining point of contact and connectivity.

Haida manga as a toponymic, or place-making, gesture is not limited to terminology; the practice is inextricable from the narrative content and technicity in Yahgulanaas's works. As Levell notes, "His studies and paintings are ripe with imagery of water in motion, seas and underwater realms are dancing with boats, fishing trawlers and canoes and teeming with supernatural and eccentric marine life forms" (*Seriousness* 43). *Carpe Fin* and *Red* both feature the water as the predominant setting for the narrative, underscoring the connection between the tree-based medium on which the stories are printed, the water-driven ink that visually materializes the works, and the narratives. *Carpe Fin* is the story of a seal-hunting expedition that ultimately relegates the carpenter, Carpe, to the depths of the sea, where supernatural creatures welcome him, and try to fit him with his own fin, before stitching him into a sealskin and casting him out. The final pages show the supernatural creatures rising in a wave from the sea and joining the humans to share food. *Red* begins and ends with the titular character's sister Jaada on a dugout canoe on the water. After Jaada is kidnapped by raiders, Red encounters the carpenter on a rock in the middle of the sea. Red and the carpenter work together to construct an artificial whale which they use to sail to the land of the raiders.

Yahgulanaas reflects directly on the correlation between water and Haida manga. His short piece *The Wave* (2014) links Haida manga practice to the imbrication of land and water. In this work, Yahgulanaas writes, "This paper is a wave. It is somewhere between the tree it was and the possibilities that haven't yet arrived." Here, Yahgulanaas literalizes the relationship between page and materiality while weaving together the realms of representation and production. This sentiment connects to the introduction for *Carpe Fin* (2019), which describes how "the ragged edges of the temperate rainforest reach far out onto an island in the western seas." Land and sea are interwoven in the language that denies their cartographic separation and establishes a new epistemology of place.[22]

As this volume repeatedly shows, questions of place and origin in comics are far more complex than they may seem: Are works associated with the author's or authors' origins? With linguistic origins? With material cultures? Yahgulanaas's Haida manga is a manifold technique of highlighting place-based encounters without sacrificing the specificity of each place. His paratextual descriptions of the settings of the stories weave land and sea as a continuous place, and the term *Haida manga* similarly takes water as a meaningful site of place-making. Yahgulanaas's text in *The Wave* compels a reader's awareness of how the material substrate—drawn from trees—works with the water-powered tool of the brush; even more, this framework implicates publishers such as Douglas and McIntyre and Locarno Press—both based in Canada—with their printers in China and South Korea. *Red* and *Carpe Fin* are both printed in China and published by Douglas and McIntyre in British Columbia; *The War of the Blink* is printed in South Korea and published by Locarno Press in BC. By attending to these connections, Yahgulanaas follows Goeman's project of "interrogat[ing] the use of historical and culturally situated spatial epistemologies, geographic metaphors, and the realities they produce" (1) while remapping for the sake of spatial justice.

---

22. Christopher Green states, "By combining calligraphy's expressive lines and the narrative conventions of manga with the stylized figures of Haida crests and the spatial ambiguity of Northwest Coast Native abstract painting and carving, Yahgulanaas creates what he considers a pan-Pacific alternative to Western art and graphic literature."

The Panel and the Frameline

Yahgulanaas's new epistemology—a form of border thinking—is reflected not only in the terminology used to describe the work but also in its formal attributes: most evidently, *Red*'s page design features no orthogonal gridding and acts as a rebuke to colonial knowledge systems and falsehoods about the emptiness of Indigenous land.[23] The role of the grid in the colonization of the Americas, as an imaginary of space and as a form of control, has a long history of scholarship (Johnson; Palmer; Brousseau; Siegert 97–120). Less well theorized is the relation between the gridding of land and the gridding of the comics page.

In *The System of Comics,* Thierry Groensteen describes the process of drawing the comics or bande dessinée image as beginning with the artist's "almost necessary" (41, "presque nécessairement" 50) construction of a mental or virtual frame (*le cadre*) for the image.[24] Groensteen describes this first "appropriation of space" as *quadrillage,* or "gridding" (41, 50). Thus, for Groensteen—as for most European and US comics theorists—the grid is taken as a virtual and or technical a priori for the visual appearance of comics. While he quotes Guy Gauthier's assertion that the preponderance of the rectangular frame is intrinsically based on its status as a "pure product of the western technocratic civilization, undoubtedly in association with the general use of perspective, geometric rationality and the imperatives of handling" (Gauthier 14, translation from Groensteen 47), Groensteen offers two alternate motives. First, he proposes that the substrate of the rectangular frame is itself rectangular, thus creating a mimetic, homologous rapport between the rectangular page (book, magazine, etc.) and the panel frame. Second, he offers that a rectangle is a shape more capably placed into series (47, 57). According to Groensteen, any panel shape other than a quadrilateral "presents a serious incon-

23. As Judith Ostrowitz writes, "Yahgulanaas is engaged with the illumination of spaces that have previously been considered empty, both in a physical sense and metaphorically. On one level, he connects his peopling of these voids with a denial of the European legend that North America was 'an empty space' when it was first encountered, because the realities of the so-called savages that inhabited this continent were 'uncivilized' and therefore negligible" (84).

24. See also Van Lier.

venience in obliging the neighboring panels to be contorted in order to make space for the intrusion" (47).[25]

Groensteen's rationale and terminology reflect a Gramscian common sense, which also coincides with Mark Rifkin's "settler common sense."[26] Thus modified, Antonio Gramsci's "conception of the world that is most widespread among the popular masses in a historical period" (360) becomes "the ways the legal and political structures that enable nonnative access to Indigenous territories come to be lived as given, as simply the unmarked, generic conditions of possibility for occupancy, association, history, and personhood" (Rifkin xvi).[27] As both Gramsci and Rifkin outline, shared values such as private property or ownership of land are forms of domination and control that shape the materiality of daily life without explicitly indexing their hegemonic influence nor their own etiology. For contemporary comics studies, the grid appears normalized to the extent that it is called "conventional" in the work of Benoît Peeters or "stereotypical" ("Navigating" 1) by Neil Cohn, who goes on to stipulate that "the most conventional layout of a comic page is a grid" ("Navigating" 3).[28] When Groensteen describes the page in terms of convenience, obligation, and intrusion, such a description reflects a widespread belief system regarding space and appropriation. As he contends, the page "express[es] a vision of the world founded on the notion of order, on Cartesian logic, on rationality" (*System* 49). The grid, in this commonsense view, forms the apotheosis for imagining the page.

In his conceptualization of the grid as a cultural technique, media theorist Bernhard Siegert asks: "Can the expansion of Western culture from the sixteenth to the twentieth century be described in terms of a growing totalitarianism of the grid?" (98). Siegert notes that cartographers have used the grid as a way to order space since Ptolemy, yet he marks the convergence of representational techniques of per-

---

25. Cf. Lefèvre: "The dominant frame model in Western art is a rectangle whose base is greater than its height, but various other shapes can be used" ("Conquest" 229).

26. There is also a correlation to be drawn with de Certeau's concept of "local authority" (106).

27. It is no coincidence that Pascal Lefèvre titles his article describing the development and continuity of the "four- and three-tier grid—the uniform waffle-iron composition" as comics evolved "towards a greater degree of standardisation of panel arrangements" ("Conquest" 252).

28. One can also see in Cohn's offhand mention of "a grid's similarity to text" ("Navigating" 3) the development of what Angel Rama calls "the lettered city."

spective and navigation by grid into "a common paradigm of image construction and early modern colonial governmentality" (103).[29] Rather than the self-contained space of the Roman *castrum* under centuriation, the colonial grid employed in the allotment of the Americas combined features such as the infinite expandability of Hippodamus's early urban planning, with "the possibility of registering the absent" (103).[30] This ability to render land vacant was inextricable from the form of the grid and its role in property.

As Hildegard Binder Johnson notes, the grid—as articulated in the Seven Ranges Survey of 1785 and thereafter—is so constitutive of settler common sense that "most Americans and Canadians accept the survey system that so strongly affects their lives and perception of the landscape in the same way that they accept a week of seven days, a decimal numerical system, or an alphabet of twenty-six letters—as natural, inevitable, or perhaps in some inscrutable way, divinely ordained" ("Preface" n. pag.). The grid as a means of governmentality and biopolitics—as when Foucault refers to the partitioning grid "le quadriller litterallement" (*Sécurité* 11)—thus becomes an "inevitable" way of seeing, one that—as Siegert notes—creates an optics of absence and presence based on colonial values.[31] Goeman explains that "the making of Indian land into territory required a colonial restructuring of spaces at a variety of scales" wherein "Native bodies . . . in relation to allotment . . . were conceived of as part of the flora and fauna" (33).[32] Little more than a century after the proliferation of allotment, in her seminal essay "Grids," Rosalind Krauss credits the grid with no less than "declaring the modernity of modern art," specifically through its antinatural capacity for "crowding out the dimensions of the real and replacing them with the lateral spread of a single surface" (50). As Krauss stipulates, "The grid is a way of abrogating the claims of natural objects to have an order particular to themselves" (50). Among these precedents, the epistemological constellation between land, grids, and art coalesces.

---

29. Benedict Anderson similarly contends that the "late colonial state's style of thinking about its domain" is characterized as "a totalizing classificatory grid" (184).

30. Siegert notes the divergent aims but identical methodologies between the gridding of South and North America (112).

31. Carlo Galli and Daniel Nemser similarly chart the "geometrization" of colonial space (Galli 51; Nemser 31).

32. See also Nemser, esp. 25–64; Brousseau 142.

Yahgulanaas's work creates a border-thinking response to the hegemonic influence of the grid. While Siegert describes the settlement fantasy of the grid as "the possibility of writing empty spaces, that is, the ability to literally reserve a space for the unknown" (107), Yahgulanaas notes the converse:

> Someone asked me a question: "Why Haida manga?" And it was a pushback against this notion of gutters, which reflects this false idea that when settler populations fled the oppression of Europe and were desperate to find something else, they imagined this place to be empty because they needed it to be empty. So they had this term called *"terra nullius"* — "the land is vacant." So that their own story was all that counted. Everything else had to be lesser than, it had to be barbaric, it had to be modified, it had to be imagined to be less than worthy. ("Guest Lecture")

In this articulation of how his own practice extends between optic and ideological approaches to the land and to the role of the grid or gutters in comics studies, Yahgulanaas conceives of Haida manga as a means by which to deconstruct the hegemonic force of the grid and its correlate, the gutter. Comics studies, especially in the US following Scott McCloud, has a long history of fetishizing the gutter as "host to much of the magic and mystery that are at the very heart of comics" (McCloud 66).[33] Thus, the reader is posed as a master over absence, invited to project their own imagined narrative in the space between panels. Yahgulanaas draws the link between this form of projection and that which segmented the land of the Americas according to a form of gridding *order* itself linked so definitively to literary order by Angel Rama (17–28).

Yahgulanaas's works from *A Tale of Two Shamans* (2001) on expose the narrowness of US and Franco-Belgian comics theory by constructing pages with "juxtaposed pictorial and other images in deliberate sequence" (McCloud 20), but without gutters. Instead, as Levell describes, Yahgulanaas developed "an alternative comic idiom that could accommodate the explosion of action and the multiplicity of play between physical and metaphysical beings and realms that are characteristic of Haida oral histories" (*Seriousness* 63) through the use

---

33. Cf. Baetens ("Une poetique"), who catalogs a number of different technical relations between image, page, and gutter (or *blanc intericonique*).

of framelines. These curving, labile lines both segment pages into sequence and draw images together into visual composition. Gray contends that Yahgulanaas's use of framelines to fill in the "gutter" of the comics page "deconstructs the very concept of the comic border in order to redefine nationhood in an Indigenous context and underscore the imposed colonial border's impact" (172). While Mauzé describes the frameline as a "kind of visual metaphor or dialectic tool to juxtapose a Haida vision of the world with Western ways of seeing, when it comes to space-time, or the connections between the people in it and their relationship to the environment."

Against the grid as an "abstract machine . . . that is nearly blind and mute even as it makes others see and speak,"[34] Yahgulanaas's framelines work as Mignolo's "machine for intellectual decolonization" (*Local Histories* 45).[35] As Yahgulanaas has stated in talks and in his short piece "In the Gutter" (2011), the whiteness of the gutter suggests a vacuum or void of space-time in between the moments of the panels (see figure 4.2). Using framelines instead provides "a more honest way of looking at, depicting the world, by filling up the time-space dividers and not pretending they're white, empty vacant spaces" ("Michael Yahgulanaas"), as colonizers did through the concept of "*terra nulius*" [*sic*] (see figure 4.2). The frameline composition also offers a "way of seeing, 'reading,' or experiencing art" (Levell, *Seriousness* 82) that is distinct from both the expectations of paginal segmentation in comics and manga and the codified study of Haida formline composition.

Many readers (Spiers, Nodelman) have relied on McCloud's insistence that manga features more of what McCloud calls "aspect to aspect transitions" between panels to interpret Yahgulanaas's work as manga. Yet McCloud's entire system is predicated on the gutters

---

34. So Gilles Deleuze summarizes Foucault's description of the *diagramme* (directly related to the grid) in *Surveiller et Punir*: "C'est une machine abstraite . . . presque muette et aveugle, bien que ce soit elle, qui fasse voir, et qui fasse parler" (42).

35. This is not to suggest that Yahgulanaas's work entirely avoids the grid. Yet the grid is used only in the transposition or transmediation between mural and codical formats: "Yahgulanaas designs the mural so it can be sliced into pages. He starts with a small sketch, scans it and enlarges it, then creates a grid to map out the pages" (Lederman). But he also calls this a "technical issue that I'm on the verge of overcoming" ("Guest Lecture") and notes: "I'm exploring Japanese scroll paper, a mulberry paper, I want to do another one similar, but I want to do it on scroll paper . . . so that I could fully eliminate the great white spaces."

FIGURE 4.2. Michael Nicoll Yahgulanaas, "In the Gutter"

that Yahgulanaas radically undoes through his framelines. Similarly, as discussed in chapter 2, Benoît Peeters's *Case, planche, récit—lire la bande dessinée* (1991), republished as *Lire la bande dessinée* in 2003, established categories of page layout. Peeters schematizes four types of page layout—conventional, decorative, rhetorical, or productive—dependent on the preponderance of either the narrative (*récit*) or the image (*tableau*). Analyzed using Peeters's categorization, *Red*'s framelines entail that every page in the book is "decorative," privileging the tabular at the expense of the linear. This would mean that each page in *Red* serves primarily as "an independent unit, whose aesthetic organization trumps any other concern" (56; "Four Conceptions" par. 12)—that is, the story is drawn to accommodate the arching black patterns of the framelines.

However, the framelines in *Red* supersede decorative function because they divide every page into panels, and they indicate and structure the totalized image formed when all the pages of *Red* are rearranged as a tableau (see figure 4.3). As a Haida artwork, *Red*'s framelines produce an image of three interlocking figures (Spiers 42). Yet, as manga, the framelines designate the differences between panels that allow a narrative to take place,[36] making the pages irresolvably decorative *and* productive—whereby "it is the organization of the page which seems to dictate the narrative" (66; "Four Conceptions" par. 30)—dependent on the cultural system and material format by which one is assessing the work. *Red*'s characters even interact with the formlines, further complicating the question of their role as decorative, extradiegetic, or diegetic elements. For example, on page 1, Jaada, *Red*'s sister, grasps a formline that stands in for the side of her boat, visible on the same page. On page 14 and elsewhere, characters use formlines to climb, hold, or lean against. Spiers contends, "Rather than the binary way in which Euro-American culture often views the world, *Red*'s organic formline erases compartmentalization" (46). Yahgulanaas has stated that he uses framelines to demonstrate other ways of seeing, and to break viewers out of traditional boxes using new "space and time lines" ("Michael Yahgulanaas").

The stipulated desire to use framelines to shake up reader expectations and practices seems to have succeeded. Reviewing *Red* for *Multiversity Comics,* Michelle White states: "The curved panel borders make determining the order of events difficult; they also blend into the art itself, making it hard to see where one panel ends and the other begins." Judith Saltman, writing for *Jeunesse: Young People, Texts, Cultures,* ties the legibility of Yahgulanaas's *Red* directly to consumption practices: "Even for consumers familiar with the conventions of comics and graphic novels, the sophisticated narrative sequencing is a stimulating challenge in logic and intuition" (142). White's and Saltman's expressed difficulty in reading *Red* exposes spatial navigation as a learned process, one inseparable from the epistemologies implicated in its development. Johanna Drucker notes that when our reading conventions become overly familiar, we fail to recognize both

---

36. As Spiers states, "Red reveals the importance of the formline to not only Haida tradition but to narrative understanding as well" (46).

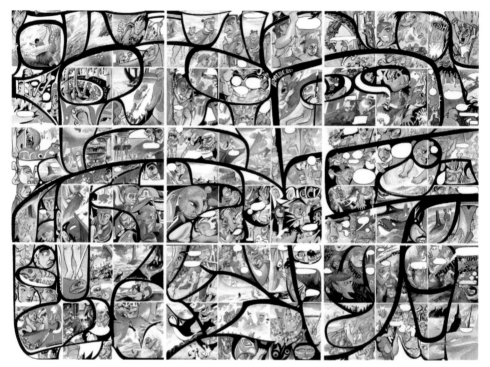

FIGURE 4.3. Michael Nicoll Yahgulanaas, *Red: A Haida Manga,* full mural (above and facing)

their rhetorical and ideological dimensions, as well as the processes by which we came to learn them (125), and Yahgulanaas states that the framelines provide a challenge or a surprise for a reader at the same time that they force the reader "to reflect on the connection of external elements" to that which is within the panel ("Re: Academic inquiry"). Thus, Haida manga, with its curving space and time lines, may seem more difficult for some readers, but this difficulty draws attention to the formal, disciplinary, and political conditions that underscore reading graphic narrative as a cultural practice.

Even his distinction between the terms formline and frameline reflects Yahgulanaas's decolonial project. *Formline* is a term popularized by American art historian Bill Holm, who wrote the now seminal study *Northwest Coast Indian Art: An Analysis of Form* (1965). Calling the terminology of "formline" both useful and "made up" (Augaitis et al. 156), Yahgulanaas has used his art to critique Holm's "somewhat rigid set of criteria or canon that continues to burden the production and evaluation of Native Northwest Coast art" (Levell, *Seriousness* 41). In his artwork, *Deconstruction of the Box* (2003), Yah-

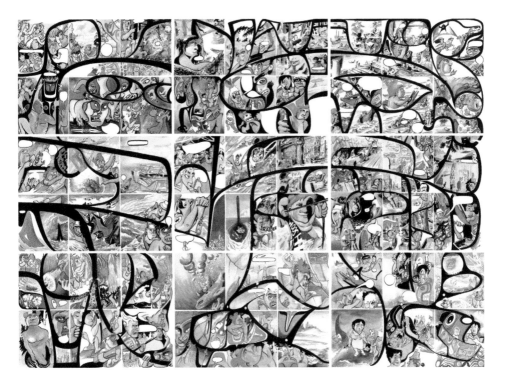

gulanaas plays with Holm's schematic and hermeneutic approach to "extract a meaning" from Haida art, finally undermining this endeavor with a panel showing a "deconstructed" Haida formline image of a bear shot for sport in disregard of its place in the larger signifying system (Yahgulanaas, "Academic inquiry").

Quibbling over artistic terminology may seem like highbrow navel-gazing, yet the issue at stake in the distinction between form-line and frameline goes well beyond the interchangeability of three vowels. Holm's study of Haida artwork reflects widespread approaches to Indigenous cultural techniques whereby the situated knowledge of the practitioners is discounted and dismissed in favor of colonial knowledge systems. It is worth quoting Holm's preface, in which he qualifies his book's sources:

Ideally, a study of this sort should lean heavily on information from Indian artists trained in the tradition that fostered the art. Unfortunately, I was unable to locate a qualified informant from the area covered, i.e., the coastal region from Bella Coola to Yakutat Bay.

> That there may be some still living is not questioned, but contemporary work seen from the area reveals *a lack of understanding by Indian craftsmen* of the principles that are the subject of this study. (xxvi–xxvii, emphasis added)

Holm's analysis thus abstracts the knowledge of artistic practice from the practice itself, and disallows Indigenous understanding of Indigenous art. Much like Peeters, Holm creates a taxonomic system for describing layout based on how images fill space, according to "configurative," "expansive," or "distributive" design principles (12), manufacturing classification as a way to extract the study and mastery of Haida art from the "Indian craftsmen" who produce it.

In Holm's taxonomy, images are delineated by black formlines: "A formline is the characteristic swelling and diminishing linelike figure delineating design units. These formlines merge and divide to make a continuous flowing grid over the whole decorated area, establishing the principal forms of the design" (29). Holm's invocation of the grid in his schematization of formline use and development implicitly marks his Eurocentric approach to space in art, wherein an artist approaches any project according to a perception of "total space" and with the requisite need to "to control the shape of the ground or negative space" (67). Even in the curvilinear design of formlines (which he distinguishes from "true lines"), Holm perceives a grid describing all potential space. The formline grid creates the a priori condition for extraction and compartmentalization as well as expansion and extension required for Holm's analytical framework.

Yahgulanaas renounces this tendency toward both abstraction and totalization in his theory and art. His development of a counter term for formline reflects the dynamic process of his art wherein "there is no prescriptive interpretation" (Levell, *Seriousness* 83). Yahgulanaas calls his lines *framelines* because "formlines suggest an all knowing ability. We see the form suggesting full understanding of the object. i use the term frameline- it suggests a way into something else- a door/window/entrance" ("Re: Academic inquiry").[37] In direct opposition to the dual centrifugal and centripetal readings Krauss ascribes to the grid (60 et passim), Yahgulanaas presents a third dimension for his compositions: rather than demarcating flat space into segments, he imagines the frameline as a matrical entrance to *other* spaces.

---

37. See also Bernardin 492; Levell, *Seriousness* 83; Green.

Yahgulanaas's framelines visually enact his antigrid, multidimensional approach to the space of the page. Beyond the ruminations in "The Wave," framelines routinely interact with the diegesis, intervening in perspectival conventions of foreground and background or form and content. In *War of the Blink* (2017), tops of totem poles flow outward and become black framelines which themselves become canoes and then the surface of the water on which the character Gunee's canoe sails. At one point the lines even become Gunee himself, filling in his eyebrow and extending around his head, creating the brim of his hat. At other points, framelines become splashing waves, denying Holm's strict division between symbolic and representative art. In *Red,* formlines make the edges of the whale ship that Red commissions the carpenter to build. When this ship is imperiled—when it runs aground or when it is deconstructed so as to rapidly surface—the framelines are drawn in crumbling pieces, sometimes with sound effects ("Snap" on page 83) written on the lines themselves (see figure 4.4). When Red decides to commit suicide after killing his brother-in-law and destabilizing his community, the great bow he uses is itself a frameline (102–3). Spiers reads this use of linework as a commentary on the connection of Haida art to the environment and the porousness of boundaries. The connections between frames and "content" blur the distinctions between human actors and environment, while the narrative stresses the responsibility that humans have for maintaining balance with these frames.[38]

At the level of the page, framelines expose the oft-overlooked techniques of the observer by challenging the naturalization of gridding and z-path reading practices, yet the framelines go beyond the page. *Red, War of the Blink,* and *Carpe Fin* are "books" that are themselves deconstructed murals—or vice versa—and each work has a life as an installation as well as a commodity object. *War of the Blink* and *Red* were displayed at the Vancouver Art Gallery in 2006 and 2009, respectively; *Carpe Fin* was commissioned by the Seattle Art Museum and has hung there since 2018. The book versions of these works include (as an image at the back of the book or a reverse print on the book jacket) a miniature print of the mural version of the works, in which the fluid framelines create continuous shapes and figures. As Perry Nodelman contends, these works, as double museum instal-

---

38. My students have repeatedly interpreted *Red* as a cautionary tale about what happens when you try to overpower your environment and wind up destroying it in the process.

FIGURE 4.4. Michael Nicoll Yahgulanaas, *Red: A Haida Manga,* page 83

lation and mechanically reproduced codex, implicate and frustrate expectations and reading strategies associated respectively with art and literature (192).

Haida Manga as Art Object

Within comics studies, the tension between the book and other formats of comics composition has been a central point of theory since at least Pierre Fresnault-Deruelle's seminal article "Du linéaire au tabulaire" (1976). In a translated version of the article, "From Linear to Tabular," Fresnault-Deruelle explains how the comic strip is often thought of in "metonymic" relation to the comics page; however, the distinct reading protocols instantiated by both the strip and the full page, as a component of magazine or book-length comics, entail a conflict between temporal and spatial dimensions, so that the linear and tabular reading practices are "bound up in a dialectic of continuity versus discontinuity" (121; cf. Baetens and Frey, *Graphic Novel* 105). Similarly, Charles Hatfield echoes this Gérard Genette–inspired attention to the "peritexte" by elaborating on the tension between "text as experience and text as object," wherein the diachronic comic is always in dynamic situation to its materiality, which "includes not only the design or layout of the page but also the physical makeup of the text, including its size, shape, binding, paper, and printing" (58). Thus, the doubling between the mural and book versions of *Red, War of the Blink,* and *Carpe Fin* both extend and wholly deconstruct the role of the book in relation to comics or graphic narrative.

The problematic set out by Fresnault-Deruelle, Hatfield, and Harry Morgan—among others—regarding the study of what Morgan calls "codexité" (61)—and which may also be thought under the rubric of Jessica Pressman's "bookishness"—departs from what we might expect to be its usual parameters in Yahgulanaas's work. As discussed in chapter 1, the introduction of the book or album was, for comics, a way of asserting the lasting value of otherwise lowbrow, ephemeral matter printed in newspapers, floppies, and magazines. In a full reversal of this formula, Yahgulanaas's mural-to-book transfer upends the high–low trajectory, reproducing a Benjaminian model of the work of art in the age of its mechanical reproducibility. As Yahgulanaas stated in an interview about *Carpe Fin,* "not everyone can get to the museum. Everyone can access the book" (Loik). And yet, even if one accepts the inversion here—comics normally become more highbrow and artlike through their inclination toward codexité, while Yahgulanaas's work as originally museal art diminishes in its book form—as an Indigenous artist, Yahgulanaas is hardly representative of standard museum valuation.

The situation of Indigenous art in the museum is never not a contentious issue, owing to the museum's origin in colonial looting (Azoulay; Onciul 4) as well as the continuous relegation of Indigenous art to either anthropology or history museums rather than fine or contemporary art museums.[39] A 2018 *New York Times* article described "the representation of Native artists" in US museums as "a trickle" (Loos). For reference, Yahgulanaas is, at the time of this

---

39. Levell, in "Site-Specificity," provides a concise overview of the "art/artefact debate" as it has inflected museology (94). See also Collison et al.'s *Indigenous Repatriation Handbook.*

writing, one of only four Indigenous artists featured in the Metropolitan Museum of Art's modern and contemporary collection (Green). The museum as a particular archival practice and the work of art as its material are inextricable from historical practices of colonial subjection. The museum is historically linked to what Glen Coulthard (Dene) describes as "the production of the specific modes of colonial thought, desire, and behavior that implicitly or explicitly commit the colonized to the types of practices and subject positions that are required for their continued domination" (16). We have considered how Yahgulanaas's works intervene in this colonial subjectivation at the levels of terminology and form; they also do so at the level of materiality.

Therefore, as Levell stresses in her study of Yahgulanaas's museum installation *Peddle to the Meddle* (2007), his compositions are "indigenized artworks that are generated as a site-specific form of institutional critique but later dislocated, mobilized and rearticulated in other disciplinary spaces" ("Site-Specificity" 93). Yahgulanaas's murals trouble normative discourses and classificatory logics that inform the consumption of visual texts. They disrupt display techniques, creating museal works that invite reading. Yet, in their installation forms, they do not include the text in word balloons or narrative boxes to facilitate the reading. By circulating as books at the same time, they challenge the sovereignty of art spaces. As Yahgulanaas has stated, "What I like about a book is you have complete authority over the story. You are the master . . . you can take this book home, the sacred text, and if you have two copies you can create your own monumental piece of Haida artwork" ("Michael Yahgulanaas"); thus, the singularity of the museum installation is disrupted by its reproducibility.

Yahgulanaas's murals *cum* books radically remap the reading spaces of graphic narrative. If comics are already understood as a hybrid of words and images, Yahgulanaas's works compel an even more historically and culturally located inquiry beyond the conceptualization of meaningful gaps between panels and "the often disjunctive back-and-forth of reading and looking for meaning" through the verbal-visual combination (Chute, "Comics as Literature?" 452). *Red, War of the Blink,* and *Carpe Fin* problematize this formal conception of graphic narrative by insisting on the material and locative components of these gaps and disjunctures. They likewise introduce material techniques and objects to resist and reimagine both the artwork and the book as they have been developed as tools for imperial domination and Indigenous suppression.

Haida Manga as Codex

At the levels of both the page and the book, Haida manga deconstructs the political and ideological values involved in navigating the spaces of comics. To take one example, *Red* multiplies the linear and tabular dimensions through its double construction as art object and book. *Red* is at once a full mural, which one may read according to methods of interpreting Haida formline composition, but which also circulates outside of the museum: as Yahgulanaas notes, "My conversation as an artist uses publications to talk with a lot of people, not just those who have money to buy an expensive commodity that reinforces what *they* think I should be" (Augaitis et al. 164). On the other hand, *Red* is sold as a book, with pages that are oriented according to the tradition of the codex. Each page has its own linear framework, but the note at the conclusion of the book specifically instructs the reader to "rip the pages out of their bindings. . . . and using the pages from two copies of this book . . . reconstruct this work of art" (109). Once fully replaced in their order as the Haida "complex of images," the relationship of linear to tabular shifts again. As Yahgulanaas contends, the double-reading of *Red* "will defy your ability to experience story as a simple progression of events" (109). Moreover, the double-materiality defies a reader's ability to experience a book as a simple object, and in doing so highlights the bound book's own history, its colonial significance, and the role it has played in simplifying the complex stories of Indigenous experience.

Yahgulanaas is acutely aware of how market considerations have determined and delimited possibilities for conceptualizing Indigenous art, and he conversely understands the formal constraints of the codex:

> I encourage people to make observations and choices arising from their own experience without relying on the authority of the artist. By extension, I'm asking that people reconsider their place in the group . . . Converting a five-metre mural into a book was a game of scale. Monumental in one manifestation, it becomes accessible to the reader who holds it in their hands. The reader is free to direct pace

and even narrative direction. If they want to go backward, they can
. . . as much as I say, "Yes, destroy the book," I really say, "Reconstruct it." I wonder, *Why are books sacred?* Are people sacred? Can we
really still afford to agree that ideology is more sacred than people?
(Sostar McClellan 39)

In the case of *Red,* transitioning from a 5 by 1.5 meter watercolor
work to a 108-page book is a form of reconstruction beyond the limits of the work itself. The codex/mural dichotomy is itself undone
and renegotiated through the interconnectivity of the works and
their constraints.

The codex, as Yahgulanaas's questions proclaim, has its own
fraught history both in the realm of Western epistemology and in
North American Indigeneity. As well attested,[40] the codex as a material form was inextricable from the spread of Christianity throughout
the Roman Empire and eventually beyond. By the third century, in
the sphere of the Roman Empire, the codex had the same popularity
for literary use as the book roll, which it would eventually supplant.
Yahgulanaas's questioning of the sacredness of books highlights the
nonsecular origins and popularization of what would serve as the
material basis for seemingly secular epistemology, its archiving, ped-
agogical use, and circulation.

The religious introduction of the codex is no secret to Indigenous
and colonized peoples worldwide, for whom "the book" directly signified the Bible as a technology of ideological discipline and control.
As Vine Deloria Jr. (Standing Rock Sioux) glibly notes, when colonial settlers "arrived they had only the Book and we had the land;
now we have the Book and they have the land" (101). However, the
book has also been recognized as a tool for Indigenous sovereignty.
Indigenous literary production is a meaningful site of negotiation,
with some scholars advocating for the subversion and reconstruction of the book by Indigenous authors, and others advocating for a
reconceptualization of "the book" outside the Christian codical tradition. Phillip Round notes how the book was mobilized by Native
authors, as it provided them "a much-needed weapon in their bat-
tles against relocation, allotment, and cultural erasure" (5). Louise

40. Colin H. Roberts and T. C. Skeat's *The Birth of the Codex* is still considered the
seminal study of the Christian codex; see also Harris, "Codex"; Skeat; Meyer; Innis
131–32; cf. Bagnall; Harnett.

Erdrich (Turtle Mountain Chippewa) claims that books have a long history in the material culture of the Americas. In her text *Books and Islands in Ojibwe Country,* she asserts that "people have probably been writing books in North America since at least 2000 B.C." (13). Furthermore, Susan Bernardin directly connects Erdrich's concept of the book's lineage in non-alphabetic, visual language to Yahgulanaas's Haida manga and "the moving practice of Indigenous literary arts" (492). These claims regarding the radical potential of Indigenous literary production reinforce how Yahgulanaas's works remap the book in both cultural and material ways.

Culturally, Yahgulanaas's Haida manga challenge how such books are recognized and consumed, while materially, the books destabilize the codex as a consumable object. Gray contends that the mural form of *Red* can be recreated by "any reader with two copies of the comic, disrupting the border between the accessible art of comics and the refined viewing space of a fine art gallery" (182). Yet I contend that a reader recreates the mural only insofar as *Red* completely remaps the place of the work of art despite its peripatetic or remediated installations. The mural, as a museum installation, recalls all the Bejaminian discussions of aura, but perhaps, most importantly, it is *not* a book. The book, *Red,* is necessarily a form that circulates outside the museum space, as portable copy. As Chute notes, "The medium of comics was marked from the beginning by its commodity status" ("Comics as Literature?" 455), and the high-art/low-art divide is intrinsic to the North American cultural history of these objects.

Thus, the challenge that *Red, War of the Blink,* and *Carpe Fin* pose to hegemonic systems of artistic and literary valuation is directed at rethinking the place of art and the book as a commodity object. For example, for the reader to recreate the nonmuseal version of *Red,* one must purchase two books. The linear containment of the narrative is then denied by its doubling. With two *Reds,* where does the story begin or end? What's more, the stability of the codex, as a reading device, is threatened by its deconstruction into nonbook form. In order to create the Haida tableau, a reader irrevocably changes how the story takes space. A new module of tabularity materializes through the destruction of the previous module. *Red, War of the Blink,* and *Carpe Fin*'s propositions serve to fundamentally displace the stability of the book as a commodity form and to provide a challenge to the literary consumer. The long association of comics and collecting leads to an aporia: the reader cannot possess both the manga and the mural as commodity objects at the same time; one can only possess their virtual duplication.

From the terminology to the page layout to the materiality of the work, Yahgulanaas's Haida manga (re)map space by mobilizing local histories for the deconstruction of global designs. *Comics, panels, gutters, murals, books* are but some of the terms and concepts put under scrutiny through Yahgulanaas's narratives. These works compel a reader to contend with the latent ideologies and ossified concepts of art and literature. This remapping project is especially evident in Yahgulanaas's use of framelines for the production of visual narrative. Goeman insists on the literary as an essential channel for

> the "imaginative" creation of new possibilities, which must happen through imaginative modes precisely because the "real" of settler colonial society is built on the violent erasures of alternative modes of mapping and geographic understandings. The Americas as a social, economic, political, and inherently spatial construction has a history and a relationship to people who have lived here long before Europeans arrived. It also has a history of colonization, imperialism, and nation-building. (2)

By using graphic narrative in innovative ways, Yahgulanaas imagines the epistemology of place, art, and story otherwise. He remaps the space of graphic narrative by implicating the role of water in the mediation of culture and cultural production. He counters the grid as the underlying logic of graphic narrative. Haida manga reasserts the materiality of art and literature: the page is not merely an insignificant vessel; it is a physical space of construction, navigation, contention, and negotiation.

CHAPTER 5

SAMANDAL
AND TRANSLATIONAL
TRANSNATIONALISM

Verbal, Visual, Amphibious

How do you make "comics" if no such word exists in your language?
This question directly addresses ongoing issues of untranslatability
and inequality in world comics. In an early interview describing the
development of the Lebanese comics magazine *Samandal,* its founders explained the title's relation to the contents: just as the magazine
printed pages between image and text, so was the Arabic word for
salamander a reference to in-between-ness, a creature between land
and water. When the interviewer asked why *Samandal*'s subtitle is
"Picture Stories," co-founder Hatem Imam replied, "There's no one
word for comics in Arabic!"[1] Whereupon co-founder the fdz inter-
jected, "But we're kind of trying to change that" (Azimi). This chapter
focuses on the Lebanese comics magazine *Samandal,* in its object-
specific permutations and alongside comparator works. In its first
fifteen issues, *Samandal* published in a unique, trilingual format that
entailed flipping each issue at various points in the reading. Without
a dominant reading orientation, issues of *Samandal* offered experimental ways to frame cultural and linguistic diversity.

1. Cf. di Ricco 200.

However, in the years since *Samandal* began publishing in 2007, its very existence as a publication has come under threat due to charges brought by the Lebanese government against three of its editors. In 2010 Lebanese organization the Catholic Media Center objected to two stories published in *Samandal* 7, the "Revenge" ("Revanche") issue, charging *Samandal* with (a) inciting sectarian strife, (b) denigrating religion, (c) publishing false news, and (d) defamation and slander (Dueben, "Interview"). After a five-year trial, the magazine was fined 30 million Lebanese liras (the equivalent of about $20,000) (Lu). Following this decision and a crowd-funding push to secure the future of *Samandal,* the editors determined that they would change the format of the magazine. From 2007 to 2013 and for fifteen issues, *Samandal* was a quarterly based on open calls and edited by committee. In 2014 it became a yearly publication under the direction of a single editor. As the collective states, the shift "presupposes a subjective choice of editorial direction (according to a theme or not), authors, working methods and printing" (Samandal, "Mission"). In 2014 Barrack Rima edited the *Généalogie* volume; in 2015 Joseph Kai edited the *Géographie* volume; in 2016 Lena Merhej edited *Ça restera entre nous* (the sexuality volume); in 2017 Raphaëlle Macaron edited the *Topie* volume on utopia; and in 2018 the *Experimentation* volume (edited by Alex Baladi) was published. The revived *Samandal* #16, signaling the return to an open-call submissions format, had its release party in early 2020.

According to a framework of reading for difference, the vicissitudes of *Samandal*'s format reveal world comics as an emergent field of objects whereby context, contingencies, and politics inflect subjective and collective choices in comics formation. This chapter traces how *Samandal* as an organization and a publication *worlds* or opens and delimits spaces for subjectivity, for expression, and for political life. Examining world comics as a site of collaboratory potential, I focus my analysis on the format(s) of *Samandal,* elucidating how they model a conceptualization of comics that resists discrete, nationalized cartographies.

The World, the Globe, and the Comic

Samandal was founded by Hatem Imam, Omar Khouri, Lena Merhej, the fdz (Fadi Baki), and Tarek Naba'a.[2] Begun in 2007, *Saman-*

---

2. Owing to idiosyncrasies in transliteration, many of these names appear in variations (e.g., Omar Khoury, The Fdz, Tarek Tabaa are all listed on *Samandal's* website); I use the spellings listed in the first issue of the journal.

dal credits itself with being "the first trilingual, amphibious comics magazine open to submissions issued in the Middle East." As glossed above, the amphibious element refers to its situation between worlds of word/image, high/low, and traditional and experimental. Based in Beirut, *Samandal* prints stories in Arabic, French, and English. As its mission statement stipulates: "Our publications are read in several languages, from right to left as from left to right and always with layout translations in several ways" (Samandal, "Mission"). This claim to layout translations is at the center of *Samandal*'s ability to reorient comics readers and challenge normative ideas about what comics are or can be.

The mission statement's invocation of layout translations is more than a reference to changing formats, which occurred when *Samandal* switched from small trim quarterly issues to larger annuals after issue 15, and again in 2020 when issue 16 heralded the original format's "comeback" [Samandal, "#16 (2019)"]. Beyond the size and shape, the form within the magazine is also translational. As a trilingual publication, *Samandal* uses what I would deem—with all admiration—a motley layout. Issues employ "flip pages" to alert readers when to rotate the magazine between a left-to-right French or English entry and a right-to-left Arabic entry. Some of the pieces published have no words, leaving a reader to attempt to discern the proper orientation either diegetically or from the context of the adjacent stories. Between and among issues, entries vary in length and narrative cohesion. Some stories are ongoing, such as Fouad Mezher's series, "The Educator," or Hachem Raslan's "John Doe"; other entries or vignettes amount to a single page, such as Matei Branea's "Bus" in issue 9. The page length of each issue varies to the extent that the notorious "Revenge" issue 7 was over 300 pages, whereas issue 13, the "Space-Time" issue, is barely eighty pages. Furthermore, the styles and layouts of comics vary considerably within a single issue according to the wide range of artists involved.

Samandal's heterogeneous collective model for publishing reflects its situation relative to the major centers of comics production. In his extensive study of urban comics, Dominic Davies highlights the value of "collaborative artistic networks" (*Urban Comics* 177) to a number of comics magazines produced and circulated outside the Europe–Japan–North America aggregation. While such networks have also informed production in the "big three" regions, Davies recognizes *Samandal*'s correlates in groups like Egypt's *Tok Tok,* and India's Pao Collective, as all three operate in urban centers (Beirut, Cairo, and Delhi, respectively) in ways that might be better understood as "networked urban social movement[s]" that "rewir[e] the otherwise discriminatory infrastructures of [emerging global cities]" (178–80). Davies's characterization of Beirut, Cairo, and Delhi as "emerging" cities gestures toward the temporal and geographic inequalities of globalization as it economically delineates centers of production, valuation, and power.

Emergence and *the global* are terms frequently conceptualized in opposition or dynamic tension relative to each other. Trying to inaugurate comics production outside established circuits of power and finance requires imagining possibilities beyond those already delineated in the US, Europe, and Japan. Davies understands "emerging" as a synonym for "aspiring" (22) in the "context of the South's aspiring 'global' cities" (20), thus situating *Samandal* within a particular group of "postcolonial" areas that have yet to realize their globality according to standards established in the North.[3] In Saskia Sassen's formative model of "global cities," the unique "combination of spatial dispersal and global integration" (*Global City* 3) that took place in the late twentieth century produced a new type of city. Focusing on New York, London, and Tokyo, Sassen contends that global cities destabilize national boundaries as nodes in global flows of information and capital.[4] However, Sassen notes widening inequalities and internal divisions within these cities, or what Stephen Graham and Simon Marvin dub "splintering urbanism." Global cities thus herald bivalent spatial vectors of increased accumulation of global capital and increased internal wealth disparity. While the networked infrastructures and urban conditions of globalization might seem to herald greater transnational comics production, such development is sporadic and often championed as a sign of growing transnational exchange without consideration of extant and emergent barriers.

---

3. As Doreen Massey phrases this critique, "they are develop*ing*, we are developed" (23).

4. A number of theorists, resistant to the seemingly neo-imperial implications of centering globalization according to how a few privileged cities determine global processes, have suggested a terminological shift from *global cities* to *globalizing cities*. As Brenda Yeoh argues, "The global city concept is often used not so much as an analytical tool but as a 'status' yardstick to measure cities in terms of their global economic linkages, to locate their place in a hierarchy of nested cities and to assess their potential to join the superleague" (608). Furthermore, Ayşe Öncü and Petra Weyland assert that "globalizing cities" is a way to acknowledge "other cities" in "other places" (2).

Conceptualizing cities as postnational, depoliticized spaces[5] of connectivity occludes how the concurrent proliferation of borders and differences established through mechanisms of privatization and state power affect localized urban cultures.

Thus, *Samandal*'s founders explain that their own censorship was surprising to those outside the area, based on the view of Lebanon, and Beirut in particular, as a liberal area with a free press. Founder the fdz explains this as a sort of aspirational view that is only true in comparison to "neighboring countries in the region," while Khouri adds:

> This image of Lebanon as a liberal place (not just for the press, but also socially) is publicly exaggerated because the country's economy is based on tourism. Being the only "liberal" island in a sea of surrounding conservative countries brings all the big spenders here. (Dueben, "Interview").

As *Samandal*'s founders express, liberalism—in both its political and economic expressions—presupposes a level playing field, but Khouri asserts that this level playing field is merely illusory in the context of globalization. Values in "common" are assumed as such according to Western ideals, and "appearances" do not always represent differences. From a visual studies standpoint, Nick Mirzoeff and others have gestured toward the ways in which

> global cities may present themselves as transparent hubs of frictionless commerce, but their residents often experience them as conflicted, dangerous, and even haunted. These are the places from which we have to see the world today and where we learn how to see. (*How to See* 166)

Yet because the global city's model for seeing the world is a learned process, it is also one that can be unlearned. Comics possess uniquely salient formal techniques for representing and contesting the global city as a visual concept.

Given the anomalous architectures of comics, their spatial practices, and their juxtaposition of scale, the formal parameters of comics have the potential to visually interrogate the simultaneous growth of

---

5. See Apter, *Against World Literature* 42.

the global city as spectacle and of the internal divisions within. Jörn Ahrens and Arno Meteling claim that "comics are inseparably tied to the notion of 'the city'" (4), while Davies specifies that "it is the *form* of graphic narrative that enables its analysis of infrastructural violence, phenomena that starkly define the urban condition of the contemporary global city" (*Urban Comics* 16). Davies adumbrates how the comics form is generally tied to the "infrastructural production of discriminatory urban environments, while simultaneously suggesting alternative—and if informal, often common—modes of urban habitation and public reconstruction" (16). The claim that comics enable an alternative visualization of urban space is especially freighted with import in the conceptualization of the global city, of which feminist geographer Doreen Massey has grimly stated, "contemporaneous multiplicities of space are denied, and 'history' is reduced to the single linearity of 'there is no alternative'" (23). Davies argues that the comics in *Samandal*'s magazines "represent Beirut's divided urban spaces in order both to challenge and reconstruct them" (247), laying conditions "for the future development of more socially and spatially just urban practices" (254). By intervening in the visual production of space, comics likewise intervene in the visual distinction between world and globe, and between worlding and globalizing.

While Sassen distinguishes global cities from world cities based on historicity—the global as a new phenomenon, the world as a type of urban center dating to Goethe ("Global City" 28)—Aihwa Ong distinguishes globalizing and worlding as practices whereby

> worlding in this sense is linked to the idea of emergence, to the claims that global situations are always in formation. Worlding projects remap relationships of power at different scales and localities, but they seem to form a critical mass in urban centers, making cities both critical sites in which to inquire into worlding projects, as well as the ongoing result and target of specific worldings. (12)

Following Davies's characterization of how Beirut—like Cairo and Delhi—is segmented into privatized spaces for neoliberal exchange, Ong's distinction allows us to conceptualize how *Samandal* resists this privatization and provides a counterhegemonic response. Reading *Samandal* as a worlding project is a way to remap "world comics" against established hierarchies of power and space. *Samandal*'s travels through time and across distance map emergent articulations of the global, not necessarily in Davies's sense of aspiring for globality but rather in Ong's sense of reimagining what such a globality would look like. The scales of *Samandal*'s map vary from the local alt-scene in twenty-first-century Beirut, to the linguistic-regional context of comics in Arabic, to the global affiliations, alliances, and influences that describe *Samandal* within broader economies of comics. This map similarly folds and unfolds at the level of the page, where it mobilizes productive tensions both familiar and novel. *Samandal* attests to the emergence of global situations at multiple levels: the commercial, the authorial, the linguistic, the formal, and the aesthetic.

Commercialism: Comics in Common

Samandal's founding ethic and distribution practice is made evident through the licensing of the work under Creative Commons. Creative Commons, in this instance, serves as a critical response both to capitalist overdetermination of artistic production and to the problematic nationalism espoused under global copyright mandates such as the Berne Convention. Creative Commons arose as a response to the increasingly oligopolistic monopolization of media, and the concomitant lack of access to creative works: "Creative Commons thus emerged as a counterpoint to open-ended copyright pushed by commercially successful creators and large media corporations" (Garcelon 1309). Publishing under a Creative Commons license is a testament to the sort of creative sharing and distribution that *Samandal* enacts. Writing about the benefits that it offers, Creative Commons senior counsel Sarah Hinchliff Pearson asserts:

> Endeavors that are made with Creative Commons thrive when community is built around what they do. This may mean a community collaborating together to create something new, or it may simply be a collection of like-minded people who get to know each other and rally around common interests or beliefs. To a certain extent, simply being made with Creative Commons automatically brings with it some element of community, by helping connect you to like-minded others who recognize and are drawn to the values symbolized by using CC. (Stacey and Pearson 33)

As an organization, Creative Commons is also cognizant of the risk of replicating US imperial practices with regard to legal infrastructure, as former CTO Mike Linskvayer notes: "Just in terms of messaging, if our default licenses are based on US law, then we're just a lackey for the United States . . . which is just bad overall" (qtd. in Garcelon 1318). *Samandal's* publication ethos—as represented by the Creative Commons license—demonstrates resistance to publishing practices, even those within Lebanon, that reproduce hegemonic and neoliberal conceptualizations of intellectual property as well as the infrastructures of copyright practices based on such ideology.[6]

Lebanon joined the Berne Convention in 1947 and only enacted its own national copyright law in 1999 ("Copyright and Permissions"). As one of the earliest attempts to regulate international copyright and intellectual property rights, the Berne Convention, which began in 1886, describes a set of rights dependent on a convoluted definition of "country of origin." While the convention was predicated on the need for copyrights to extend beyond the country of origin, this concept—delineated in Article 5 of the Convention—is at once anathema to *Samandal's* international collaboratory and problematic for its imperial underpinnings. The Berne Convention's fundamental purpose is the establishment of a "union" of countries that would uphold the worldwide "protection of the rights of authors in their literary and artistic works" (World Intellectual Property Organization). However, the rules and regulations of ownership are determined by European ideals of creativity, property, and authorship. Further, country of origin is always determined by country of publication, with works published in both Union and non-Union countries defaulting to the Union.

From an example of ongoing cultural imperialism such as the Berne Convention, one can surmise how even the seemingly liberal conception of transnational exchanges of cultural objects reproduces systems of power and greater inequities of cultural wealth and distribution. Further, attention to precedents in transnational copyright illuminates the resistance in *Samandal's* publishing approach. For example, *Samandal's* "some rights reserved" publishing model stands in stark contrast to the excessive litigiousness of Moulinsart. Two antipolar approaches to local and global comics production are delineated: on the one hand, Moulinsart is invested in shoring up as property any and all *Tintin* reproductions as a way to consolidate power

---

6. *Samandal's* use of the Creative Commons license preceded the establishment, in 2010, of the Lebanese Creative Commons Chapter. In an article heralding the event, Lebanese NGO Social Media Exchange (SMEX) listed six "well-known examples" of CC licenses already in existence, with *Samandal* as one of the six ("Lebanon Launches").

in the hands of a few Europeans. On the other hand, *Samandal*'s collective founders espouse the necessity of expanding the influence of comics published in the Middle East by "open[ing] them up" to readers elsewhere as a form of creative conversation and co-action. In a Creative Commons grant submitted in 2010, the fdz describes *Samandal* as "a non-governmental organization dedicated to the proliferation of comic art production in the Arab region" but laments that the current distribution of *Samandal* comics is limited by its print condition. The grant would allow for a website whereby *Samandal* comics would be translated into three languages and published online, "thus creating a hub were [*sic*] comic book readers from everywhere can read, share, critique and remix the works." The proposal imagines a network for Arab comics that would "bridge the localized comics scene" and "connect an emerging genre with the comics medium worldwide, encouraging exposure, feedback and exchange" (Samandal Organization for Comics). Advocating for a comics practice in which ownership is not limited to publishers but instead articulated through relationships among artists, readers, translators, and remixers, *Samandal*'s grant is a mode of worlding that imagines comics as a form of community-building and collaboration.

Samandal's acute attention to the co-determination of local conditions and global networks is evident in its publisher collaborations as well. While all of *Samandal* has been published under a Creative Commons license, the first four issues were published through xanadu*, itself founded as "a non-profit art collective" (El Khalil). Begun in 2003 by Zena El Khalil, a Lebanese expatriate living in New York, xanadu* was founded as a response to the 9/11 attacks. As an "ungallery space" in New York, xanadu* featured work from Arab artists "during a time of extreme xenophobia in NYC" (El Khalil). El Khalil imagined xanadu* as a way to provide creative opportunities for Arab artists in the US. Upon her return to Lebanon, El Khalil, via xanadu*, partnered with *Samandal* as well as other Lebanese artists and poets, to publish works in Lebanon (Zalzal). Although El Khalil may be historicized as the founder of xanadu*, her efforts should be understood as woven within partnerships and collectives, and her travels—and the travels of xanadu*—describe a specific and mutable relationship between Arab art and place.

In becoming "a part of the Samandal family," as noted in a press release for *Samandal* issue 0, xanadu* brings together local Lebanese arts collectives invested in a bivalent movement to make Arab arts well known to a wider audience, and to bring artists from around the world into the "beautiful place" created by xanadu* for artistic production. Yet the rationale for this collaboration also stems from lack, or an unequal playing field. As El Khalil describes, xanadu* was a response to the ill treatment of and dearth of opportunities for Middle Eastern artists in the US. As *Samandal*'s founders conversely explain, *Samandal* was a response to the lack of adult comics in the Arab world. "Xanadu" is, of course, not only a reference to a historic Mongolian city but also inextricable from its Orientalist exoticization by Marco Polo and later romanticization by Samuel Taylor Coleridge. To bring together a new word for *comics*—which is actually an old word for a fire-born amphibian—with a word for an old place made mythic through European imaginaries, xanadu* and *Samandal* assert a material presence and future for an imagined Other (Said, *Orientalism* 1–2) that has been delimited by conditions of scarcity and underrepresentation.

In this material presence, publishing and copyright are imagined not in the terms of the *capital* of the West but instead within the filiations of a rhizomatic family. Through this structure of fluctuating yet material affinities, *Samandal,* xanadu*, and other families recombine in self-determinant centers of production. By articulating its own means of publication in concert with other entities (under the license of Creative Commons), *Samandal* addresses the "here and there" in its subtitle ("pictures stories from here and there") as oriented around a *here* in Beirut, and a *there* in the commons of graphic narratives published through its collaborative practices.

Authorship: The Right to Draw

Collectives and local–global scalar dynamics continually inflect emergent developments (and regressions) in Lebanese comics. As Massimo di Ricco and Jonathan Guyer note, *Samandal* finds a direct precedent in the Mouhtaraf JAD (JAD Workshop), founded by George Khoury (Jad)[7] in 1986 (di Ricco 188; Guyer, "War" 83). In the workshop, Jad/Khoury brought together cartoonist Edgar Aho, artist

---

7. Jad's self-naming is itself a verbal-visual and locally inflected event. As he explains, realizing that George Khoury was a name that "projected sectarianism"— "No way that George would be Muslim, or Khoury which means priest"—Jad sought "a neutral name" (Guyer, "Beirut"). And yet, he qualifies Jad as both a name that would be easily pronounced by Western audiences and that looks good when drawn on the page.

Wissam Beydoun, artist and art teacher Choghig Der-Ghougassian, graphic designer and director May Ghaibeh, and her sister Lina Ghaibeh, who would go on to be a professor of comics and animation at the American University of Beirut, where she is also founding director of the Mu'taz and Rada Sawwaf Arabic Comics Initiative (Guyer, "Beirut"). The final publication that this group put forth in 1989, *Min Beirut* [*From Beirut*], included six narrative accounts of the Lebanese Civil War, or what Khoury calls "the sectarian war" (qtd. in Guyer, "Beirut"), and modeled a collaborative anthology of Lebanese comics for adults.

JAD Workshop set the conditions of possibility for *Samandal* in a number of ways. Khoury's belief in adult comics is reflected in *Samandal*'s cover indication of the audience reading age: 18+ (di Ricco 190). Also, Omar Khouri recounts meeting with Khoury at AUB and discussing plans for *Samandal* (Azimi). So too, Lina Ghaibeh's role in establishing the cultural legitimacy and possibility for comics in the Arab world extends from her founding of the first archive dedicated to these materials, to her role as a professor who teaches Arabic comics, to her directorship of the Arabic Comics Initiative.[8] In each capacity, Ghaibeh consecrates these comics as works with an established history, pedagogically relevant present, and promising future. The archive is "dedicated to early examples of caricature and cartooning from the 19th century, and the various spheres of underground cartooning they evolved into" (Guyer, "War" 83), while the Mu'taz and Rada Sawwaf Arabic Comics Initiative offers workshops, symposia, exhibitions, and awards to "promote comics, editorial cartoons and illustration in the Arab world" ("Mu'taz and Rada Sawwaf Arabic Comics Initiative"). Likewise, JAD Workshop's focus on collaboration illustrates the interplay between local, Beirut-based comics and global connectivities, in relation to art collectives.

Beyond the precedent of the JAD Workshop and the influence of the Arabic Comics Initiative, *Samandal*'s founders weave together global sites and sights in the narrativization of the magazine's genesis. An article in *Bidoun* cites the Japanese anime *Grendizer* as a primary influence on their youthful imaginations, before noting the fdz's London-based education in film, Imam's UK-based fine arts education, Khouri's travel to the US to become a painter, and Merhej's US-based design education. Each member lists additional com-

---

8. See also Morayef on the academic embrace of Arab comics through Ghaibeh and Mu'taz Sawwaf.

ics influences, from *Batman* and *Superman* (Khouri notes that in Arabic translation the "S" on Superman's costume was backwards) to *Asterix* and *Tintin,* as well as Middle East–based comics magazines *Majid* and *Samir.* Drawing from separate sensibilities and transnational art experiences, the friends "came together to create a comic book of their own—in, of, and for Lebanon" (Azimi).

Describing the genesis of *Samandal,* Khouri and the fdz contextualize the double-edged devastating and generative impact of the Lebanese Civil War on the development of its local comics scene. Years earlier, Jad Khoury characterized the war as "the major if not decisive factor in shaping my artistic choices, and making this comic path, and helped comics as a genre of art to flourish" (qtd. in Guyer, "Beirut"). Given its role as the theme for JAD workshop's publication, war features as both a destructive, ongoing, thematic element and a formally generative component, necessitating adult-oriented comics capable of handling the maturity of the topic. As the inheritors of JAD workshop's mature form, *Samandal's* adult comics uniquely reflect the experiences of the next generation of Lebanese artists during the war. As the fdz explains, the civil war led to massive displacement of Lebanese peoples, creating both a shared history of sectarian violence and disparate but common diasporic experiences:

> Lebanon specifically, because of the civil war, there's a history . . . and you have a lot of people, maybe second generation people who are returning. Because the civil war got so bad you have to relocate to a different place. There is very much that history that binds us together, but at the same time it brings in so many different influences whether it's people that have grown up in the States, or they grew up in the gulf, or they grew up in France. Each one comes with a completely different background. ("Lebanese Comics")

The founders and artists of *Samandal* map inward and outward trajectories of worlding comics. *Samandal* is always situated in an exchange between the local experiences and aesthetics of the Beirut comics scene and its transnational vectors.

Originally, the magazine was published through both a network of known associates and an open call for contributions. The submission guidelines contain advice for illustrators and writers (or a team) who have produced a comic, and for illustrators who "have no script to work from" and for writers "who have no illustrator to work with." Both latter groups are advised to submit samples so that they can be matched "with an appropriate writer [or illustrator] from our *Samandal* database" (*Samandal* 2, 149). The magazine itself thus functions as a major hub, connecting disparate nodes of comics producers around the world. Although it was only printed in the three main languages of Lebanon (Arabic, French, and English), Merhej noted that contributors also come from Brazil, Bulgaria, and the Czech Republic. As Merhej stipulates:

> Our authors come from a bit of everywhere, especially in the Arab countries of Egypt, Syria, Jordan . . . We think it is important that a publication like *Samandal* exists in the Arab world. In addition, we had no shortage of contacts abroad from the start: in Brazil [Flab, designer of the *El Perceptor* series (published by Nucléa)] or in the United States (Andy Warner). We have also developed partnerships with foreign collectives: l'Employé du moi, with whom we published our number 7. And we have exchanges with Bulgaria, the Czech Republic, Serbia . . . These are often areas that have also known war, which allows us to compare our experiences. Being an illustrator also helps to meet other authors at workshops held abroad. We want to develop collaborations wherever possible. ("Lena Merhej")

As Merhej explains, from its inception, *Samandal* acted as a network-building collective and publication center, one attuned to the inequalities of neoliberal globalization. Merhej's description of *Samandal*'s inclusivity is couched in her attention to its role as a publication in the Arab world, a world which is further qualified as one that has "known war"[9] along with other areas from which artists contribute. Thus, the "bit of everywhere" that *Samandal* represents and delineates as a global network of artistic collaboration is also situated according to specific areas of shared experience and greater or lesser control and authority in the global economies of graphic narrative.

From its inception to its current formation, *Samandal*'s contributors have espoused a belief in the importance of operating "beyond the demarcated and official boundaries, promoting dialogue between peoples using words and pictures to tell stories of

---

9. Jonathan Guyer quotes *Samandal* contributor Sandra Ghosn in his article about Lebanese comics and commonalities among Lebanese and Arab artists: "War. War is common. The memory of war, more precisely. I was born in the war; everything I do goes back to this phase that I blocked out completely" ("War" 88).

their own" ("Samandal Comics Magazine: Issue One Press Release"). One can read this transnational inclusivity as a centrifugal, outward-facing embrace of likeminded artists around the world regardless of national, linguistic, or cultural borders. Indeed, considering Huda Terki's original-English-language yaoi manga piece in *Samandal* 2 — "It's My Love Letter" — which is a manga story in English read from right to left and drawn by a young woman in Tripoli,[10] *Samandal*'s panels seem to evoke a borderless world.

The dialogue that *Samandal* promotes implicates not only space but time as well. In his editorial for *Généalogie* (2014), the first *Samandal* volume published after the switch to an annual publication model, editor Rima notes that typically one imagines genealogy vertically, drawing together ancestors and descendants (n. pag.). Instead, he offers, why not approach the titular concept of the volume "horizontally, and from the vantage of the language of visual narration?" (n. pag.). In doing so, Rima collects artists across generations and geographic locations, according to visual and narrative relations. Rima literally positions *Samandal* as it looks outward, drawing a web of international artists into its assemblage: "The starting point is Lebanon and the horizon is the whole world" ("Le point de départ est le Liban et l'horizon est le monde entier"; n. pag.).

However, recent *Samandal* addition Karen Keyrouz qualifies that the collective is also rooted in centripetal exigence. As Nina Morelli — who interviewed Keyrouz for *Middle East Monitor* — describes it, Keyrouz "points out that in a country where the government doesn't support culture, it's natural for artists to come together. 'After all, any kind of collective is created because people know that together they have a louder voice.'" Thus, the role of the collective, while still operating as a form of decentralized and democratic production, is also inflected by the lack of support for comics in Lebanon (see also Khoury 13–15). Further, Joseph Kai stipulates that the collective approach does not necessarily behoove local self-determination. Of the small Lebanese comics scene, Kai avers that "it's super-difficult for me to think of one aspect that is Lebanese . . . It has very, very different and various references, and inspirations" (qtd. in Guyer, "War" 87). Keyrouz and Kai both make clear that the desire to transcend the bounds of nationalism is not necessarily coterminous with a project of liberation or even neoliberalism. Rather, in working toward the

---

10. Or perhaps wom*en* (Azimi).

creation of a Lebanese comics scene, *Samandal*'s creators came to see that Lebanese national culture did not have a place for a dedicated comics culture, necessitating a search for recognition and legibility in a global comics scene.

However, despite its global network, *Samandal* could not avoid being implicated in local frames of interpretation. Issue 7—a collaborative issue produced with L'employé du Moi, a Belgian comics publisher—aroused the objection of the Catholic Media Center in Lebanon, which ultimately led to charges and a fine against three of the editors. The charges were based on two stories, one by Merhej (who was out of the country at the time) and one by French artist Valfret.[11] Thus, an issue produced as a transnational publication around a shared theme was read and adjudicated against based on legal and religious strictures in Lebanon. The editors do not understand why charges were brought against only three of four editors, none of whom were the artist for the offending stories; nor do they grasp the rationale for fining *Samandal* without preventing its publication or even censoring issue 7 (Muhanna; Dueben, "Interview"; Dabaie). The editors *do* understand that the case itself was representative of deeply sectarian laws in what is "not a secular country" (qtd. in Dueben, "Interview").

The case against *Samandal* demonstrates the risks and complex relations involved in the project of using comics to construct transnational, translingual, and transcultural coalitions. As recounted by the editors singled out for charges, Khouri, the fdz, and Imam, when they were first summoned to answer to Lebanese censorship authorities, the censors' lack of familiarity with comics was an impediment in questioning. Rather than being read for its own logics and poetics, *Samandal* was scrutinized according to international events. The General Security men took the issue's title, "Revanche" ("Revenge"), as an indication that it was meant as a retaliation for the Danish newspaper *Jyllands Posten*'s publication of comics depicting the prophet Muhammad (Muhanna; Dueben, "Interview"), thus misreading the theme of the issue. Further misreading attended the comics structure itself: Merhej decries the deliberate graphic illiteracy enacted by offended readers in her metacomic describing the outrage over her "offending" comic (Dabaie). Here she stipulates that

---

11. Also known as Valfret Aspératus, also known as Cyprien Mathieu; born in France, Valfret went to school and lives in Belgium (Delmas).

> the image that upset Samandal's readers is not complete and was isolated in its context . . . Because the art of comics is based on the narration in sequential images and is often accompanied by a text, cutting or removing (or understanding) a picture of a comic story is equivalent to cutting a word from a text. (qtd. in Dabaie)

As shown through the example of *Metro*'s banning as well, a lack of widespread comics culture in a specific area can lead to reading practices predicated on unfamiliarity, and even bad faith.

Both *Samandal* stories that were singled out speak to the untranslatability inherent not only in comics form but also in religious imagery. Merhej's piece is a particular exercise in translational poetics, as she takes regional insults from Lebanon and visually translates them. Merhej explained that the purpose of the piece was to show the violence at work in the literal expression of some commonly used phrases (Dabaie). "May God burn your religion," illustrated through a priest and an imam being lit on fire, was the translation singled out for its denigration of religion. The calculus in the selection of two works, one by a Lebanese artist and one by a French artist, links creators from differential national locations of visual production in an overlapping frame of juridical interpretation. Furthermore, in Elias Muhanna's analysis, "It was unusual that the suit was directed against the editors, rather than the artists." As Muhanna reveals, "Khouri suspected that this was motivated by the fact that one of the artists, Valfret, was a foreign national, and the other, Merhej, was the daughter of a former minister." For his part, Khouri did not see the choice of offense as indicative of a complicated plot by the General Security office, saying, "I think they probably just looked at the names of everyone involved and decided who could be sued without any hassle" (qtd. in Muhanna).

Valfret's comment on the ruling was, "I was shocked . . . in Europe you can say whatever you want" (qtd. in Muhanna), a claim that begs further qualification. It is tempting to presume, as Valfret does, that a secular approach to freedom of speech has no limits. Yet this presumption rests on a facile distinction between nations as well as juridical and lay readers. While Bienvenu Mbutu Mondondo's case may seem to indicate that all manner of racist representation is permitted in Belgium, David Enright's case against *Tintin in the Congo* demonstrates that the same imagery will not be tolerated in the same way in England. In a far more horrifying example, French citizens

Chérif and Saïd Kouachi perpetrated the massacre of twelve people at the *Charlie Hebdo* offices, putatively in retaliation for Islamophobic cartoons. These brothers operated outside established French law, yet their murderous outrage and the ensuing debates regarding *Charlie Hebdo*'s satirical targets demonstrates that nationally delimited readerships are not homogeneous.[12] Furthermore, *Charlie Hebdo* itself was born as a result of government censorship and the outlawing of its predecessor, the graphic satire magazine *Hara-Kiri* (Gautheron). The banning of *Hara-Kiri,* following a 1970 cover comparing the death of French hero Charles de Gaulle with a tragic fire at a dancehall in Saint-Laurent-du-Pont that killed 146 people, indicates that in Europe you cannot necessarily "say whatever you want." In response to Minister of the Interior Raymond Marcellin's interdiction against the magazine, one of the first issues of *Charlie Hebdo,* assembled by the same editorial staff as *Hara-Kiri,* bore the ironic headline "There is no censorship in France!" Some figures, be they a burning priest or a World War II resistance leader and president, enter a localized realm of the sacred, even in the most secular of democracies.

Frames for censorship as well as frames for reading and recognizing comics vary according to linguistic, religious, and national borders. Yet, while the case against *Samandal* demonstrates the precarity involved in trying to break out of these borders, its aftermath reasserts the dynamic tension between national and transnational collectives. Facing fines that nearly shut down the organization, *Samandal*'s editors responded with a crowd-funding campaign that brought in donors from around the world, as well as an anthology, *Muqtatafat,* bringing together "artists from Arabic-speaking regions of the Middle East, including Lebanon, Egypt, and Jordan" (Lewis et al.). Although editors A. David Lewis, Anna Mudd, and Paul Beran had planned to release *Muqtatafat* before *Samandal*'s legal censure, they were able to donate all profits to the continued existence of *Samandal* thanks to a delay in publication.[13]

---

12. In this regard, Emmanuel Todd's *Qui est Charlie?* critically examines the racialization of "freedom of speech" as it has been used in France to delimit citizenships into hierarchies of exclusion and belonging.

13. Lewis attributes said delay to "short-sightedness": "Those in the American comics industry didn't necessarily know what to make of these Middle Eastern works, and they couldn't count on there being a US market for them" (qtd. in *Arab-Lit Quarterly,* "Ground Breaking Middle Eastern Anthology").

Feedback networks between global and local comics concerns both imperiled and galvanized *Samandal*. As a way of reading for difference, the case and the role of transnational collectives in its unfolding is indicative of what Emily Apter dubs "translational transnationalism," an approach to world comics (or literature, in her use) "that responds to the dynamics of geopolitics without shying away from fractious border wars" (*Against World Literature* 42). Valfret is not wrong to assert differences between national policies of censorship, yet the case against *Samandal* reminds us that national differences presuppose transnational frames of comparison and interaction. Collaborations across national borders conditioned the possibility of issue 7, and they also reflected its adjudication in Lebanese court. While the court's ruling was localized, in that it targeted Khouri, the fdz, and Imam for fines, the threat to *Samandal* as a publication unfolded along global and local lines simultaneously. Transnational fundraising networks worked to sustain *Samandal*, while its editors avowed their enhanced commitment to publish comics in Lebanon following the court case. Khouri avows that "the best resistance to censorship is to make more comics" (qtd. in Dueben, "Interview"), especially given the terms of the case brought against *Samandal*. Because the title given to the suit is "The People vs. Samandal Comics," the editors felt a need to publicize the magazine's persecution so that "the people" might know "what the state is doing in their name" (qtd. in Dueben, "Interview").

Language: Thinking in Opposite Directions

Apter has clarified that she uses the term *translational transnationalism* to "emphasize translation among small nations or minority language communities" (*Translation Zone* 5). While Lebanon may indeed be considered a small nation, it is also a sort of minority-language community given its trilingualism. In what follows, I consider the ways in which conditions of linguistic possibility—trilingual French, Arabic, and English publishing—engender *Samandal*'s appeal to transnational contributors and readers as well as its unique formal characteristics.

Translation studies has long debated the politics of translating between and among Western and non-Western languages, with opponents such as Apter famously advocating for "untranslatability" as a strategy "against World Literature." Apter contends that to introduce questions of equality and the uneven distribution of linguistic shares in world languages and literatures is to foreground the political in translation theory. Nonequivalence, the right not to translate, cultural incommensurability: these problematics not only anchor the problem of untranslatability in world literature (and comparative literature more generally), they also engender the broader question of what it means "to relate to" literarily. ("Untranslatability" 199)

Following the claims of those who, like Apter, hold that untranslatability functions as a tactic for resisting the Scylla and Charybdis of monocultural homogenization or rampant pluralism attending the globalization of culture (not to mention the culture of globalization), one can read in *Samandal*'s linguistic structure a radical reimagining of how to physically foreground relations of translation and untranslatability.

Since its inception, *Samandal* has been published in Arabic, French, and English. While di Ricco and Davies describe *Samandal*'s "multilingualism" as "pragmatic" (di Ricco 199; Davies, *Urban Comics* 249), Merhej notes that the trilingualism actually "limits the readership" ("Lena Merhej"). Indeed, although di Ricco and Davies read the trilingualism in terms of the public the artists want to reach, rather than as a product of colonial history, Merhej reminds us that these three languages have a specific relationship to Lebanon, showing the trilingualism's dual centripetal and centrifugal valences. Arabic, French, and English are specific to Lebanon and also represent what Tejaswini Niranjana refers to as "unequal languages" (48) in the determination of linguistic and aesthetic reading practices in the nation. Myriem El Maïzi describes them: "the three languages spoken in Lebanon—Arabic (the official language of the country), French (the language of the mandate and the number one foreign language currently in use in Lebanon), and English" ("'Real News from Beirut'" 200). These languages draw the reader's attention to the violence and colonial influence underlying their co-presence in the work. The co-presence does not imply parity or an equal footing among the languages; it gestures instead to sites of struggle in the practices of recognition and literacy.[14]

---

14. Interviewer Negar Azimi notes: "Language seems very important to you guys. As far as I can tell, *Samandal* is the first trilingual comic ever. Very Lebanese."

Although comics in Arabic can be traced back to *karikatur* in the 1880s (Guyer, "Arab Page" 12) or to the autonomic development of Arabic-language comics magazines in the 1950s (Douglas and Malti-Douglas; Merhej, "Introduction"; di Ricco), Arabic is not a "language of comics" of the same magnitude as French and English. The co-presence of all three in *Samandal* reflects both lived, material usage and parlance in the region, and the influence of French and US comics on the development of comics in Arabic. Hatem Imam describes this trilingual comics situation in his article on comics in Arabic, "Tongue-Tied—The Evasiveness of Language in Today's Arab Comics":

> We have always translated, lettered, reprinted and read American, European, and Japanese comics, and in comparison rarely made indigenous Arab comics. The rate and scale of production has been in fits and starts, never really sustained or cogent, mostly targeting children and often propounding dominant political ideologies from pan-Arabism to Islamism. Few attempts struggled with forging a native genre that transcended the barriers of sub-cultural differences and dialects.

Imam gestures both outward and inward to show how languages delimit comics production. English and French are two of the primary linguistic registers oversaturating the market for comics in the Middle East, while the dialects in the region create "barriers." In his introduction to the catalog for the Angoulême exhibit, "The New Generation: Arabic Comics Today," Jad (as Georges Khoury) notes the issue of language as the conundrum at the heart of the development of Arab comics. He explains that classical Arabic (*fusha*) "has traditionally dominated the literary sphere," while "under the influence of Pan-Arab ideology, dialects have progressively gained ground thanks to the social and political interests of the Arab revolutions" (15). Arabic-language comics expose multiple interwoven negotiations and revisions at the levels of local and global forms of expression.[15] Yet Jad sees in *Samandal* an emergent dedication to breaking out of hegemonic traditions of expression while also championing linguistic diversity and self-determination. The title is a Latinized Arabic word (i.e., *Samandal*, not *Salamandre* or *Salamander*), with

---

15. On this point, see Douglas and Malti-Douglas 224–27.

which *Samandal* asserts its local situation in Lebanon, at the same time featuring two of the languages most associated with globalized comics—French and English.

Samandal uniquely brings together three languages in order to imagine new situations of global-local interactivity. The editors even wrote the editorial for issue 3 in *fusha* (Azimi), serving as a meta-commentary on the strangeness of literary language in this context while drawing attention to its absence elsewhere in the work. For editor Rima, such language play is itself a component of all comics production and reading. In the *Généalogie* volume, he stipulates: "Comics is a language of associations based on the creation of links and ruptures, and characterized by permanent tensions, as much in its inscription as in its reading." These linguistic links and ruptures that Rima identifies as the basis of comics are also reflected in formal continuities and discontinuities. It is possible to qualify Davies's description of *Samandal*'s trilingualism as "pragmatic" by way of his use of the *Géographie* volume as his primary source text. As he notes of this work, translations in French, Arabic, and English are provided as "footnotes" in the volume (*Urban Comics* 248); the same cannot be said of all *Samandal* volumes. While I consider the page form in more detail in the following section, *Samandal*'s translational approaches have changed between issues. Issue 1 was republished originally on *Samandal*'s website and subsequently on the platform https://issuu.com with accompanying translations; other issues were published with partial translations or booklets that accompanied the magazine.

Samandal demonstrates translation as a media-specific and emergent practice. In his grant proposal for a trilingual website, the fdz notes that "the translations, unlike the print versions, will be integrated into the comics themselves to allow a non-disruptive reading experience (something that would be practically impossible in the print magazine short of reprinting every issue three times)" (Samandal Association for Comics). Amusingly, the *Topie* volume of *Samandal was* published in three distinct versions, "allowing each reader to be fully submerged in the stories and making it 'the first Arabic publication of its kind' according to [editor] Macaron" (Morley). In creating linguistically distinct versions, the volume is actually—as noted on *Samandal*'s website—three distinct books, each with its own title: *Topie* in French, *Toupya* in Arabic, and *Topia* in English (https://samandalcomics.org). However, the fdz gestures toward precisely the frictions engendered by a trilingual comic. While any translation theorist is familiar with Walter Benjamin's championing of the interlinear scriptures as the ideal of translation (82), a commensurate model for comics is perhaps only achievable as the fdz describes it, through entirely separate publications. *Samandal*'s numerous translation approaches and strategies thus draw attention to the strangeness of comics and translation.[16]

As Niranjana reminds us, translation is always a situated practice, one responsive to history, power, and cultural differences. As an example of translational idiosyncrasies, *Samandal*'s volume *Ça Restera Entre Nous,* or "This Stays Between Us," has a different title in Arabic. Merhej explains that in Arabic the title is "Behind the Door," but this title would have a different connotation in French, given that in France, "*Derrière la porte* refers too much to the porn film *Derrière la porte verte*" (Samandal, "Samandal, deuxième rencontre"). Capitulations and compromises are often made in translation based on local cultures, yet frequency does not evacuate these negotiations of differentials in power, money, and influence. By producing a cover with two distinct titles sharing the same space, *Ça Restera Entre Nous / Behind the Door* provides yet another model for reading difference in comics production.

Of course, as demonstrated in chapter 2, it is the imbrication of image and text that creates an existential barrier for translation. To consider a counterexample, L'Association's massive anthology *Comix 2000* collected 2,000 pages of comics by 324 authors from twenty-nine countries. Aspiring to collect the best comics art from around the world, the editors determined that all pieces should be wordless in order to skip "the agonies of translation" and so that "anyone in any country will be able to read the same book. A universal comic tome!" (Menu, "Preface"). Without discounting the significance and innovation of *Comix 2000,* one can see this claim to a cosmopolitical universality as a mode of subsuming difference. Taken for granted are the precepts that everyone is able to read the same way without words, and that the tome affords universal access. A contrapuntal reading considers that the book, formatted for left-to-right reading, has already delimited the readers oriented in this direction. Further, with only one contributor from a country whose official language is Arabic, the book establishes the universality of comics in rather unilateral ways, so that artists from French- and English-speaking countries represent the majority of the best comics from around the world.

---

16. See Reyns-Chikuma; Zannetin.

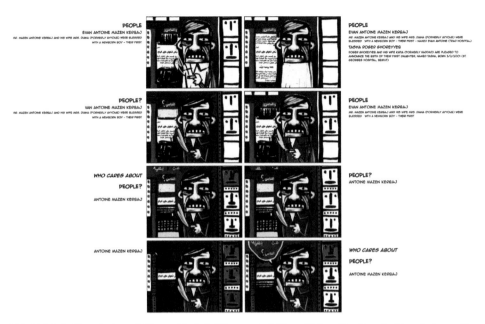

FIGURE 5.1. Translation of Mazen Kerbaj, "Suspended Time Vol. 1: The Family Tree," shows the panels as originally printed on the page, with columns adjacent to the comic showing translations formatted to accompany the panels

Samandal's experimental approach to translation offers a counter to *Comix 2000* by continually negotiating with and foregrounding translation as a generative point for creative engagement.

Through reading one of the first comics published in *Samandal*, Mazen Kerbaj's "Suspended Time Vol. 1: The Family Tree," we can see the political potential of the "agonies of translation." "Suspended Time" constructs a narrative through a series of minor changes between panels (see figure 5.1). From panel to panel a word or image is altered or erased so that a new expression emerges. The text and image are united within the picture plane so that each modifies the other. A print announcement for Evan Antoine Mazen Kerbaj's birth is painted over, panel by panel, until only his grandfather's name— Antoine Kerbaj ("The First Generation")—remains, beside a painting of Antoine himself. This painting will shift first into the Holiday Inn made famous in the Battle of Hotels in 1975, and then into Mazen Kerbaj (the second generation), before shifting again into Evan Antoine Mazen Kerbaj (the third generation), as all the while different word combinations revise and reshape how the images are read and their relations to preceding and subsequent panels. The specific combination of image and text makes the work explicitly untranslatable in the way that Apter uses this term to foreground incommensurability (*Against World Literature* 3). The same effect cannot be achieved by replacing the Arabic text with English and flipping the orientation of the pages. Therefore, in order to "translate" the online version of the comic, the editors of *Samandal* displayed a translation alongside the comic but external to the panels (see figure 5.1). In this way, the translation of "Suspended Time" can only appear as translated work by denaturing that which it is designed to translate. The comic as a paginal composition is no longer visually cohesive, now distended from a portrait layout into a wider format without the same rectilinear organizing principle. The translation is a supplement: that which supplants the visual coherence of the page layout while it supplements the linguistic decoding of the text.

"Suspended Time" functions in my reading as a metaphor, object, and agent. It is a metaphor for comics' relationship to literature: comics might be added to world literature, but only by disfiguring the unexamined textuality of literature and disorienting those readers whose mastery has been established through literary means. It is an object in that I read it at a particular moment in space and time and my reading of the work shifts depending on the material substrate of the edition I read. This object demands that I attend to the historical and literary specificity of global print cultures. While I read, I feel the reading as it reorients my eyes and hands in unfamiliar ways. It is also an agent, in that as I read "Suspended Time," it becomes an instrument for cultivating disorienting reading practices. It spurs me to question how certain works appear in the world. What possibilities does the translation open? What does it foreclose? What possibilities do global comics as a media technology offer for reorienting world reading and world readers?

Kerblog versus *Beyrouth juillet-août 2006* versus *Beirut Won't Cry*

A necessary point of comparison for how a format handles trilingualism and translation is found in the travels of one of Kerbaj's other works, originally published on his blog, *Kerblog*. In July 2006 Kerbaj began documenting the thirty-three-day Israeli bombardment of Beirut with a series of cartoons and comics which he published online.

These pieces are frequently satirical with text in Arabic, French, and English throughout. A year after their posting, L'Association acquired the rights to publish the entries in book form as part of their Côtelette imprint. As noted in chapter 3, Côtelette was conceived as the more "literary" of L'Association's imprints, featuring a standardized ivory cover and rectangular *roman* or novelesque trim size. The book was titled *Beyrouth: juillet-août 2006* and published with accompanying French subtitles for any post originally written in English or Arabic. A decade later, in 2017, Fantagraphics published a book version entitled *Beirut Won't Cry* with the subtitle *Lebanon's July War: A Visual Diary.* This version was released through the Fantagraphics Underground imprint, with English translations and an introduction from Joe Sacco.

These three versions of a work demonstrate how commercial print practices can delineate readerships in time and space. The blog format engendered a formal punctuation correspondent to posting times while creating a contiguous scroll in which the past rolls out behind the latest entries. Though Ghenwa Hayek describes the narrative structure as a "social contract, which in the 'Kerblog' case is the reader's volition to keep on clicking" (179), the digital format of immediate publication also creates the possibility of a reader who is not clicking back through past entries but instead waiting for a post in real time. Because many of the entries are Kerbaj's drawn responses to events as he is living them, *Kerblog* becomes an instance of what Charles Hatfield calls "radical synchronism" (52), whereby at any point in time, the frame of the computer screen and the blog scroll may present multiple moments in time within a single space.

Readership for the blog is also conversational such that it becomes part of *Kerblog*. Readers may post comments to any of Kerbaj's drawings, and he in turn admonishes or thanks readers at times in text-only posts such as one from July 26, 2006: "please do not contact me for any interview anymore.//i am beginning to freak out repeating 5 times a day the same things. if your interested in what i am doing, please write yourself a story about it (it's easy, you'll see)" ("i am sorry"). Commenters self-locate in a range of places and through multiple languages. Some describe having found the blog through local newspapers or friends; others attest that they do not know how they stumbled upon Kerbaj's work.

L'Association's 264-page volume *Beyrouth* or Fantagraphics's 266-page *Beirut* shift the temporal relations of the work and delimit the books' readership through both paratextual and translational cues. The tonnage of entries effected by the blogroll is formally renegotiated according to the thickness of page stock along with the number of pages. By taking each image as a discrete paginal entry, the L'Association and Fantagraphics books create a sort of capsular aesthetic wherein each post is its own enunciation rather than a participant in a long, vertical strand of visual responses. The brief length of the bombardment—thirty-three days—is undermined by the blog's inclusion of far more entries, connoting the feeling of waiting for bombs to fall in a drawn-out, moment-to-moment approach. The books distend the period July 14, 2006–August 14, 2006[17] into thick stacks of pages. Moreover, the reverse chronology of a blog, wherein the latest post is the first that a reader encounters, is reversed in the book, which begins with posts from July 14, 2006, and progresses past the purported August 14 end of the war, until August 27, 2006.

As opposed to *Kerblog*—and to *Samandal*—these books are rhetorically situated vis-à-vis an intended audience, and a monolingual one at that. This situating is evident in the print orientation of the books; both are read left-to-right, in keeping with French and English readerships. It is also clear from the linguistic realignment; both are titled in French or English, and all corresponding captions and prose are in the same language. The text-only blog entries—originally in English—are translated into French throughout *Beyrouth*. More importantly, for the sake of Comics Studies, both books are also aesthetically oriented in a distinct way that diverges from the blog.

Beyrouth is visually recognizable as a Côtelette book, and *Beirut Won't Cry* bears a number of paratextual trappings of not only a highbrow graphic novel but also a particular kind of Fantagraphics book. These aesthetic sensibilities are likewise evident in the delineation of readerships that the books produce, such that in 2017 the UK music magazine *Wire* can title an article about *Beirut Won't Cry* "Mazen Kerbaj Inks *New* Graphic Novel" (emphasis added), and Davies can describe the book's "temporal immediacy" and "resoundingly presentist documentation" (*Urban Comics* 39). The newness perceived by these readers of English is a result of the commercial and aesthetic repackaging of decade-old contents. That is, the contents are "new" or "immediate" only for a reader who has not read *Kerblog* or

---

17. As noted by El Maïzi, the end date of the "war" is disputed, as are many related details (199).

Beyrouth ten years prior. Similarly, when Paul Love reviewed *Beirut Won't Cry* for US-based publication *World Literature Today,* he pointed out that "the print publication of the book is actually the *second* time these images have been shared with the world" (emphasis in original), explaining that they were originally published in blog format without noting the existence of *Beyrouth.*

The counterexample of Kerbaj's texts is provided not as a rebuke to book publishing, which has its own constraints and exigencies, but instead as a reminder of why *Samandal*'s process was and continues to be distinct. *Beyrouth* and *Beirut Won't Cry* are books oriented toward a specific, linguistically delineated readership. They reduce a trilingual text to a dominant linguistic regime, which in turn determines formal aspects of the text. While each claims the cultural capital corresponding to the "indie" publishers, L'Association[18] and Fantagraphics—not to mention the specifically rarefied imprints, Côtelette and Fantagraphics Underground—they are rendered for convenient consumption according to recognizable aesthetic and cultural expectations. Further, they literally do not make a reader work in the same way that any of the first fifteen issues of *Samandal* forces a reader to move, to exert energy in the act of reading the magazine. On the one hand, a reader of *Beyrouth* or *Beirut Won't Cry* will always encounter a left-to-right orientation, uniform extradiegetic elements, and translations; on the other hand, a reader of *Samandal* may open a magazine at random only to realize they must reorient the work in order to read it.

Form: Trilingualism and the Heterotopia of the Flippy Page

Samandal's approach to trilingualism conjugates all the medial aspects of comics: as Hatfield schematizes these tensions, they are the interplay between word and image, between single panel and sequence, between sequence and surface, and between text as object and text as experience (32–67). By using a "flippy page" (see figure 5.2) as a way to delimit and orient a reader to the reading direction in a given section of *Samandal,* the magazines exemplify the multifaceted nature of what Hatfield calls image-text tension. Comics engender a jockeying between the image and the text, but also—as in the case of *Saman-*

18. See Beaty.

FIGURE 5.2. Assorted "flippy pages" from *Samandal*

dal—between images and texts, creating linguistic zones for a reader to experience frictions and border crossings. At any point, a narrative in *Samandal* might end and be followed—or preceded—by a page that suddenly changes the orientation of narrative progression. Similarly, the flippy page as a bidirectional reading plane rubs up against the comics page, imparting linear–tabular tension with another dimension.[19] Unlike *Comix 2000, Samandal* magazines do not presume a universal legibility; instead, the format explicitly marks and materially enacts differential readerships.

The flippy page acts in conjunction with the many other ways in which *Samandal* abrogates world literature as a means of shoring up objects, authors, languages, aesthetics. It is a checkpoint both between languages and between readerly sensibilities. It is also a checkpoint through which one passes into a different space, which in turn necessitates that the reader move herself. Like a Foucauldian heterotopia ("Other Spaces"),[20] the flippy page is a specific form of nonplace that exists only in relation to the two places it conjoins, yet it takes space as its own—named—place, one with a unique set of rules informing its construction and use.

As noted in a 2015 announcement for Merhej's workshop at the British Library, "the Flippy Page is an upside-down technique invented by *Samandal* to deal with the two opposite reading directions of Arabic and English" ("Flippy Page"). Some of these pages feature characters from stories, while others are *sui generis,* merely verbally instructing or visually suggesting that a reader flip the magazine. The act of flipping the magazine while reading forces a reader to confront the physical orientations of literacy. Even a trilingual reading subject must physically resituate the work in order to move between languages. Flippy pages function as translation zones, in which a reader is disoriented and reoriented in meaningful ways. To juxtapose the global to the local, *Samandal* is especially indicative of the processual makeup of form. The protean shifts in the work describe a space that is at once virtual, subject to emergent contexts and constraints, and actual, limned and delimited by material concatenations of history, politics, and power.

Aesthetics: Experimental Salamanders

From the magazines to the volumes of *Samandal,* formats shift in emergent ways. The volumes have a larger trim size and handle translation differently from volume to volume, and compared with

19. Even the material format of Samandal creates translational effects: Khouri chose the trim size based on his preference for manga (Azimi), so the issues are Lebanese-produced emulations of Japanese objects.

20. The page is also comparable to Mark McKinney's discussion of the interplay between the *affrontier* and the *afrontier* (*Redrawing* 3, 33).

the magazines. Besides the radical pluralism of *Topie,* volumes like *Géographie* and *Généalogie* have a central meeting point so that left-to-right and right-to-left stories come to a border or divide midway through these larger works. Rather than the frequent negotiations of the heterotopic flippy page, these volumes suggest a formal détente. While readers might begin from either cover, their decision will ultimately lead to a limit point where they must start again from the opposite side.

All these changes evince an approach to the global as always in formation. Languages, formats, and even aesthetics are consistently in flux, and *Samandal's* shifting approaches express this mutability. The open-call submissions of the magazines led to a wide variety of styles from a heterogenous field of producers. Some of the artists were professionally trained, with graduate degrees in art or design. Some were high school students. Even the shift to a single editor for each volume of *Samandal* entailed a unique aesthetic sensibility each year. The heterogeneity of aesthetic styles and topics throughout the print history of *Samandal* makes a reader critically aware of how graphic works are judged and evaluated. As an American scholar, I must always contend with the violence that my own reading practices do to texts by inscribing them within what theorist Rey Chow calls "hierarchical frames of comparison—and judgment—that have long been present, that stand in the way, as it were, as universals subsuming otherness" (88). *Samandal's* differences are reminders of the need to be cognizant of how expectations derived from financially dominant centers of production in global networks come to overdetermine how we imagine "comics."

As the field of Comics Studies expands to consider works in a more global cast, it is paramount that it likewise rethink alterity and orientation in its approach. To return to Ong's formulation of worlding as "situated everyday practices," how can the study of comics conceptualize "practices that creatively imagine and shape alternative social visions and configurations—that is, 'worlds'—than what already exists in a given context" (12)? Such practices may involve collectivities that broker local and global conditions for artistic and creative production, constellating emergent and even risky zones of interactivity. Such practices may involve modes of publication that eschew predatory and exclusionary traditions of property and nationalism. Such practices may involve reading in ways that are physically disruptive to our conditioned physicality. To shape a world in which unlearning imperialism is possible, and in which the politics of location is an intrinsic reading modality for image-texts, we must allow our expectations, our literacies, and even our books to be flipped from time to time, that they may flip us in return.

BIBLIOGRAPHY

Abedinifard, Mostafa. "Graphic Memories: Dialogues with Self and Other in *Persepolis* and *Persepolis 2*." *Familiar and Foreign: Identity in Iranian Film and Literature,* edited by Veronica Thompson and Manijeh Mannani, Athabasca UP, 2015, pp. 83–109.

Abirached, Zeina. "Artist's Statement." *European Comic Art* 8.1 (Spring 2015): 69–86.

———. *A Game for Swallows: To Die, to Leave, to Return.* Translated by Edward Gauvin, Graphic Universe, 2012.

———. *Mourir partir revenir. Le jeu des hirondelles.* Paris: Cambourakis, 2007.

Abomo, Marie-Rose Maurin. "Tintin au Congo: ou La nègrerie en clichés." *Images de l'Afrique et du Congo-Zaïre dans les lettres belges de langue française et alentour. Actes du colloque de Louvain-la-Neuve, 4–6 février,* edited by Pierre Halen and János Riesz, Textyles-Éditions, 1993, pp. 151–62.

Abdalla, Iskandar and Stefan Winkler, translators. *Metro: Kairo Underground.* By Magdy El Shafee, Edition Moderne, 2012.

Ahmed, Sara. *Queer Phenomenology: Orientations, Objects, Others.* Duke UP, 2006.

———. *Strange Encounters: Embodied Others in Post-Coloniality.* Routledge, 2000.

Ahrens, Jörn, and Arno Meteling, editors. "Introduction." *Comics and the City: Urban Space in Print, Picture, and Sequence,* Continuum Books, 2010, pp. 1–16.

Allan, Michael. *In the Shadow of World Literature: Sites of Reading in Colonial Egypt.* Princeton UP, 2016.

Allison, Anne. *Millennial Monsters: Japanese Toys and the Global Imagination.* U of California P, 2006.

Anderson, Benedict. *Imagined Communities: Reflections on the Origin and Spread of Nationalism*. Verso, 1991.

Apostolidès, Jean-Marie. *The Metamorphoses of Tintin, Or, Tintin for Adults*. Translated by Jocelyn Hoy, Stanford UP, 2010.

———. *Tintin et le mythe du surenfant*. Moulinsart, 2004.

Appadurai, Arjun. "Disjuncture and Difference in the Global Cultural Economy." *Theory, Culture and Society* 7.2 (1990): 295–310.

Appiah, Kwame Anthony. "Is the Post- in Postmodernism the Post- in Postcolonial?" *Critical Inquiry* 17.2 (Winter 1991): 336–57.

Appollo. "Persepolis [t1] de Marjane Satrapi." *du9: l'autre bande dessinée*, Mar. 2001. https://www.du9.org/chronique/persepolis-t1/.

Apter, Emily. *Against World Literature: On the Politics of Untranslatability*. Verso, 2013.

———. *The Translation Zone: A New Comparative Literature*. Princeton UP, 2006.

———. "Untranslatability and the Geopolitics of Reading." *PMLA* 134.1 (2019): 194–200.

———. "Untranslatables: A World System." *New Literary History* 39.3 (Summer 2008): 581–98.

ArabLit Quarterly. "Ground-Breaking Middle Eastern Comics Anthology Launches; Proceeds to Support 'Samandal.'" *ArabLit Quarterly*, 18 Dec. 2015. https://arablit.org/2015/12/18/ground-breaking-middle-eastern-comics-anthology/.

L'Association. "Petite histoire pour néophytes." *L'Association*, https://www.lassociation.fr/infos/.

Assouline, Pierre. *Hergé: The Man Who Created Tintin*. Translated by Charles Ruas, Oxford UP, 2009.

Augaitis, Daina, et al. *Raven Travelling: Two Centuries of Haida Art*. Vancouver Art Gallery, 2006.

Azimi, Negar. "*Samandal*: Super Friends." *Bidoun* 18 (2009). https://www.bidoun.org/articles/samandal.

Azoulay, Ariella Aïsha. *Potential History: Unlearning Imperialism*. Verso, 2019.

Baetens, Jan. "From Black and White to Color and Back: What Does It Mean (Not) to Use Color?" *College Literature* 38.3 (Summer 2011): 111–28.

———. "Hommage à Pierre Fresnault-Deruelle: Pour relire « Du linéaire au tabulaire »." *Les cahiers du GRIT* 1 (2011): 122–28.

———. "Pour une poétique de la gouttière." *Word & Image* 7.4 (1991): 365–76.

Baetens, Jan, and Hugo Frey. *The Graphic Novel: An Introduction*. Cambridge UP, 2015.

———. "Modernizing Tintin: From Myth to New Stylizations." *The Comics of Hergé: When the Lines Are Not So Clear*, edited by Joe Sutliff Sanders, UP of Mississippi, 2016, pp. 98–112.

———. "'Layouting' for the Plot: Charles Burns and the Clear Line Revisited." *Journal of Graphic Novels and Comics* 8.2 (2017): 193–202.

Baetens, Jan, et al. "Introduction." *The Cambridge History of the Graphic Novel*, edited by Jan Baetens, Hugo Frey, and Stephen E. Tabachnick, Cambridge UP, 2018, pp. 1–18.

Bagnall, Roger S. *Early Christian Books in Egypt*. Princeton UP, 2009.

Bahrampour, Tara. "Tempering Rage by Drawing Comics; A Memoir Sketches an Iranian Childhood of Repression and Rebellion." *New York Times,* 21 May 2003. https://www.nytimes.com/2003/05/21/books/tempering-rage-drawing-comics-memoir-sketches-iranian-childhood-repression.html.

Barthes, Roland. *Mythologies.* Translated by Annette Lavers, Hill and Wang, 1972.

Bassnett, Susan, and Harish Trivedi. "Introduction: Of Colonies, Cannibals and Vern aculars." *Post-colonial Translation: Theory and Practice,* edited by Susan Bassnett and Harish Trivedi, Routledge, 1999, pp. 1–18.

Beaty, Bart. *Unpopular Culture: Transforming the European Comic Book in the 1990s.* U of Toronto P, 2007.

B[eauchard], David. *L'Ascension du haut mal* tomes 1–6. L'Association, 1996–2003.

——. *Epileptic.* Translated by Kim Thompson, Pantheon, 2005.

Benjamin, Walter. "The Task of the Translator" [first printed as introduction to a Baudelaire translation, 1923]. *Illuminations,* translated by Harry Zohn and edited by Hannah Arendt, Harcourt Brace Jovanovich, 1968, pp. 69–82.

Benoît-Jeannin, Maxime. *Le Mythe Hergé.* Villeurbanne: Éditions Golias, 2001.

Bentahar, Ziad. "Tintin in the Arab World and Arabic in the World of Tintin." *Alternative Francophone* 1.5 (2012): 41–54.

Bernardin, Susan. "Future Pasts: Comics, Graphic Novels, and Digital Media." *The Routledge Companion to Native American Literature,* edited by Deborah L. Madsen, Routledge, 2016, pp. 480–93.

Berndt, Jaqueline, and Bettina Kümmerling-Meibauer. "Introduction: Studying Manga across Cultures." *Manga's Cultural Crossroads,* edited by Jaqueline Berndt and Bettina Kümmerling-Meibauer, Routledge, 2013, pp. 1–15.

Berninger, Mark, et al., editors. *Comics as a Nexus of Cultures: Essays on the Interplay of Media, Disciplines and International Perspectives.* McFarland & Company, 2010.

"Beirut Partita: Zeina Abirached's Lecture at Duke University on 25 Sep. 2013." Center for French and Francophone Studies at Duke. *YouTube,* 7 Oct. 2013. https://www.youtube.com/watch?v=nPBTZ8kegjI.

Bhabha, Homi. *The Location of Culture.* Routledge, 1994.

——. "Remembering Fanon: Self, Psyche and the Colonial Condition." *Colonial Discourse and Post-Colonial Theory: A Reader,* edited by Patrick Williams and Laura Chrisman, Columbia UP, 1994, pp. 112–23.

Bisson, Julien. "Zeina Abirached: La bande dessinée qui pose un regard drôle et décalé sur l'horreur . . . et la nostalgie d'une nuit de conflits." *L'Express,* 11 Jan. 2007. http://www.lexpress.fr/culture/livre/zeina-abirached_813223.html.

Bourdil, Pierre-Yves, and Bernard Tordeur. *Bob de Moor: 40 ans de bande dessinéee, 35 ans au côtés d'Hergé.* Editions Lombard, 1986.

Bredehoft, Thomas. *The Visible Text: Textual Production and Reproduction from Beowulf to Maus.* Oxford UP, 2014.

Brienza, Casey E. "Books, Not Comics: Publishing Fields, Globalization, and Japanese Manga in the United States." *Pub Res Q* 25 (2009): 101–17.

——, editor. "Introduction." *Global Manga: "Japanese" Comics without Japan?* Ashgate, 2015, pp. 1–21.

——. *Manga in America: Transnational Book Publishing and the Domestication of Japanese Comics.* Bloomsbury, 2016.

Brousseau, Marcel. "Allotment Knowledges: Grid Spaces, Home Places, and Story-scapes on the Way to Rainy Mountain." *NAIS: Journal of the Native American and Indigenous Studies Association* 5.1 (2018): 136–67.

Burns, Charles. *The Hive.* Pantheon, 2012.

——. *Incubation.* Pigeon Press, 2015.

——. *Johnny 23.* Le Dernier Cri, 2010.

——. *Last Look.* Pantheon, 2016.

——. *Sugar Skull.* Pantheon, 2014.

——. *Vortex.* Cornélius, 2016.

——. *X'ed Out.* Pantheon, 2010.

Callison, Camille, and Candida Rifkind. "Introduction: 'Indigenous Comics and Graphic Novels: An Annotated Bibliography.'" *Jeunesse: Young People, Texts, Cultures* 11.1 (2019): 139–55.

Cambourakis, Frédéric. "Frédéric Cambourakis." *LM: Art & Culture,* 16 Feb. 2013. http://www.lm-magazine.com/blog/2013/02/16/frederic-cambourakis/.

Carrier, Mélanie. "Persepolis et les révolutions de Marjane Satrapi." *Belphégor* 4.1 (2004). https://dalspace.library.dal.ca//handle/10222/47691.

Casanova, Pascale. "Literature as a World." *New Left Review* 31 (2005): 71–90.

——. *The World Republic of Letters.* Translated by M. B. Debevoise. Harvard UP, 2004.

Cascone, Sarah. "Publisher Strips Hergé's Heirs of Millions of Dollars in Rights to Tintin Drawings." *Art Net News,* 9 June 2015. https://news.artnet.com/art-world/tintin-rights-court-ruling-306273.

Cates, Isaac. "Comics and the Grammar of Diagrams." *The Comics of Chris Ware: Drawing Is a Way of Thinking,* edited by David Ball and Martha Kuhlman. UP of Mississippi, 2010, pp. 90–104.

Caumery, and J.-P Pinchon. *L'enfance de Bécassine.* Gautier et Languereau, 1913. *MSU Libraries Digital Repository.* https://d.lib.msu.edu/gnn/1122#page/4/mode/2up.

Celotti, Nadine. "The Translator of Comics as a Semiotic Investigator." *Comics in Translation,* edited by Federico Zanettin, St. Jerome Publishing, 2008, pp. 33–49.

Chalmers, Robert. "Marjane Satrapi: Princess of Darkness." *Independent,* 30 Sep. 2006. https://www.independent.co.uk/arts-entertainment/books/features/marjane-satrapi-princess-of-darkness-417932.html.

Chavanne, Renaud. *Composition de la bande dessinée.* PLG, 2010.

Cheah, Pheng. *What Is a World?: On Postcolonial Literature as World Literature.* Duke UP, 2016.

——. "World against Globe: Toward a Normative Conception of World Literature." *New Literary History,* 45.3 (2014): 303–29.

Chow, Rey. *The Age of the World Target: Self-Referentiality in War, Theory, and Comparative Work.* Duke UP, 2006.

Chute, Hillary. "Comics as Literature? Reading Graphic Narrative." *PMLA,* 123.2 (Mar 2008): 452–65.

——. *Graphic Women: Life Narrative and Contemporary Comics.* Columbia UP, 2010.

———. "An Interview with Charles Burns." *Believer Magazine*, 1 Jan. 2008. https://believermag.com/an-interview-with-charles-burns/.

———. "The Popularity of Postmodernism." *Twentieth Century Literature* 57.3/4 (2011): 354–63.

———. "The Texture of Retracing in Marjane Satrapi's Persepolis." *Women's Studies Quarterly* 36.1/2 (2008): 92–110.

Cohn, Neil. "Navigating Comics: An Empirical and Theoretical Approach to Strategies of Reading Comic Page Layouts." *Frontiers in Psychology* 4.186 (2013): 1–15.

———. *Who Understands Comics?: Questioning the Universality of Visual Language Comprehension*. Bloomsbury Academic, 2021.

Collison, Jisgang, et al. *Indigenous Repatriation Handbook*. Royal British Columbia Museum, 2019.

Conley, Tom. *Cartographic Cinema*. U of Minnesota P, 2007.

Cooke, Rachel. "Riad Sattouf: not French, not Syrian . . . I'm a Cartoonist." *Guardian*, 27 Mar. 2016. https://www.theguardian.com/books/2016/mar/27/riad-sattouf-arab-of-the-future-interview.

"Copyright and Permissions: Lebanese Law." American University of Beirut: University Library, Library Guides. Jan. 26, 2021. https://aub.edu.lb.libguides.com/copyright/Lebanese-Law.

Coulthard, Glen Sean. *Red Skin, White Masks: Rejecting the Colonial Politics of Recognition*. U of Minnesota P, 2014.

Couch, Chris. "The Publication and Formats of Comics, Graphic Novels, and Tankobon." *Image [&] Narrative: Online Magazine of the Visual Narrative* 1 (Dec. 2000). http://www.imageandnarrative.be/narratology/chriscouch.htm.

Council of the Haida Nation. *Haida Land Use Vision*. Apr. 2005. http://www.haidanation.ca/wp-content/uploads/2017/03/HLUV.lo_rez.pdf.

La cour d'appel de Bruxelles, 9ème chambre. *Mbutu Mondondo et Le Conseil Représentatif des Associations Noires contra Moulinsart et Éditions Casterman*. 28 Nov. 2012. *Tintin.com*, https://www.tintin.com/tintin/actus/actus/003918/jugement_tintinCongo_MONDONDO.pdf.

Cowan, Alison Leigh. "A Library's Approach to Books That Offend." *New York Times*, 19 Aug. 2009. https://cityroom.blogs.nytimes.com/2009/08/19/a-librarys-approach-to-books-that-offend.

Crucifix, Benoît. "Cut-Up and Redrawn: Reading Charles Burns's Swipe Files." *Inks: The Journal of the Comics Studies Society* 1.3 (2017): 309–33.

Dabaie, Marguerite. "Help Samandal Speak." *Hooded Utilitarian*, Nov. 2015. https://www.hoodedutilitarian.com/2015/11/help-samandal-speak/.

Damluji, Nadim. *Majalat: The Art of Arab Comics*. https://majalat.tumblr.com/.

———. "An Introduction." *Tintin Travels*, 3 June 2010. https://tintintravels.com/post/662020335/introduction.

———. "Samir Magazine and the Art of Bootlegging Tintin." *Tintin Travels*, 16 Apr. 2011. https://tintintravels.com/post/4655671320/samir-magazine-and-the-art-of-bootlegging-tintin.

Davies, Catriona. "Egypt's Banned Graphic Novel to Be Published in English." *CNN*, 23 Mar. 2011. http://www.cnn.com/2011/WORLD/meast/03/23/egypt.graphic.novel/index.html.

Davies, Dominic. "Comics and Graphic Narratives: A Global Cultural Commons." *Words Without Borders*, Feb. 2017. https://www.wordswithoutborders.org/article/february-2017-international-graphic-novels-volume-xi-comics-and-graphic.

——. *Urban Comics: Infrastructure and the Global City in Contemporary Graphic Narratives*. Routledge, 2019.

Davies, Dominic, and Candida Rifkind, editors. *Documenting Trauma in Comics: Traumatic Pasts, Embodied Histories, and Graphic Reportage*. Palgrave Macmillan, 2020.

Davies, Humphrey, translator. "from *Metro*." By Magdy El Shafee. *Words Without Borders* (Feb. 2008). https://www.wordswithoutborders.org/graphic-lit/from-metro.

——. "Humphrey Davies Recommends the Best of Contemporary Egyptian Literature." *Five Books* (2011). https://fivebooks.com/best-books/egyptian-literature-humphrey-davies/.

Davis, Rocío G. "A Graphic Self: Comics as Autobiography in Marjane Satrapi's Persepolis." *Prose Studies* 27.3 (2005): 264–79.

de Certeau, Michel. *Heterologies: Discourse on the Other*. Translated by Brian Massumi, U of Minnesota P, 1986.

——. *The Practice of Everyday Life*. Translated by Stephen Randall, U of California P, 1984.

Debord, Guy, and Gil Wolman. "A User's Guide to Détournement (1956)." *Situationist International Anthology*, edited and translated by Ken Knabb, Bureau of Public Secrets, 2006, pp. 14–21.

Deloria, Vine Jr. *Custer Died for Your Sins: An Indian Manifesto*. U of Oklahoma P, 1969.

Deleuze, Gilles. *Foucault*. Les Éditions de Minuit, 1986.

Delisle, Philippe. *Bande Dessinée Franco-Belge Et Imaginaire Colonial: Des Années 1930 Aux Années 1980*. Éditions Karthala, 2016.

——. "Le Reporter, Le Missionnaire Et L'« Homme-Léopard ». Réflexions sur les stéréotypes coloniaux dans l'œuvre d'Hergé." *Outre-mers: Revue D'histoire* 96.362 (2009): 267–81.

Delmas, Gabriel. "Delmas x Valfret Asperatus." *du9: l'autre bande dessinée*, Mar. 2017. https://www.du9.org/entretien/delmas-x-valfret-asperatus/.

Denson, Shane. "Afterword: Framing, Unframing, Reframing: Retconning the Transnational Work of Comics." *Transnational Perspectives on Graphic Narratives: Comics at the Crossroads*, edited by Shane Denson et al., Bloomsbury Academic, 2014, pp. 271–84.

Denson, Shane, et al., editors. *Transnational Perspectives on Graphic Narratives: Comics at the Crossroads*. Bloomsbury Academic, 2014.

Detournay, Charles-Louis. "Pour le 90e anniversaire de Tintin, Moulinsart affirme son leadership sur Casterman." *ActuaBD*, 9 Jan. 2019. https://www.actuabd.com/Pour-le-90e-anniversaire-de-Tintin-Moulinsart-affirme-son-leadership-sur#nh1.

——. "Tintin quitterait Casterman?" *ActuaBD*, 30 Apr. 2009. https://www.actuabd.com/Tintin-quitterait-Casterman.

di Ricco, Massimo. "Drawing for a New Public: Middle Eastern 9th Art and the Emergence of a Transnational Graphic Movement." *Postcolonial Comics: Texts, Events, Identities*, edited by Binita Mehta and Pia Mukherji, Routledge, Taylor and Francis, 2014, pp. 187–203.

Dine, Philip. "The French Colonial Empire in Juvenile Fiction: From Jules Verne to Tintin," *Historical Reflections / Réflexions Historiques* 23.2 (Spring 1997): 177–203.

Dony, Christophe. "Postcolonial Theory: Writing and Drawing Back (and Beyond) in 'Pappa in Afrika' and 'Pappa in Doubt.'" *More Critical Approaches to Comics: Theories and Methods,* edited by Matthew Brown, Matthew J. Smith, and Randy Duncan, Taylor and Francis, 2019, pp. 20–36.

———. "What Is a Postcolonial Comic?" *Chronique de Littérature Internationale* (7 Nov. 2014): 12–13.

Douglas, Allen, and Fedwa Malti-Douglas. *Arab Comic Strips: Politics of an Emerging Mass Culture.* Indiana UP, 1994.

Drucker, Johanna. "Graphic Devices: Narration and Navigation." *Narrative* 16.2 (May 2008): 121–39.

Dueben, Alex. "'I Was Convinced That Beirut Stopped at the Wall': An Interview with Zeina Abirached." *Comics Journal,* 25 Nov. 2013. http://www.tcj.com/i-was-convinced-that-beirut-stopped-at-that-wall-an-interview-with-zeina-abirached/.

———. "An Interview with Samandal." *Comics Journal,* 18 Dec. 2015. http://www.tcj.com/an-interview-with-samandal/.

———. "Kidd Designs Alex Ross' 'Rough Justice.'" *Comic Book Resources,* CBR.com, 23 Mar. 2010. https://www.cbr.com/kidd-designs-alex-ross-rough-justice/.

Eberstadt, Fernanda. "God Looked Like Marx." *New York Times,* 11 May 2003. https://www.nytimes.com/2003/05/11/books/god-looked-like-marx.html.

Edwards, Brian T. *After the American Century: The Ends of US Culture in the Middle East.* Columbia UP, 2016.

———. "Jumping Publics: Magdy El Shafee's Cairo Comics." *Novel* 47.1 (2014): 67–89.

Eggers, Dave. "Why Knopf Editor in Chief Sonny Mehta Still Has the 'Best Job in the World.'" *Vanity Fair,* 15 Sep. 2015. https://www.vanityfair.com/culture/2015/09/sonny-mehta-knopf-editor-in-chief.

Eisner, Will. *Graphic Storytelling and Visual Narrative.* Poorhouse, 1996.

El Hak, Maha Gad. "Remarques sur le discours de *Persepolis* (Bande dessinée et film d'animation)." *Revue Dilbilim XIX,* İstanbul 2009: 75–89.

El Khalil, Zena. "About Zena." *Zena El Khalil.* http://www.zenaelkhalil.com/zena#:~:text=Zena%20is%20also%20the%20founder,of%20extreme%20xenophobia%20in%20NYC.

El Maïzi, Myriem. "'Real News from Beirut': Blog BD et témoignage de guerre." *French Cultural Studies* 27.2 (2016): 199–215.

El Shafee, Magdy (مجدي الشافعي). *Metro* (مترو). Malamih (دار ملامح للنشر), 2008.

Elder, Josh. "Comics: The Universal Language." *Medium,* 31 May 2015. https://medium.com/@joshelder/comics-the-universal-language-a940213ad83c.

Elsworth, Peter C. T. "Tintin Searches for a US Audience." *New York Times,* 24 Dec. 1991, p. C9.

Emmerich, Karen. *Literary Translation and the Making of Originals.* Bloomsbury, 2017.

Enright, David. "Tintin in the Congo Should Not Be Sold to Children." *Guardian,* 4 Nov. 2011. https://www.theguardian.com/commentisfree/2011/nov/04/tintin-in-the-congo.

Erdrich, Louise. *Books and Islands in Ojibwe Country.* National Geographic, 2003.

Evans-Bush, Katy. "An Animated Dispute in Egypt." *Guardian,* 17 Apr. 2009. https://www.theguardian.com/commentisfree/libertycentral/2009/apr/17/egypt-freedom-of-speech.

Evenson, Brian. "'Catalog of an Impossible Library': A Conversation with David B." *World Literature Today,* Mar. 2016. https://www.worldliteraturetoday.org/2016/march/catalog-impossible-library-conversation-david-b-brian-evenson.

Exem. *Zinzin, maître du monde.* Éditions Tchang, 1984.

Farr, Michael. *Tintin: The Complete Companion.* Last Gasp, 2011.

"Flippy Page Comic Workshop." *British Library,* 26 July 2015. https://www.bl.uk/events/flippy-page-comic-workshop#.

Foucault, Michel. "Of Other Spaces: Utopias and Heterotopias." *Diacritics* 16 (Spring 1986): 22–27.

——. *Sécurité, territoire, population: Cours au Collège de France (1977–78),* edited by François Ewald, Alessandro Fontana, and Michel Senellart, Gallimard, 2004.

——. "What Is an Author?" *Aesthetics, Method, and Epistemology: Essential Works of Foucault 1954–1984,* edited by James D. Faubion and translated by Robert Hurley and others, The New Press, 1998.

Fresnault-Deruelle, Pierre. "Du linéaire au tabulaire." *Communications* 24 (1976): 7–23.

——. "From Linear to Tabular." *The French Comics Theory Reader,* edited by Ann Miller and Bart Beaty, Leuven UP, 2014, pp. 121–38.

——. *Hergé, ou, Le secret de l'image: essai sur l'univers graphique de Tintin.* Casterman, 2000.

——. "The Moulinsart Crypt." *European Comic Art* 3.2 (2010): 119–37.

Frey, Hugo. "Contagious Colonial Diseases in Hergé's *The Adventures of Tintin.*" *Modern & Contemporary France* 12.2 (2004): 177–88.

——. "History and Memory in Franco-Belgian Bande Dessinée (BD)." *Rethinking History: The Journal of Theory and Practice* 6.3 (2002): 293–304.

Frome, Jonathan. "Identification in Comics." *The Comics Journal* 211 (1999): 82–87.

Gabilliet, Jean-Paul. "A Disappointing Crossing: The North American Reception of Asterix and Tintin." *Transnational Perspectives on Graphic Narratives: Comics at the Crossroads,* edited by Daniel Stein, Shane Denson, and Christina Meyer, Bloomsbury Academic, 2014, pp. 257–70.

——. "Sutures génériques et fêlures intérieures chez Charles Burns." *Sillages critiques* 28, 1 May 2020. http://journals.openedition.org/sillagescritiques/9579.

Gagliano, Maria. "#SLWC17: Meet the Speakers—An Interview with Ayesha Pande Literary Agent Anjali Singh." *Slice,* 15 June 2017. https://slicemagazine.org/slwc17-meet-the-speakers-an-interview-with-ayesha-pande-literary-agent-anjali-singh/.

Galal, Mona, Mónica Carrión, and Pedro Rojo, translators. "Extracto del cómic 'Metro' de Magdy el Shafee." *Fundación Al Fanar para el Conocimiento Árabe,* 18 Sep. 2015. http://www.fundacionalfanar.org/extracto-del-comic-metro-de-magdy-el-shafee/.

Galli, Carlo. *Spazi politici: L'età moderna et l'età globale.* Il Mulino, 2001.

Ganguly, Debjani. *This Thing Called the World: The Contemporary Novel as Global Form.* Duke UP, 2016.

Garcelon, Marc. "An Information Commons? Creative Commons and Public Access to Cultural Creations." *New Media and Society* 11(8): 1307–26.

Gautheron, Agnès. "« Charlie Hebdo » : la première fois que « Le Monde » l'a écrit." *Le Monde,* 18 Sept. 2020. https://www.lemonde.fr/m-le-mag/article/2020/09/18/charlie-hebdo-la-premiere-fois-que-le-monde-l-a-ecrit_6052740_4500055.html.

Gauthier, Guy. *Vingt leçons sur l'image at le sens.* Edilig, 1982.

Gauvin, Edward. "*A Game for Swallows* by Zeina Abirached." *Edward Gauvin blog,* 24 July 2012. http://www.edwardgauvin.com/blog/?p=1067.

——. "Re: Katherine Kelp wants to get in touch with you." Received by Katherine Kelp-Stebbins, 28 July 2017.

Ghosh, Bishnupriya. *Global Icons: Apertures to the Popular.* Duke UP, 2011.

Gikandi, Simon. "Globalization and the Claims of Postcoloniality." *The South Atlantic Quarterly* 100.3 (Summer 2001): 627–58.

Gill, Ian. *All That We Say Is Ours: Guujaaw and the Reawakening of the Haida Nation.* Douglas & McIntyre, 2009.

Gilmore, Leigh. "Witnessing *Persepolis*: Comics, Trauma, and Childhood Testimony." *Graphic Subjects: Critical Essays on Autobiography and Graphic Novels,* edited by Michael Chaney, U of Wisconsin P, 2011, pp. 157–63.

Glissant, Édouard. *Philosophie de la Relation: Poésie en étendue.* Gallimard, 2009.

Goddin, Philippe. *The Art of Hergé: Vol. 1, 1907–1937.* Translated by Michael Farr, Last Gasp, 2008.

——. *The Art of Hergé: Vol. 2, 1937–1949.* Translated by Michael Farr, Last Gasp, 2009.

——. *Hergé and Tintin Reporters: From Le Petit Vingtième to Tintin Magazine.* Translated by Michael Farr, Sundancer, 1987.

Goeman, Mishuana. *Mark My Words: Native Women Mapping Our Nations.* U of Minnesota P, 2013.

Good, Oliver. "Gold Ring: The UAE's First Manga." *The National* (United Arab Emirates), 20 July 2009. https://www.thenational.ae/arts-culture.

Goodman, Nelson. *Ways of Worldmaking.* Hackett, 1978.

Graham, Stephen, and Simon Marvin. *Splintering Urbanism: Networked Infrastructures, Technological Mobilities and the Urban Condition.* Routledge, 2001.

Gramsci, Antonio. *Prison Notebooks Volume 3.* Edited and translated by Joseph A. Buttigieg. Columbia UP, 2007.

Gravett, Paul. "Hergé & The Clear Line: Part 1." *Paul Gravett,* 20 Apr. 2008. http://paulgravett.com/articles/article/herge_the_clear_line.

Gray, Brenna Clarke. "Border Studies in the Gutter: Canadian Comics and Structural Borders." *Canadian Literature* 228/229 (Spring/Summer 2016): 170–87.

Green, Christopher. "Fluid Frames: The Hybrid Art of Michael Nicoll Yahgulanaas." *Art in America,* 2 Nov. 2017. https://www.artnews.com/art-in-america/features/fluid-frames-the-hybrid-art-of-michael-nicoll-yahgulanaas-60076/.

Grewal, Inderpal. *Transnational America: Feminisms, Diasporas, Neoliberalisms.* Duke UP, 2005.

Grewal, Inderpal, and Caren Kaplan. "Introduction: Transnational Feminist Practices and Questions of Postmodernity." *Scattered Hegemonies: Postmodernity and Trans-*

national Feminist Practices, edited by Inderpal Grewal and Caren Kaplan, U of Minnesota P, 1994, pp. 1–33.

Griffin, Kevin. "Michael Nicoll Yahgulanaas: The Politics Behind Haida Manga." *Vancouver Sun,* 20 Apr. 2011. https://vancouversun.com/news/staff-blogs/michael-nicoll-yahgulanaas-the-politics-behind-haida-manga.

Groensteen, Thierry. "The Art of Braiding: A Clarification." *European Comic Art* 9.1 (Spring 2016): 88–98.

———. *Comics and Narration.* Translated by Ann Miller, UP of Mississippi, 2013.

———. "Definitions." *The French Comics Theory Reader,* edited by Ann Miller and Bart Beaty, Leuven UP, 2014, pp. 93–114.

———. *The System of Comics.* Translated by Bart Beaty and Nick Nguyen, UP of Mississippi, 2007.

———. "Why Are Comics Still in Search of Cultural Legitimation?" *A Comics Studies Reader,* edited by Jeet Heer and Kent Worcester, U of Mississippi P, 2007, pp. 3–11.

Groth, Gary. Telephone interview with the author. 15 Aug. 2019.

Grove, Laurence. *Comics in French: The European Bande Dessinée in Context.* Berghahn Books, 2010.

"Guest Lecture: Michael Nicoll Yahgulanaas." The Bill Reid Centre at SFU. *YouTube,* 6 May 2016. https://www.youtube.com/watch?v=pri3SCalWPY.

Guilbert, Xavier. "The Inner Worlds of Charles Burns." *du9: l'autre bande dessinée,* 6 Aug. 2015. https://www.du9.org/en/entretien/the-inner-worlds-of-charles-burns/.

Guyer, Jonathan. "From Beirut: The Origin Story of Arab Comix." *Institute of Current World Affairs,* 9 Sept. 2015. https://www.icwa.org/from-beirut-the-origin-story-of-arab-comix/.

———. "On the Arab Page." *Le Monde Diplomatique* (Jan. 2017): 12–13.

———. "War, Romance, and Everyday Life in Beirut's Emerging Alt-Comix Scene." *International Journal of Comic Art* 21.2 (2019): 74–90.

Haines, Robert. "Red: A Haida Manga by Michael Nicoll Yahgulanaas." *The Joe Shuster Awards,* 22 Feb. 2010. https://joeshusterawards.com/2010/02/22/red-a-haida-manga/.

Hajdu, David. "Persian Miniatures." *Artforum* (Oct./Nov. 2004). https://www.mutual-art.com/Article/Persian-Miniatures/66A209E1F044F4EA.

Hanafy, Iman. "Revolutionizing the Graphic Novel." *symploke* 24.1–2 (2016): 421–34.

Harnett, Benjamin. "The Diffusion of the Codex." *Classical Antiquity* 36.2 (Oct. 2017): 183–235.

Harris, Susan. "Graphic Censorship." *Words Without Borders,* 17 Apr. 2008. https://www.wordswithoutborders.org/dispatches/article/graphic-censorship/.

Harris, William V. "Why Did the Codex Supplant the Book-Roll?" *Renaissance Society and Culture: Essays in Honor of Eugene F. Rice, Jr.,* edited by J. Monfasani and R. G. Musto, Italica, 1991, pp. 71–85.

Harrison, Richard. "Seeing and Nothingness: Michael Nicoll Yahgulanaas, Haida Manga, and a Critique of the Gutter." *Canadian Review of Comparative Literature / Revue Canadienne de Littérature Comparée,* 43.1 (Mar. 2016): 51–74.

Hatfield, Charles. *Alternative Comics: An Emerging Literature.* UP of Mississippi, 2005.

Hatheway, Cameron. "Review: A Game for Swallows." *Bleeding Cool,* 12 Jan. 2013. http://www.bleedingcool.com/2013/01/12/review-a-game-of-swallows/.

Hayek, Ghenwa. *Beirut: Imagining the City.* I. B. Tauris, 2015.

Helou, Samanta. "Native Superheroes Are the Norm at This All-Indigenous Comics Store." *Good,* 5 June 2018. https://www.good.is/features/native-american-indigenous-comic-store-red-planet-albuque.

Hergé. *The Black Island.* Translated by Michael R. Turner and Leslie Lonsdale-Cooper, Methuen Books, 1966.

———. *The Blue Lotus.* Translated by Leslie Lonsdale-Cooper and Michael R. Turner, Little, Brown, 1984.

———. *Le Lotus Bleu.* Casterman, 1974 (1946).

———. *Le Secret de La Licorne.* Casterman, 1943.

———. *L'Île Noire.* Casterman, 1938.

———. *Objectif Lune.* Casterman, 1953.

———. *On a marché sur la lune.* Casterman, 1954.

———. *Prisoners of the Sun.* Translated by Michael R. Turner and Leslie Lonsdale-Cooper, Methuen Books, 1971.

———. *Red Rackham's Treasure.* Translated by Michael R. Turner and Leslie Lonsdale-Cooper, Methuen Books, 1959.

———. *The Secret of the Unicorn.* Translated by Michael R. Turner and Leslie Lonsdale-Cooper, Methuen Books, 1965.

———. *The Seven Crystal Balls.* Translated by Michael R. Turner and Leslie Lonsdale-Cooper, Methuen Books, 1962.

———. *The Shooting Star.* Translated by Michael R. Turner and Leslie Lonsdale-Cooper, Methuen Books, 1972.

———. *Tintin au Congo.* Casterman, 1974.

———. *Tintin au Pays des Soviets.* Casterman, 1981.

———. *Tintin in American.* Translated by Michael R. Turner and Leslie Lonsdale-Cooper, Methuen Books, 1978.

———. *Tintin in the Land of the Soviets.* Translated by Leslie Lonsdale-Cooper and Michael Turner, Little, Brown, 2007.

———. *Tintin in Tibet.* Translated by Michael R. Turner and Leslie Lonsdale-Cooper, Methuen Books, 1972.

Hergé and Numa Sadoul. *Entretiens Avec Hergé.* Casterman, 2011.

Hodapp, James, and Deema Nasser. "The Complications of Reading Egypt as Africa: Translation and Magdy el-Shafee's المترو (Metro)." *ALT 35: Focus on Egypt: African Literature Today,* edited by Ernest N. Emenyonu et al., Boydell & Brewer, pp. 22–38.

Holland, Jessica. "Graphic Novel about Egyptian Life Gets English Publication." *The National* (United Arab Emirates), 6 June 2012. https://www.thenational.ae/arts-culture/books/graphic-novel-about-egyptian-life-gets-english-publication-1.406735.

Holm, Bill. *Northwest Coastal Indian Art: An Analysis of Form.* U of Washington P, 1965.

Howes, Franny. "Imagining a Multiplicity of Visual Rhetorical Traditions: Comics Lessons from Rhetoric Histories." *ImageTexT: Interdisciplinary Comics Studies* 5.3 (2010). http://www.english.ufl.edu/imagetext/archives/v5_3/howes/

Hunt, Nancy Rose. "Tintin and the Interruptions of Congolese Comics." *Images and Empire: Visuality in Colonial and Postcolonial Africa*, edited by Paul S. Landau and Deborah Kaspin, U of California P, 2002.

Huntington, Samuel. "The Clash of Civilizations?" *Foreign Affairs* 72.3 (1993): 22–49.

———. *The Clash of Civilizations and the Remaking of World Order*. Simon and Schuster, 1996.

Iadonisi, Rick. "Bleeding History and Owning His [Father's] Story: *Maus* and Collaborative Autobiography." *CEA Critic* 57.1 (1994): 41–56.

Imam, Hatem. "Tongue-Tied—The Evasiveness of Language in Today's Arab Comics." *ArteEast: The Global Platform for Middle East Arts*, summer 2008. http://arteeast.org/quarterly/summer-2008-tongue-tied/.

Innis, Harold. *Empire and Communications*. Rowman & Littlefield, 2007.

Italie, Hillel. "Andre Schiffrin: A Gadfly within the Publishing World." *Arizona Daily Sun*, 19 May 2001. https://azdailysun.com/andre-schiffrin-a-gadfly-within-the-publishing-world/article_93c2673e-ac09-55b4-bb83-54b5af8eb3e1.html.

Jaggi, Maya. "The Godfather of Egyptian Graphic Novelists: Magdy El Shafee." *Newsweek*, 25 June 2012.

Jakaitis, Jake and James F. Wurtz. "Introduction: Reading Crossover." *Crossing Boundaries in Graphic Narrative*, edited by Jake Jakaitis and James F. Wurtz. McFarland & Company, 2012, pp. 1–22.

Jaquette, Elisabeth. "Formerly Banned Graphic Novel 'Metro' Now Available in Cairo." *Arabic Literature (In English)*, 28 Jan. 2013. http://arablit.wordpress.com/2013/01/28/formerly-banned-graphic-novel-metro-now-available-in-cairo/.

Jarno, Stéphane. "Mourir, partir, revenir, Le jeu des hirondelles." *Télérama* 3037, 29 Mar. 2008. https://www.telerama.fr/livres/mourir,-partir,-revenir,-le-jeu-des-hirondelles,26937.php.

jock123. "English editions re-lettered? #9." *Tintin Forums, Tintinologist.org*, 23 Feb. 2006. https://www.tintinologist.org/forums/index.php?action=vthread&forum=8&topic=1280.

Johnson, Hildegard Binder. *Order Upon the Land: The US Rectangular Land Survey and the Upper Mississippi Country*. Oxford UP, 1976.

Kannemeyer, Anton. *Pappa in Afrika*. Michael Stevenson, 2010.

Kaplan, Caren. "The Politics of Location as Transnational Feminist Critical Practice." *Scattered Hegemonies: Postmodernity and Transnational Feminist Practices*, edited by Inderpal Grewal and Caren Kaplan, U of Minnesota P, 1994, pp. 137–52.

Kashtan, Aaron. *Between Pen and Pixel: Comics, Materiality, and the Book of the Future*. The Ohio State UP, 2018.

Kerbaj, Mazen. *Beirut Won't Cry: Lebanon's July War: A Visual Diary*. Fantagraphics Underground, 2017.

———. *Beyrouth: juillet-août 2006*. L'Association, 2007.

———. "i am sorry to decline your proposition." *Kerblog*, 27 July 2006. http://mazenkerblog.blogspot.com/2006/07/i-am-sorry-to-decline-your-proposition.html.

———. "Suspended Time, Number 1: The Family Tree." *Samandal* 1 (2008): 15–34.

Khoury, Georges (Jad). "Rebellion Resuscitated: The Youth's Will Against History." *Catalogue: The New Generation: Arabic Comics Today,* Alifbata, 2018.

King, C. Richard. "Alter/Native Heroes: Native Americans, Comic Books, and the Struggle for Self-Definition." *Cultural Studies* ↔ *Critical Methodologies* 9.2 (Apr. 2009): 214–23.

Kirk, Mimi. "Graphic (Novel) Repression in Egypt." *Foreign Policy,* 9 Oct. 2013. https://foreignpolicy.com/2013/10/09/graphic-novel-repression-in-egypt/.

Koutsoukis, Jason. "Banned Egyptian Writer Fights for Comic Relief." *Sydney Morning Herald,* 28 Nov. 2009. https://www.smh.com.au/entertainment/books/banned-egyptian-writer-fights-for-comic-relief-20091128-gdttfz.html.

Krauss, Rosalind. "Grids." *October* 9 (1979): 50–64.

Labio, Catherine. "The Inherent Three-Dimensionality of Comics." *Yale French Studies,* 131/132 (2017): 84–100.

Langford, Rachel. "Photography, Belgian Colonialism, and Hergé's *Tintin au Congo.*" *Journal of Romance Studies* 8.1 (Spring 2008): 77–89.

Le Monde.fr and AFP. "Justice belge refuse d'interdire 'Tintin au Congo.'" *Le Monde,* 12 Oct. 2012. https://www.lemonde.fr/europe/article/2012/02/10/la-justice-belge-refuse-d-interdire-tintin-au-congo_1641919_3214.html.

"Lebanese Comics w/ Omar Khouri and Fadi 'the fdz' Baki." Podcast. May 2019. Ventures by UChicago Center for Middle Eastern Studies. *Soundcloud.* https://soundcloud.com/uchicago-cmes/lebanese-comics-omar-khouri-fdz.

"Lebanon Launches Creative Commons Chapter." *SMEX,* 10 Nov. 2010. https://smex.org/lebanon-launches-cc-chapter/.

Lecigne, Bruno. *Les Héritiers d'Hergé.* Magic Strip, 1983.

Lederman, Marsha. "Michael Nicoll Yahgulanaas Seeks Solutions to Environmental Mayhem in New Work *Carpe Fin: A Haida Manga.*" *Globe and Mail,* 26 Nov. 2019. https://www.theglobeandmail.com/arts/books/article-michael-nicoll-yahgulanaas-seeks-solutions-to-environmental-mayhem-in/.

Lee, Wendy. "Anjali Singh: Combing the Edges." *Guernica,* 15 July 2014. https://www.guernicamag.com/combing-the-edges/.

Lefèvre, Pascal. "The Conquest of Space: Evolution of Panel Arrangements and Page Layouts in Early Comics Published in Belgium (1880–1929)." *European Comic Art* 2.2 (2009): 227–52.

———. "The Importance of Being 'Published': A Comparative Study of Different Comics Formats." *Comics and Culture: Analytical and Theoretical Approaches to Comics,* edited by Anne Magnussen and Hans-Christian Christiansen, Museum Tusculanum, 2000, pp. 91–105.

Leservot, Typhaine. "Occidentalism: Rewriting the West in Marjane Satrapi's 'Persépolis.'" *French Forum,* 36.1 (Winter 2011): 115–30.

Levell, Nicola. "Beyond Tradition, More Than Contemporary: Four Northwest Coast Artists and Citizens Plus." *Urban Thunderbirds: Ravens in a Material World,* authored and co-curated by Rande Cooke, Francis Dick, lessLie, and Dylan Thomas, Art Gallery of Greater Victoria, 2013, pp. 38–49.

———. "*Coppers from the Hood*: Haida Manga Interventions and Performative Acts." *Museum Anthropology* 36.2 (Sept. 2013): 113–27.

——. *The Seriousness of Play: Michael Nicoll Yahgulanaas.* Black Dog, 2016.

——. "Site-Specificity and Dislocation: Michael Nicoll Yahgulanaas and His Haida Manga *Meddling.*" *Journal of Material Culture* 18.2 (2013): 93–116.

Lewis, David A., Anna Mudd, and Paul Beran, editors. *Muqtatafat: A Comics Anthology Featuring Artists from the Middle East Region.* Ninth Art Press, 2015.

Libération. "«Ten» Inspire Marjane Satrapi." 12 Feb. 2003. https://www.liberation.fr/cinema/2003/02/12/ten-inspire-marjane-satrapi_430673/.

Link, Alex. "Tulips and Roses in a Global Garden: Speaking Local Identities in *Persepolis* and *Tekkon Kinkreet.*" *Representing Multiculturalism in Comics and Graphic Novels,* edited by Carolene Ayaka and Ian Hague, Routledge, 2015, pp. 240–55.

Lofficier, Randy, and Jean-Marc Lofficier. *The Pocket Essential Tintin.* Pocket Essentials, 2007.

Loft, Steve. "Who, Me? Decolonization as Control." *Decolonize Me,* Ottawa Art Gallery; Oshawa: Robert McLaughlin Gallery, 2012.

Loik, Louise. "Using Art to Blur the Line between 'Us' and 'Them.'" *Canada's National Observer,* 15 Oct. 2017. https://www.nationalobserver.com/2017/10/15/news/using-art-blur-line-between-us-and-them.

Loos, Ted. "A Canadian Museum Promotes Indigenous Art. But Don't Call It 'Indian.'" *New York Times,* 13 July 2018. https://www.nytimes.com/2018/07/13/arts/design/art-gallery-of-ontario-indigenous-art.html.

Love, Paul. "*Beirut Won't Cry: Lebanon's July War: A Visual Diary* by Mazen Kerbaj." *World Literature Today,* Mar. 2018. https://www.worldliteraturetoday.org/2018/march/beirut-wont-cry-lebanons-july-war-visual-diary-mazen-kerbaj.

Lu, Alexander. "Samandal, a Beirut-based Anthology Targeted by the Lebanese Government, Needs Your Help." *The Beat: The Blog of Comics Culture,* 23 Dec. 2015. https://www.comicsbeat.com/samandal-a-beirut-based-anthology-targeted-by-the-lebanese-government-needs-your-help/.

Lyotard, Jean-François. *Le Différend.* Les Éditions de Minuit, 2013.

Maher, Robert. "Local Action & Geomatics: The Gowgaia Institute on Haida Gwaii." *GoGeomatics Canada,* 27 Nov. 2015. https://gogeomatics.ca/local-action-geomatics-the-gowgaia-institute-on-haida-gwaii/.

Malek, Amy. "Memoir as Iranian Exile Cultural Production: A Case Study of Marjane Satrapi's *Persepolis* Series." *Iranian Studies* 39.3 (Sep. 2006): 353–80.

Mangles, Alex. "Stitching Out a Life in Graphic Memoir." *Los Angeles Review of Books,* 8 June 2015. https://lareviewofbooks.org/article/stitching-out-a-life-in-graphic-memoir-baddawi/.

Marks, Clifford. "Wise Beyond Her Years: How Persepolis Introjects the Adult into the Child." *Picturing Childhood: Youth in Transnational Comics,* edited by Mark Heimermann and Brittany Tullis, U of Texas P, 2017, pp. 163–80.

Marion, Jean-Luc, and Michael Syrotinski. "Terrifying, Wondrous Tintin." *Yale French Studies* 131/132 (2017): 222–36.

Marion, Philippe. *Traces en Cases.* Académia, 1993.

Massey, Doreen. *World City.* Polity Press, 2007.

Mauzé, Marie. "Haida Manga: An Artist Embraces Tragedy, Beautifully." *The Conversation,* 12 July 2018. https://theconversation.com/haida-manga-an-artist-embraces-tragedy-beautifully-99543.

May, Elizabeth. *Paradise Won: The Struggle for South Moresby.* McLelland & Stewart, 1990.

"Mazen Kerbaj Inks New Graphic Novel *Beirut Won't Cry.*" *The Wire,* 17 Aug. 2017. https://www.thewire.co.uk/news/47782/mazen-kerbaj-inks-new-graphic-novel-beirut-won-t-cry.

Mazhari, Shadi. "Marjane Satrapi's *Persepolis* and the Overarching Problematic of Totalitarianism and Democracy in Postrevolutionary Iran." *Persian Language, Literature and Culture: New Leaves, Fresh Looks,* edited by Kamran Talattof, Routledge, 2015, pp. 287–301.

Mazur, Dan, and Alexander Danner. *Comics: A Global History, 1968 to the Present.* Thames and Hudson, 2014.

McCarthy, Tom. *Tintin and the Secret of Literature.* Granta, 2011.

McCloud, Scott. *Understanding Comics: The Invisible Art.* Kitchen Sink Press, 1993.

McKinney, Mark. *The Colonial Heritage of French Comics.* Liverpool UP, 2013.

——. *Postcolonialism and Migration in French Comics.* Leuven UP, 2020.

——. *Redrawing French Empire in Comics.* The Ohio State UP, 2013.

Medley, Mark. "Pacific Notion: The Convergence of B.C.'s Haida with Japan's Manga." *National Post,* 17 Oct. 2009. https://mny.ca/en/article/2/2009-10-17-pacific-notion.

Mehta, Binita and Pia Mukherji. "Introduction." *Postcolonial Comics: Texts, Events, Identities,* edited by Binita Mehta and Pia Mukherji Routledge, 2015, pp. 1–26.

Menu, Jean-Christophe. "Preface." *Comix 2000.* L'Association, 1999.

——. "Stay Off My Patch." *The French Comics Theory Reader,* edited by Ann Miller and Bart Beaty, Leuven UP, 2014, pp. 327–33.

Menu, Jean-Christophe and Sammy Harkham. "Interview." *Comics Journal* 300, Nov. 2009.

Merhej, Lena Irmgard. "Introduction: New Comics in the Arab Countries." *Muqtatafat: A Comics Anthology Featuring Artists from the Middle East Region,* edited by A. David Lewis, Anna Mudd, and Paul Beran, Ninth Art Press, 2015, pp. 7–10.

——. "Lena Merhej." Interview with Voitachewski. *du9: l'autre bande dessinée,* Dec. 2011. https://www.du9.org/entretien/lena-merhej/.

——. "Men with Guns: War Narratives in New Lebanese Comics." *Postcolonial Comics: Texts, Events, Identities,* edited by Binita Mehta and Pia Mukherji, Routledge, 2015, pp. 204–222.

——. "What Happened." In "Help Samandal Speak," by Marguerite Dabaie, *The Hooded Utilitarian,* Nov. 2015. https://www.hoodedutilitarian.com/2015/11/help-samandal-speak/.

Meyer, E. A. "Roman Tabulae, Egyptian Christians, and the Adoption of the Codex." *Chiron* 37 (Jan. 2007): 295–331.

"Michael Nicoll Yahgulanaas (Haida) on the Charles Edenshaw." Bard Graduate Center. *YouTube,* 3 May 2019. https://www.youtube.com/watch?v=CKiwF2e2OqQ.

"Michael Yahgulanaas—Red: A Haida Manga." University of British Columbia. *YouTube,* 4 Oct. 2010. https://www.youtube.com/watch?v=dBbLiEqUZ-g.

Mickwitz, Nina. *Documentary Comics: Graphic Truth-Telling in a Skeptical Age.* Palgrave Macmillan, 2016.

Mignolo, Walter D. "I Am Where I Think: Epistemology and the Colonial Difference." *Journal of Latin American Cultural Studies* 8.2 (1999): 235–45.

———. *Local Histories/Global Designs: Coloniality, Subaltern Knowledges, and Border Thinking.* Princeton UP, 2000.

Miller, Ann. "*Les héritiers d'Hergé*: The Figure of the Aventurier in a Postcolonial Context." *Shifting Frontiers of France and Francophonie,* edited by Yvette Rocheron and Christopher Rolfe, Peter Lang, 2004, pp. 307–24.

———. *Reading Bande Dessinée: Critical Approaches to French-Language Comic Strip.* Intellect, 2007.

———. "Marjane Satrapi's *Persepolis*: Eluding the Frames." *L'Esprit Créateur* 51.1 (Spring 2011): 38–52.

Miller, Nancy K. "Out of the Family: Generations of Women in Marjane Satrapi's *Persepolis*." *Life Writing* 4.1 (2007): 13–29.

Mirzoeff, Nick. *How to See the World: An Introduction to Images, from Self-Portraits to Selfies, Maps to Movies, and More.* Basic Books, 1996.

———. *The Right to Look: A Counterhistory of Visuality.* Duke UP, 2011.

Mitchell, W. J. T. *Iconology, Image, Text, Ideology.* U of Chicago P, 1986.

Miyoshi, Masao. "A Borderless World? From Colonialism to Transnationalism and the Decline of the Nation-State." *Critical Inquiry* 19.4 (1993): 726–51.

Morayef, Soraya. "Arab Comics: Fit for Academic Exploration." *Al-Fanar Media,* 18 Nov. 2014. https://www.al-fanarmedia.org/2014/11/arab-comics-fit-academic-exploration/.

Morelli, Nina. "Samandal: Lebanese Graphic Novelists Rise from the Ashes." *Middle East Monitor,* 18 Nov. 2020. https://www.middleeastmonitor.com/20201118-samandal-lebanese-graphic-novelists-rise-from-the-ashes/.

Moretti, Franco. "Conjectures on World Literature." *New Left Review* 1 (2000): 54–68.

———. "World-Systems Analysis, *Weltliteratur*." *Review* 28.3 (2005): 217–28.

Morley, Madeleine. "After a Controversial Lawsuit, Lebanese Comic Publisher *Samandal* Has Returned Stronger Than Ever." *Aiga: Eye on Design,* 8 June 2018. https://eyeondesign.aiga.org/after-a-controversial-lawsuit-lebanese-comic-publisher-samandal-has-returned-stronger-than-ever/.

Morgan, Harry. *Principes des littératures bandes dessinées.* Éditions de l'An 2, 2004.

Mouchart, Benoît. *À l'ombre de la ligne claire: Jacques van Melkebeke, le clandestin de la BD.* Vertige Graphic, 2002.

Mouchart, Benoît, and François Rivière. *La damnation d'Edgar P. Jacobs: biographie.* Seuil/Archimbaud, 2003.

Mountfort, Paul. "'Yellow skin, black hair . . . Careful, Tintin': Hergé and Orientalism." *Australasian Journal of Popular Culture* 1.1 (2012): 33–50.

Mufti, Aamir. *Forget English!: Orientalisms and World Literatures.* Harvard UP, 2016.

Muhanna, Elias. "The Fate of a Joke in Lebanon." *New Yorker,* 26 Sep. 2015. https://www.newyorker.com/news/news-desk/the-fate-of-a-joke-in-lebanon.

"The Mu'taz and Rada Sawwaf Arabic Comics Initiative: About Us." *American University of Beirut,* n.d. https://www.aub.edu.lb/saci/Pages/default.aspx.

Nadel, Dan. "The Comics Pantheon Likes." *Publishers Weekly*, 20 Oct. 2003. https://www.publishersweekly.com/pw/by-topic/industry-news/comics/article/22455-the-comics-pantheon-likes.html.

Naghibi, Nima, and Andrew O'Malley. "Estranging the Familiar: 'East' and 'West' in Satrapi's *Persepolis*." *ESC: English Studies in Canada* 31.2–3 (June/Sept. 2005): 223–47.

Nemser, Daniel. *Infrastructures of Race: Concentration and Biopolitics in Colonial Mexico*. U of Texas P, 2017.

Niranjana, Tejaswini. *Siting Translation: History, Post-Structuralism, and the Colonial Context*. U of California P, 1992.

Nodelman, Perry. "Michael Nicoll Yahgulanaas's *Red* and the Structures of Sequential Art." *Seriality and Texts for Young People: The Compulsion to Repeat*, edited by Mavis Reimer et al., Palgrave Macmillan, 2014, pp. 188–205.

Onciul, Bryony. *Museums, Heritage and Indigenous Voice: Decolonising Engagement*. Routledge, 2015.

Öncü, Ayşe, and Petra Weyland. *Space, Culture and Power: New Identities in Globalizing Cities*. Zed Books, 1997.

Ong, Aihwa. "Introduction: Worlding Cities or the Art of Being Global." *Worlding Cities: Asian Experiments and the Art of Being Global*, edited by Ananya Roy and Aihwa Ong, Wiley-Blackwell, 2011, pp. 1–25.

Ostby, Marie. "Marjane Satrapi's *Persepolis*, Persian Miniatures, and the Multifaceted Power of Comic Protest," *PMLA* 132.3 (May 2017): 558–79.

Ostrowitz, Judith. "Michael Nicoll Yahgulanaas: It Looks Like Manga." *Objects of Exchange: Social and Material Transformation on the Late Nineteenth-Century Northwest Coast*, edited by Aaron Glass, Yale UP, 2011, pp. 79–89.

Owens, Chris. "Tintin Crosses the Atlantic: The Golden Press Affair." *Tintinologist.org*, Jan. 2007. https://www.tintinologist.org/articles/goldenpress.html.

Pagano, Ernesto, translator. *Metro*. By Magdy El Shafee. il Sirente, 2010.

Palmer, Mark. "Theorizing Indigital Geographic Information Networks." *Cartographica* 47.2 (2012): 80–91.

Park, Liz, editor. *Old Growth: Michael Nicoll Yahgulanaas*. Red Leaf, 2011.

Pasamonik, Didier, editor. *L'Affaire Tintin au Congo*. Actuabd.com, 2016.

——. "Bienvenu Mbutu Mondondo: 'Cette bande dessinée est raciste.'" *ActuaBD*, 31 Aug. 2007. https://www.actuabd.com/Bienvenu-Mbutu-Mondondo-Cette-bande-dessinee-est-raciste.

——. "Frédéric Cambourakis (éditeur): 'La bd est en crise depuis une petite année.'" *ActuaBD*, 12 Sep. 2011. http://www.actuabd.com/Frederic-Cambourakis-editeur-La-BD.

——. "Hergé: une ligne claire." *De Georges Remi à Hergé*. Institut Saint Boniface, 1984.

Paul, Pamela. "Life under Siege: 'A Game for Swallows,' by Zeina Abirached." *New York Times*, 14 Nov. 2012. https://www.nytimes.com/2012/11/14/books/a-game-for-swallows-by-zeina-abirached.html.

Peeters, Benoît. "Four Conceptions of the Page: From *Case, planche, récit: lire la bande dessinée* (Paris: Casterman, 1998, pp. 41–60)." Translated by Jesse Cohn. *ImageText* 3.3 (Spring 2007). http://imagetext.english.ufl.edu/archives/v3_3/peeters/.

——. *Hergé, Son of Tintin*. Translated by Tina A. Kover, Johns Hopkins UP, 2012.

——. *Lire la bande dessinée.* Flammarion, 2003.

——. *Tintin and the World of Hergé: An Illustrated History.* Translated by Michael Farr, Bullfinch Press, 1992.

Pilcher, Tim and Brad Brooks. *The Essential Guide to World Comics.* Collins & Brown, 2005.

Place-Verghnes, Floriane. "Instruction, distraction, réflexion: lecture de *Persepolis.*" *French Cultural Studies* 21.4 (2010): 257–65.

Pleban, Dafna. "Investigating the Clear Line Style." *Comic Foundry,* 7 Nov. 2006. https://web.archive.org/web/20160305161452/http://comicfoundry.com/?p=1526 .

Pratt, Mary Louise. *Imperial Eyes: Travel Writing and Transculturation.* Routledge, 1992.

Pressman, Jessica. "The Aesthetic of Bookishness in Twenty-First-Century Literature." *Michigan Quarterly Review* 48.4 (Fall 2009): 465–82.

Qualey, M. Lynx. "'Metro' Available to Friends, Not Family." *Egypt Independent,* 31 July 2012. http://www.egyptindependent.com/news/metro-available-friends-not-family.

Rama, Angel. *The Lettered City.* Edited and translated by John Charles Chasteen, Duke UP, 1996.

Repetti, Massimo. "African Wave: Specificity and Cosmopolitanism in African Comics." *African Arts* 40.2 (Summer 2007): 16–35.

Reyns-Chikuma, C[h]ris. "Introduction: Translation and Comics." *TranscUlturAl* 8.2 (2016): 1–7.

Rich, Adrienne. "Notes Toward a Politics of Location." *Blood, Bread, and Poetry: Selected Prose 1979–1985,* Norton, 1994, pp. 210–31.

Rifas, Leonard. "Ideology: The Construction of Race and History in Tintin in the Congo." *Critical Approaches to Comics: Theories and Methods,* edited by Matthew J. Smith and Randy Duncan, Routledge, 2012, 221–34.

Rifkin, Mark. *Settler Common Sense: Queerness and Everyday Colonialism in the American Renaissance.* U of Minnesota P, 2014.

Rima, Barrack. "Éditorial." *Samandal: Généalogie.* 53 Dots, 2014.

Roberts, Colin H., and T. C. Skeat. *The Birth of the Codex.* Oxford UP, 1983.

Roberts-Farina, Jessica. "Thirty Years of 'Old Growth.'" *The Tyee,* 10 Mar. 2012. https://thetyee.ca/Books/2012/03/10/Old-Growth/.

Roche, Olivier, and Dominique Cerbelaud. *Tintin: bibliographie d'un mythe.* Les impressions nouvelles, 2014.

Rossetti, Chip. Telephone interview with author. 23 Oct. 2019.

——, translator. *Metro: A Story of Cairo.* By Magdy El Shafee. Metropolitan Books, 2012.

——. "Translating Cairo's Hidden Lines: The City as Visual Text in Magdy El Shafee's *Metro.*" *The City in Arabic Literature,* edited by Nizar F. Hermes and Gretchen Head, Edinburgh UP, 2018, pp. 306–325.

Rota, Valerio. "Aspects of Adaptation: The Translation of Comics Formats." *Comics in Translation,* edited by Federico Zanettin. St. Jerome, 79–91.

——. "The Translation's Visibility: David B.'s L'Ascension du Haut Mal in Italy." *Belphégor* 4.1 (Nov. 2004). https://dalspace.library.dal.ca/bitstream/handle/10222/47698/04_01_Rota_davidb_en_cont.pdf?sequence=1&isAllowed=y.

Round, Phillip H. *Removable Type: Histories of the Book in Indian Country, 1663–1880.* U of North Carolina P, 2010.

Royal, Derek Parker. "Foreword; or Reading within the Gutter." *Multicultural Comics: From Zap to Blue Beetle,* edited by Frederick Luis Aldama, U of Texas P, 2010, pp. ix–xi.

———. "Introduction: Coloring America: Multi-Ethnic Engagements with Graphic Narrative." *Melus* 32.3 (2007): 7–22.

Sacco, Joe. *Palestine.* Fantagraphics Books, 2001.

———. *Palestine: A Nation Occupied.* Fantagraphics Books, 1993.

———. *Palestine: In the Gaza Strip.* Fantagraphics Books, 1996.

Said, Edward. "The Clash of Ignorance." *The Nation,* 4 Oct. 2001. https://www.thenation.com/article/clash-ignorance/.

———. *Culture and Imperialism.* Knopf, 1993.

———. *Orientalism.* Penguin Classics, 1978.

———. *The World, the Text, and the Critic.* Harvard UP, 1983.

Saltman, Judith. "A Publisher's Legacy: The Children's Books of Douglas & McIntyre." *Jeunesse: Young People, Texts, Cultures* 5.1 (2013): 132–48.

Samandal. "#16 (2019)." *Samandal Comics.* https://samandalcomics.org/project/16/.

———. "Mission and Activities." *Samandal Comics.* http://new.samandalcomics.org/about/#mission.

———. *Samandal 13.* 53 Dots, 2012.

———. *Samandal 9.* Dar al Kotob, 2010.

———. *Samandal 7.* Dar al Kotob, 2009.

———. *Samandal 2.* xanadu*, 2008.

———. *Samandal 1.* xanadu*, 2007.

———. "Samandal, deuxième rencontre." Interview with Voitachewski. *du9: l'autre bande dessinée,* July 2017. https://www.du9.org/entretien/samandal-deuxieme-rencontre/.

Samandal Association for Comics. "Grants/Samandal: Publishing Comics Online in Three Languages under CC Licenses." *Creative Commons Wiki,* last edit 30 June 2010. https://wiki.creativecommons.org/wiki/Grants/Samandal_:_Publishing_Comics_Online_in_Three_Languages_Under_CC_Licenses.

"Samandal Comics Magazine: Issue One Press Release." *Xanadu Productions,* 28 Mar. 2008. http://www.xanaduproductions.net/salamander/pr-samandal1.html.

Sanders, Joe Sutliff, editor. *The Comics of Hergé: When the Lines Are Not So Clear.* UP of Mississippi, 2016.

Sante, Luc. "The Clear Line." *Give Our Regards to the Atom Smashers,* edited by Sean Howe, Pantheon, 2004, pp. 24–33.

———. "She Can't Go Home Again." *New York Times,* 22 Aug. 2004. https://www.nytimes.com/2004/08/22/books/she-can-t-go-home-again.html.

Sassen, Saskia. "The Global City: Introducing a Concept." *The Brown Journal of World Affairs* 11.2 (Winter/Spring 2005): 27–43.

———. *The Global City: New York, London, Tokyo.* Princeton UP, 1991.

Satrapi, Marjane. *Persepolis* tome 1. *L'Association,* 2000.

——. *Persepolis* tome 2. L'Association, 2001.

——. *Persepolis* tome 3. L'Association, 2002.

——. *Persepolis* tome 4. L'Association, 2003.

——. *Persepolis: The Story of a Childhood.* Translated by Mattias Ripa and Blake Ferris, Pantheon, 2003.

——. *Persepolis 2: The Story of a Return.* Translated by Anjali Singh, Pantheon, 2004.

——. "Persepolis: A State of Mind." *Literal: Latin American Voices / Voces Latinoamericanas* 13. http://literalmagazine.com/persepolis-a-state-of-mind/.

Schiffrin, André. *The Business of Books: How the International Conglomerates Took Over Publishing and Changed the Way We Read.* Verso, 2001.

——. *Words and Money.* Verso, 2010.

Schodt, Frederik L. "The View from North America: Manga as Late-Twentieth-Century Japonisme?" *Manga's Cultural Crossroads,* edited by Jaqueline Berndt and Bettina Kümmerling-Meibauer, Routledge, 2013, pp. 19–26.

Screech, Matthew. "Introduction." *European Comic Art* 3.2 (2010): v–xiii.

——. *Masters of the Ninth Art: Bandes Dessinées and Franco-Belgian Identity.* Liverpool UP, 2005.

Serrano, Nhora Lucía, editor. *Immigrants and Comics: Graphic Spaces of Remembrance, Transaction, and Mimesis.* Routledge, 2021.

Serres, Michel. *Hergé, Mon Ami: Études et portrait.* Moulinsart, 2000.

Shatz, Adam. "Drawing Blood: A French Graphic Novelist's Shocking Memoir of the Middle East." *New Yorker,* 12 Oct. 2015. https://www.newyorker.com/magazine/2015/10/19/drawing-blood.

Sheyahshe, Michael A. *Native Americans in Comic Books: A Critical Study.* McFarland, 2008.

Shih, Shu-Mei. "Global Literature and the Technologies of Recognition." *PMLA* 119.1 (2004): 16–30.

Siegert, Bernhard. *Cultural Techniques: Grids, Filters, Doors, and Other Articulations of the Real.* Fordham UP, 2015.

Singer, Mark. *Breaking the Frames: Populism and Prestige in Comics Studies.* U of Texas P, 2018.

Singh, Anjali. Telephone interview with the author. 14 July 2017.

——. Skype interview with the author. 25 Sep. 2019.

Sitterson, Aubrey. "The Adventures of Tintin and the Case of the Too-Convincing Pirates, or How Apple and Comic Fans Got Fooled." *IFC blog,* 3 Nov. 2011. https://web.archive.org/web/20130327024017/http://www.ifc.com/fix/2011/11/tintin-apple-app-store-piracy.

Skeat, T. C. "The Origin of the Christian Codex." *Zeitschrift für Papyrologie und Epigraphik* 102 (194): 263–68.

Smith, Sidonie. "Human Rights and Comics." *Graphic Subjects: Critical Essays on Autobiography and Graphic Novels,* edited by Michael Chaney. U of Wisconsin P, 2011, pp. 61–72.

Smolderen, Thierry. *The Origins of Comics: From William Hogarth to Winsor McCay.* Translated by Bart Beaty and Nick Nguyen, UP of Mississippi, 2014.

Sorrell, Traci. "Interview: Lee Francis IV on Native Publishing, Bookstores & Indigenous Comic Con." *Cynthia Leitich Smith*, 4 Apr. 2018. https://cynthialeitichsmith.com/2018/04/interview-lee-francis-iv-on-native/.

Sostar McLellan, Kristine. "Mythic Proportions" Interview. *Suburbia* 16/17 (2015): 38–39.

Soumois, Frédéric. *Dossier Tintin: Sources, Versions, Thèmes, Structures.* Jacques Antoine, 1987.

Spiegelman, Art. *Maus: A Survivor's Tale.* Pantheon, 1986.

———. *MetaMaus.* Pantheon, 2011.

Spiers, Miriam Brown. "Creating a Haida Manga: The Formline of Social Responsibility in *Red*." *Studies in American Indian Literatures* 26.3 (Fall 2014): 41–61.

Spivak, Gayatri. *Death of a Discipline.* Columbia UP, 2003.

———. "The Rani of Sirmur: An Essay in Reading the Archives." *History and Theory* 24.3 (1985): 247–72.

———. "Three Women's Texts and a Critique of Imperialism." *Critical Inquiry* 12.1 (1985): 243–61.

Spurgeon, Tom. "*CR* Holiday Interview #3: Bart Beaty on *Persepolis*." *Comics Reporter*, 22 Dec. 2009. http://www.comicsreporter.com/index.php/cr_holiday_interview_03/.

Stacey, Paul, and Sarah Hinchliff Pearson. *Made with Creative Commons.* Ctrl+Alt+Delete Books, 2017.

Stanbridge, Nicole. "Introduction." *Urban Thunderbirds: Ravens in a Material World,* authored and co-curated by Rande Cooke et al., Art Gallery of Greater Victoria, 2013, pp. 11–19.

Storace, Patricia. "A Double Life in Black and White." *New York Review of Books*, 7 Apr. 2005. https://www.nybooks.com/articles/2005/04/07/a-double-life-in-black-and-white/.

"Student Sues Publishers over 'Racist' Tintin au Congo Book." *YouTube,* uploaded by AP Archive, 30 July 2015. https://www.youtube.com/watch?v=Q-4UncCa5pI&ab_channel=APArchive.

Stulik, Dusan C., and Art Kaplan. *The Atlas of Analytical Signatures of Photographic Processes.* Getty Conservation Institute, 2013. https://www.getty.edu/conservation/publications_resources/pdf_publications/atlas.html.

Takeda, Louise. *Islands' Spirit Rising: Reclaiming the Forests of Haida Gwaii.* UBC Press, 2015.

Tensuan, Theresa M. "Comic Visions and Revisions in the Work of Lynda Barry and Marjane Satrapi." *Modern Fiction Studies* 52.4 (Winter 2006): 947–64.

Thompson, Harry. *Tintin: Hergé and His Creation.* Hodder & Stoughton, 1991.

Thompson, Kim, and Tom Spurgeon. "CR Holiday Interview #8—Kim Thompson." *The Comics Reporter*, 22 Mar. 2012. http://www.comicsreporter.com/index.php/resources/interviews/37008/.

Todd, Emmanuel. *Qui est Charlie?: Sociologie d'une crise religieuse.* Éd. du Seuil, 2015.

Tornare, Alain-Jacques. *Tint'Interdit: Pastiches et Parodies.* Éditions Cabedita, 2014.

Townsend-Gault, Charlotte. "Art Claims in the Age of *Delgamuukw*." *Native Art of the Northwest Coast: A History of Changing Ideas*, edited by Charlotte Townsend-Gault, Jennifer Kramer, and Ḳi-ḳe-in, UBC Press, 2013, pp. 864–935.

Tuck, Eve, and K. Wayne Yang. "Decolonization Is not a Metaphor." *Decolonization: Indigeneity, Education & Society* 1.1 (2012): 1–40.

Tully, Annie. "An Interview with Marjane Satrapi." *Bookslut,* Oct. 2004. https://web.archive.org/web/20161129163704/http://www.bookslut.com/features/2004_10_003261.php.

Valenti, Kristy. "Translation Roundtable—Part One of Three." *Comics Journal,* 2 June 2010. https://web.archive.org/web/20160329021608/http://classic.tcj.com/international/translation-roundtable-part-one-of-three/.

Valium, Henriette. *1000 Rectums, It's an Album Valium.* H. Valium, 1996.

Van Lier, Henri. "La bande dessinée, une cosmogenie dure." *Bande dessinée, récit et modernité,* edited by Thierry Groensteen, Futuropolis, 1988, pp. 5–24.

Venuti, Lawrence. *Contra Instrumentalism: A Translation Polemic.* U of Nebraska P, 2019.

——. *The Scandals of Translation: Towards an Ethics of Difference.* Routledge, 1998.

——. *The Translator's Invisibility: A History of Translation.* Routledge, 1995.

——. "World Literature and Translation Studies." *The Routledge Companion to World Literature,* edited by Theo D'haen, David Damrosch, and Djelal Kadir, Routledge, 2011, pp. 180–93.

Versaci, Rocco. *This Book Contains Graphic Language: Comics as Literature.* Continuum, 2007.

Voitachewski. "Zeina Abirached." *du9: l'autre bande dessinée,* Aug. 2011. http://www.du9.org/entretien/zeina-abirached/.

Vrielink, Jogchum. "Effort to Ban Tintin Comic Book Fails in Belgium." *Guardian,* 14 May 2012. https://www.theguardian.com/law/2012/may/14/effort-ban-tintin-congo-fails.

Walkowitz, Rebecca. *Born Translated: The Contemporary Novel in the Age of World Literature.* Columbia UP, 2015.

Wanzo, Rebecca. *The Content of Our Caricature: African American Comic Art and Political Belonging.* New York UP, 2020

White, Michelle. "Red: A Haida Manga." *Multiversity Comics,* 23 Aug. 2016. http://www.multiversitycomics.com/reviews/red-a-haida-manga/.

Whitlock, Gillian. "Autographics: The Seeing 'I' of the Comics." *Modern Fiction Studies* 52.4 (Winter 2006): 965–79.

——. *Soft Weapons: Autobiography in Transit.* U of Chicago P, 2007.

Winkler, Stefan, and Kerstin Pinther. "Metro: Magdy El Shafee." *Afropolis: City/Media/Art,* edited by Kerstin Pinther, Larissa Förster, and Christian Hanussek, Jacana, 2012, p. 102.

Wivel, Matthias. "A House Divided: The Crisis at L'Association (Part 1 of 2)." *Comics Journal,* 3 Nov. 2011. http://www.tcj.com/a-house-divided-the-crisis-at-l%E2%80%99association-part-1-of-2/.

Wolk, Douglas. "The GN Imprint That Isn't." *Publishers Weekly,* 7 Mar. 2005. https://www.publishersweekly.com/pw/print/20050307/25390-the-gn-imprint-that-isn-t.html.

——. "This Sweet Sickness." *New York Magazine,* 6 Jan. 2005. http://nymag.com/nymetro/arts/books/reviews/10851/.

World Intellectual Property Organization. "Berne Convention for the Protection of Literary and Artistic Works (as amended on September 28, 1979)." *WIPO IP Portal.* https://wipolex.wipo.int/en/text/283693.

Worth, Jennifer. "Unveiling: *Persepolis* as Embodied Performance." *Theatre Research International* 32.2 (2007): 143–60.

Yahgulanaas, Michael Nicoll. "Academic inquiry about your work." E-mail to the author. 11 July 2020.

——. *Carpe Fin: A Haida Manga.* Douglas & McIntyre, 2019.

——. *A Lousy Tale.* Rocking Raven Comix, 2000.

——. "Notes on Haida Manga." *Geist* 70 (Fall 2008): 54–56.

——. "Re: Academic Inquiry about your work." E-mail to the author. 21, 22, 24, 26 Aug. 2018.

——. *Red: A Haida Manga.* Douglas & McIntyre, 2009.

——. *A Tale of Two Shamans.* Theytus Books Ltd. and Haida Gwaii Museum at Qay'llnagaay, 2001.

——. *A Tale of Two Shamans.* Locarno Press, 2018.

——. *War of the Blink: A Haida Manga.* Locarno Press, 2017.

——. "The Wave" (2014). *Haida Manga.* http://haidamanga.com/series/1/the-wave.

Yamanaka, Chie. "Domesticating Manga? National Identity in Korean Comics Culture." *Reading Manga: Local and Global Perceptions of Japanese Comics,* edited by Jaqueline Berndt and Steffi Richter, Leipziger Universitätsverlag, 2006, pp. 193–204.

——. "*Manhwa* in Korea: (Re-)Nationalizing Comics Culture." *Manga's Cultural Crossroads,* edited by Jaqueline Berndt and Bettina Kümmerling-Meibauer, Routledge, 2013, pp. 85–99.

Yeoh, Brenda. "Global/Globalizing Cities." *Progress in Human Geography* 23.4 (1999): 607–16.

Yuste Frías, José. "Traduire l'image dans les albums d'Astérix: À la recherche du pouce perdu en Hispanie." *Le tour du monde d'Astérix,* edited by Bertrand Richet, Presses Sorbonne Nouvelle, 2011, pp. 255–71.

Zalzal, Zéna. "Le feu et les mantras de Zena el-Khalil." *L'Orient Le Jour,* 21 Aug. 2017. https://www.lorientlejour.com/article/1068291/le-feu-et-les-mantras-de-zena-el-khalil.html.

Zanettin, Federico. "Comics in Translation: An Overview." *Comics in Translation,* edited by Federico Zanettin, St. Jerome Publishing, 2008, pp. 1–32.

INDEX

Abdalla, Isakandar, 77, 78n6, 88, 88 fig.
2.2, 94 fig. 2.5, 102

Abedinifard, Mostafa, 108n4, 130n25

Abirached, Zeina, 106, 136–47, 138n29,
143n31; Atelier de Recherche ALBA,
studied *graphisme* at, 142; David B.,
Jacques Tardi, Emmanuel Guibert
cited as influences, 142; École nationale supérieure des Arts Décoratifs,
attended, 142

Abomo, Marie-Rose Maurin, 25, 48

*After the American Century: The Ends
of US Culture in the Middle East*
(Edwards), 80

Ahmed, Sara, 16, 147

Aho, Edgar: member of Mouhtaraf JAD,
198

Alaidy, Ahmed, 83

albums, 4, 5, 32, 36, 39, 44–46, 58, 59, 67,
79, 117–19, 124, 126–27; format, 32;
lack of success in US, 4, 5, 58. See
also *bandes dessinées*

Aldama, Frederick Luis, 3, 8

Alternative Comics: An Emerging Literature
(Hatfield), 115

Anderson, Benedict, 33

anti-Semitism, 48

anticolonialism, 11, 48, 61, 166

Apostolidès, Jean-Marie, 30, 31, 43,
47n23, 48

Appadurai, Arjun, 135

Appiah, Kwame Anthony, 26, 54–56, 58,
66; cultural syncretism as imperialism, 160

Appollo (Olivier Appollodorus), reviewing *Persepolis*, 110, 111

Apter, Emily, 6n8, 10, 18, 193n5, 206,
207, 212

Arab Spring, 79–81, 83. *See also* #Jan25

Arabic dialects, 208. *See also* fusha

*Ascension du haut mal, L'. See L'Ascension
du haut mal*

Association, l'. *See* L'Association

Assouline, Pierre, 31, 35n15, 41, 44n21

authenticity, 152–156. *See also* Haida manga

Azoulay, Ariella, 152n8

Baetens, Jan, 11, 31n10, 57, 60–62, 84n9, 117, 118, 174n33, 183; cites black-and-white as an artistic choice, 145, 146

Baki, Fadi. *See* the fdz

bandes dessinées, 4, 10, 11, 13, 14, 23, 33, 34, 37–39, 113, 115, 117, 119. *See also* albums; comics

Barthes, Roland, 31

Bassnett, Susan, 15, 16

Beauchard, David. *See* David B.

Bécassine, 33, 37

Beaty, Bart, 3, 32n13, 46, 109, 110, 113, 115, 116, 119, 121, 124, 144, 145, 215n18

Beirut, 137, 141, 143n31, 191–95, 198–200, 212

Beirut Won't Cry, 213–15; reformatting of *Kerblog*, 214. *See also Beyrouth: juillet-août 2006*

Benoît-Jeannin, Maxime, 48

Berenboom, Alain, 52

Berndt, Jaqueline, 166n20

Berne Convention, 195, 196

Between Pen and Pixel: Comics, Materiality, and the Book of the Future (Kashtan), 101

Beydoun, Wissam: member of Mouhtaraf JAD, 199

Beyrouth [Catharsis] (Abirached), 142, 143

Beyrouth: juillet-août 2006 (Kerbaj), 213–15; format, 213; reformatting of *Kerblog*, 214; subtitles, 213. *See also Beirut Won't Cry*

Bhabha, Homi, 63, 64, 106, 107, 154

Bitterkomix (Kannemeyer), 57

Black Hole (Burns), 58

bonelliano. See format

border thinking, 151, 174. *See also* Mignolo, Walter

braiding, 66, 94, 98

Breaking the Frames (Singer), 113

Bredehoft, Thomas A., 87n10

Brienza, Casey, 162–65

Bringing up Father (McManus), influence on *Tintin*, 6

Broadhead, John, 153–54, 153n11

Burke, Laurie, 51

Burns, Charles, 19, 25–27, 57, 58–61, 62n33, 62n34, 63, 64, 66, 120. *See also* Nitnit trilogy

Cairo, 70, 71, 73–7, 80–82, 84, 90, 96, 99, 192

Callison, Camille, 158

Cambourakis, Frédéric, 142, 143

Canada: Canadian identity, 160

captions, 36–39, 67, 81

Carpe Fin (Yahgulahnaas), 151, 168 fig. 4.1, 169; experienced as a mural, 183, 187; habitation of the water, 166; original art commissioned by and displayed at Seattle Art Museum, 181

Carrión, Mónica, 78

Casterman, 36, 46, 46n22, 51, 52, 68; ordered standardized font for *Tintin*, 44

Celotti, Nadine, 86

Chaland, Yves, 56

Charlie Hebdo, 205

Chute, Hillary, 2n1, 3, 11, 12, 104, 105n2, 130, 145, 187

Ciboulette collection, 118, 119, 124

clash of civilizations, 105, 105n1

codexité, 183

Coeurs Vaillants, 35, 39n20, 45

Cohn, Neil, 6n9, 172, 172n28

colonialism, 13, 23, 24, 28, 29, 31, 34, 45, 47–51, 53, 54, 149, 158, 171; use of gridding, 172. *See also* decolonization; postcolonialism; anticolonialism

comics *auteur*, 105, 113, 116

comic strips, 5, 6. *See also* comics

comics: distribution, 5; form, 4, 5, 12, 40, 194; global, 4, 136, 196, 203, 212; racism in, 25, 29; semiotics of, 9, 11, 76; term used as imperializing nomenclature, 165; untranslatability of, 189, 204; See also *bandes dessinées*; comic strips; comics scholarship; graphic novels

comics scholarship, 11, 13, 14, 24, 84, 91, 126, 148, 166n20, 172, 174, 182, 214, 218

Comic Shop, 77, 78n6

Comix 2000, 210, 211, 217; format, 211

Conley, Tom, 93

Cornélius, 64

Creative Commons, 195, 196–98, 196n6

Crucifix, Benoît, 60

cultural appropriation, 108, 153

cultural identity, 109, 158

Damluji, Nadim, 50, 51, 142n30

Danner, Alexander, 14, 118

David B. (David Beauchard), 105, 106, 110–14; Satrapi, influence on, 113, 118

Davies, Dominic, 8, 76, 89, 191, 192, 194, 207, 214; highlights importance of collaborative networks, 191

Davies, Humphrey: translation of *Metro* into English, 77, 78n6, 80, 83, 88, 95, 100, 102

Davis, Rocío G., 107

de Moor, Bob, 56

Debord, Guy, 17, 17n4, 55n31

decolonial mapping, 17, 18, 150, 168, 169, 188

Decolonize Me: Ottawa art gallery exhibition (2012), 152

decolonization, 7n10, 53, 148, 149, 152; Haida manga as a tool for, 20, 175

Delisle, Philippe, 14, 29, 29n6, 30n8, 33–35, 47, 51n29

Denson, Shane, 7, 14

Der-Ghougassian, Choghig: member of Mouhtaraf JAD, 199

Dernier Cri, Le, 64

di Ricco, Massimo, 142n30, 189n1, 198, 207

digitization, 101

Dirks, Rudolph, 37

détournement, 17, 55–57

Dony, Christophe, 29n6, 57

Douglas, Allen, 71n3, 142n30, 208n15

Douglas and McIntyre, 170

Eberstadt, Fernanda, 111, 130

Edenshaw, Charles, 149, 153

Éditions Cambourakis, 142

Edition Moderne, 77, 79, 101, 102

Edwards, Brian T. 70, 73, 75, 76, 80–84, 102

Egmont, 53

Ego comme X, 118

Egypt, 5–8, 70, 75–82, 201. *See also* Cairo

El Khalil, Zena, found of xanadu*, 197, 198

El Shafee, Magdy, 3, 5, 18, 19, 69–71, 73, 76, 77n4, 78, 79, 80–83, 87, 90 figure 2.3, 96, 97 figure 2.6, 102, 136; arrested, 76; Libyan by birth, 78. *See also Metro*

Emmerich, Karen, 87

Enright, David, 51, 53

Epileptic. See *L'Ascension du haut mal*

Exem, 56

Fantagraphics, 71, 120, 121, 135, 213–15

Farr, Michael, 61

Fili, Louise, 117

flippy pages, 17, 18, 20, 215–18

Fondation Moulinsart. *See* Moulinsart

format, 4, 5, 17, 32–34, 44, 46, 58, 59, 64, 73, 74, 84, 101–03, 119, 126, 143, 144, 146, 164, 165, 182, 189–91, 212, 213, 217, 217n19; album, 4, 32; blog, 213, 215; *bonelliano*, 101; codex, 175n35; graphic novel, 118; *lianhuanhua*, 64

formlines, 20, 154, 154n12, 155, 175, 177–80, 177n36, 185

Foucault, Michel, 114, 116, 144, 173, 175n34

framelines, 155, 175–81

France, 19, 37n16, 105–07, 110, 113–16, 118, 120, 121, 124, 126, 129, 130, 133–37, 141, 142, 144, 147, 205

Francis, Lee, IV, 158, 164

Frank, Dan, 122, 123, 123n19

Fresnault-Deruelle, Pierre, 11, 11n13, 12, 23n3, 43, 73, 84, 182, 183

Frey, Hugo, 29n6, 31n10, 48, 57, 60–62, 117, 118, 183

Fundación al Fanar, 77, 78

fusha, 208, 209

Gabilliet, Jean-Paul, 14, 58, 59, 62n34

Galal, Mona, 78

Game for Swallows, A. See Mourir, partir, revenir: Le jeu des hirondelles

Gauvin, Edward, translator of *Mourir, partir, revenir: Le jeu des hirondelles* into English, 144, 146

Gauthier, Guy, 171

Gerner, Jochen, 56, 66n36

Ghaibeh, Lina: member of Mouhtaraf JAD, 199; American University of Beirut professor of comics and animation, 199; Mu'taz and Rada Sawwaf Arabic Comics Initiative, director of, 199

Ghaibeh, May: member of Mouhtaraf JAD, 199

global cities, 8, 191, 192, 192n4; comics relation to, 193, 194

Goddin, Philippe, 23, 31, 34, 63

Goeman, Mishuana, 150, 150n6, 151, 161, 166, 170, 173, 188

Goethe, Johann Wolfgang von, 5, 5n7, 194

Golden Press, 44

Goodman, Nelson, 22

Ghosh, Bishnupriya, 22

Graphic Novel: An Introduciton, The (Baetens and Frey), 117

graphic novels, 2, 4, 19, 59, 74, 80, 82, 102, 109, 110, 113, 117, 118, 120, 124, 126n22, 135, 140, 141, 143–46, 164, 165, 166, 166n20. *See also* comics

Graphic Universe: *Mourir, partir, revenir: Le jeu des hirondelles* as *A Game for Swallows*, US publisher of, 144

Gramsci, Antonio, 172

Gray, Brenna Clark, 157, 158, 163, 167, 175, 187

Grewal, Inderpal, 16, 17

gridding, 171, 173n30, 174, 181; based on Cartesian logic, 172; colonialist tool, 172–74; Western concept, 172, 173

Groensteen, Thierry, 3, 10, 11n12, 12, 73, 84, 85, 94–96, 98, 171, 172; gridding as a priori for comics creating, 171

Groth, Gary, 120, 121

Haida Gwaii, 149, 156, 159, 161, 166

Haida manga, 20, 149–52, 154–61, 163–70, 174, 178, 178 fig. 4.3, 182 fig. 4.4, 185, 187, 188; as Canadian art, 160; as decolonial mapping, 167–69; challenges how books are recognized and consumed, 187; cultural "hybridity," 153, 154, 159, 166n20; defines a difference between Haida and Western ways of seeing, 175; gridding, a new idiom replacing, 174; Japan directly connected to Haida Gwaii, 166; on cover of *The Last Voyage of the Black Ship*, 154; what defines it, 160, 164. *See also* Indigenous art; Indigenous comics; Yahgulanaas, Michael Nicholl

Hanafy, Iman, 75, 76, 80, 84

Hara-Kiri, censored and outlawed, 205

Harrison, Richard, 159–61

Hatfield, Charles, 2n1, 3n2, 11, 34, 42, 73, 74, 84, 85, 91–94, 100, 115, 183, 215; "radical synchronism," 213

Hayek, Ghenwa, 213

Henry Holt and Company: *Metro*, first book-length English language edition of, 77, 78n6

Hergé (Georges Remi), 4, 23, 31, 33, 35, 37, 38–42, 38n17, 44–46, 48–52, 55, 56, 61, 63, 65; Orientalism, 50; research, 61; use of word balloons, 37, 38

Hive, The (Burns), 58, 59, 64

Hodapp, James, 75, 76, 78, 82–84, 92, 95

Holm, Bill, 153n10, 178–81; dismissal of Indigenous artists in favor of colonial knowledge system, 179; Eurocentric approach to space, 180

Hunt, Nancy Rose, 49–51
Hyslop, Neil, 44

Imam, Hatem, 189, 203, 206, 208; co-founder of *Samandal*, 190; fine arts education, 199
Incubation (Burns), 64
Indigenous art, 152, 153, 158, 180; in museums, 183–84. *See also* Haida manga
Indigenous comics, 158, 159, 164
Innis, Harold, 36
Iran, 104, 105, 108–10, 127, 131–34, 136n28, 140, 141, 146, 147
Islamophobia in the US, 133

#Jan25, 81, 102
Jijé, 56
Johnny 23 (Burns), 64–66, 65 fig. 1.3; ciphers in, 65, 66

Kannemeyer, Anton, 57
Kaplan, Caren, 19, 137
Kashtan, Aaron, 101
Kerbaj, Mazen, 211–15, 211 fig. 5.1
Keyrouz, Karen, 202
Khouri, Omar, 190, 193, 199, 200, 203, 204, 206, 217n19
Kerblog, 212–14
Khoury, George, 198–200, 208; founder of Mouhtaraf JAD, 198; "Jad" used as pseudonym, 198n7; Lebanese Civil War as major influence on, 200
Kidd, Chip, 122
King, C. Richard, 159
Kroll, Pierre, 54
Kümmerling-Meibauer, Bettina, 166n20

Labio, Catherine, 33
Lapin, 118
L'Ascension du haut mal (David B.), 106, 110, 112, 113, 115, 118, 127, 135, 137
L'Association, 111, 113, 113n9, 115, 118–21, 124, 126, 127, 132; *Beyrouth:*

juillet-août 2006, publisher of, 213; *Comix 2000*, publisher of, 210; *Persepolis*, first success of, 118n13, 123
Last Look (Burns), 59, 64
Last Voyage of the Black Ship, The (Yahgulanaas), 151, 155
layout, 73–76, 84, 85, 96, 98, 100, 180, 191, 212; Peeters classifications of, 172, 176–78. *See also* panels; sequence
Lebanese Civil War, 137, 143n31, 199, 200
Lebanon, 77, 137, 140–42, 146, 147, 193, 196, 200–207, 209
Lecigne, Bruno, 24, 42, 56. See also *ligne claire*
Lefèvre, Pascal, 4n5, 32n13, 126, 172n25, 172n27
Leservot, Typhaine, 109, 130, 133
lettering, 44
Levell, Nicola, 151, 155, 169, 174, 183n39, 184
lianhuanhua format, 64
ligne claire, 6, 23–25, 27, 28, 30, 40–43, 56, 61, 62, 62n34, 67; masks complication and confusion, 43; practicality for reproduction, 40; semiotic effects, 42; trains readers to see the world as a legible text, 24; visual imperialism, 24, 42
Link, Alex, 109
Little, Brown & Co., 4
Locarno Press, 170
Loik, Louise, 150n7
Lousy Tale, A (Yahgulanaas), 167, 168

Majid, 200
Malamih, 76
Malek, Amy, 108, 112
Malti-Douglas, Fedwa, 71n3, 142n30, 208n15
manga, 13, 14, 101, 156, 158–67, 163n19, 166n20, 175. *See also* Haida manga
maps, 89, 91–99, 156, 161. See also *Metro*
Martin, Jacques, 56
masks, 27, 66
Massey, Doreen, 192n3, 194
Masson, Pierre, 11

Maus (Spiegelman), 5, 111–20, 116n12, 122–24; comparison to *Persepolis*, 119, 136–45; first collection publication, 122; published in two volumes, 126n21

Mauzé, Marie, 150n7, 175

Mazur, Dan, 8, 14, 118

McCloud, Scott, 11, 13, 19, 27–31, 28 fig. 1.1, 29, 35, 42, 49, 57, 60, 63, 66, 67, 84, 163, 164, 174, 175; describes *ligne claire*, 27, 28; gutters, privileging of, 174; viewer identification with Tintin, 31, 42, 63; Tintin as a stereotype, 26, 30; used by Spiers in close reading of *Red*, 163, 164; uncritical reading of *Tintin*, 57; Western, white, anticonquest reading of *Tintin*, 43

McKinney, Mark, 14, 29n6, 30, 35, 42, 217n20

McManus, George, 6, 37

Mehta, Binita, 14

Mehta, Sonny, 123, 123n18

Menu, Jean-Christophe, 118, 119, 127, 135, 144

Merhej, Lena, 190, 201, 203, 204, 207, 208; co-founder of *Samandal*, 190

Metro (El Shafee), 3, 6–8, 17–20, 69–71, 74–76, 78–81, 83, 86; banned in Egypt, 5, 4, 69, 75, 76; "first" Egyptian graphic novel, 75, 78, 102; layout, 70, 85, 99; maps in, 88, 89, 90 fig. 2.3, 91, 92 fig. 2.4, 94 fig. 2.5, 94–99, 97 fig. 2.6; newspapers in, 93; qualification as an African work, 75; sound effects in, 87, 89; translated into Spanish, 77, 88, 101; untranslatability outside of Egypt, 75, 79, 81–86

Metro, 3, 5–8, 17–9, 69–71, 74, 76–86, 88 fig. 2.2, 89, 90, 90 fig. 2.3, 92 fig. 2.4, 93–96, 94 fig. 2.5, 97 fig. 2.6, 99 fig. 2.7, 100–103

Meyer, Christina, 14, 15, 186n40

Mignolo, Walter, 7, 7n10, 16, 31, 151, 159, 161, 166, 175; decolonization through "border thinking," 151

Miller, Ann, 3, 14, 29n6, 42, 47n23, 146

Mirzoeff, Nick, 26, 29, 47, 52, 67, 193

Mitchell, W. J. T., 87

Mondodo, Bienvenu Mbutu, 19, 25–27, 25n5, 43, 51–54, 57, 68

Monsieur Jabot (Töpffer), 37

Morgan, Harry, 11, 183

Mossieu Réac, 37

Moulinsart, 46, 46n22, 51–53, 65, 68, 196

Mourir, partir, revenir: Le jeu des hirondelles (Abirached), 106, 136; compared to *Persepolis*, 137–46; format, 143; format changes between French and US editions, 144

Mountfort, Paul, 48, 49

Mouhtaraf JAD, 198–200

Mu'taz and Rada Sawwaf Arabic Comics Initiative, 199

Mubarak, Hosni, 5, 79, 80, 83

Mufti, Aamir, 3, 8, 17, 105n3

Mukherji, Pia, 14

Muqtatafat, 205; profits donated to *Samandal*, 205

Naba'a, Tarek: co-founder of *Samandal*, 190

Naghibi, Nima, 108, 128

narration, 37, 38, 94

Nasser, Deema, 75, 76, 78, 82–84, 92, 95, 96

Native Realities, 158

Niranjana, Tejaswini, 16, 207, 210

Nitnit in Otherland (Valium), 56

Nitnit trilogy (Burns), 25, 57–64, 66; swiping in, 60

No Tankers, T'anks (Yahgulanaas), 149, 153

Old Growth (Yahgulanaas), 153

O'Malley, Andrew, 108, 128

Ong, Aihwa, 194, 195, 218

Orientalism, 19, 50, 51, 105, 106, 109, 114, 140, 147, 198; Indigenous, 109

Ostby, Marie, 105n2, 108, 112n7, 127

Ostrowitz, Judith, 163; Yahgulanaas's illumination of empty space, 171n23

Outcault, Richard F., 37

Pagano, Ernesto, 77, 87, 89, 91, 94 fig. 2.5, 95, 102

Palestine (Sacco): Cairo, depiction of, 71, 72 fig. 2.1, 73, 75; format, 74; influence on Metro, 70, 73

Palestine: A Nation Occupied (Sacco), 71

Palestine: In the Gaza Strip (Sacco), 71

panels, 11, 20, 38, 39, 62, 71, 73, 85–87, 94, 95, 96–103, 171, 172, 174, 175, 177, 184, 211. See also layout; sequence

Pantheon, 2, 5, 59, 113, 117, 120–24, 120n15, 126, 127, 132, 133, 135

Papagaio, O, 35

Pappa in Afrika (Kannemeyer), 57

Pasamonik, Didier, 25n5, 40, 52

Peddle to the Meddle (Yahgulanaas), museum exhibit, 184

Peeters, Benoît, 12, 37, 37n16, 38, 39n19, 40, 41, 46, 73, 84; page layout classification, 172, 176

Persepolis (Satrapi), 5, 13, 18, 19, 104–13, 116–32, 118n13, 125 fig. 3.1, 134, 135, 136n27, 136n28, 138, 140–42, 144, 145, 147; as a cultural object, 105; avant-garde comics, credited with the rise of, 115; compared to L'Ascension du haut mal, 111, 112, 127; compared to Maus, 111, 112, 123, 124; compared to Mourir, partir, revenir: Le jeu des hirondelles, 137–46; comparison to Persian miniature, 114; association with Shahnameh, 105, 127; English translation, 120–24; French edition covers, 127–30, 128 fig. 3.2; format, 124–30, 125 fig. 3.1; introductions to, 132, 133; narrative alterations between French and US edition, 130–32; narrative progression of the French covers, 127; reviews of, 110–113; title of, 130; translation of, 133; US edition, 104, 105, 110, 124; US edition aligns with Maus, 132; US edition cover, 129, 129 fig. 3.3, 130; US edition volumes given subtitles, 130, 131

Persian miniatures, 105, 109, 114

Petit Vingtième, Le, 33, 35, 38, 45

photogravure printing, 40–42

Pieds Nickelés, 37

Pigeon Press, 64

postcolonialism, 9, 14–16, 25, 26, 54, 57, 63. See also colonialism; anticolonialism

postmodernism, 25, 26, 55–58

Pratt, Mary Louise, 24

Pressman, Jessica, 4, 5, 183

quadrillage. See gridding

Qualey, M. Lynx, 78

RAW, 113, 117

reading for difference, 1, 6, 7, 12, 21, 25, 28, 29, 84, 129, 158, 190, 206; definition, 28, 29; Haida manga, 158; Hergé's works, 49; in production, 211; opposed to consumption practice, 28; role of transnational collectives in Samandal, 206

Red: A Haida Manga (Yahgulanaas), 16, 20, 151, 155, 159, 163–65, 169, 170, 176, 177, 178 fig. 4.3, 181, 182 fig. 4.4, 183, 185–87; duality as book and mural, 183, 185–87; experienced as a mural, 164, 181, 185–87; framelines interact with diegesis, 181, 182 fig. 4.4; full mural, 178–79 fig. 4.3; Haida manga, 159, 163; layout defies Peeters' classifications, 175–77; layout, reviews of, 177; story summary, 169–70

revisionism, 26, 29, 42–46

Rich, Adrienne, 15

Rifkin, Mark, 172

Rifkind, Candida, 8, 158

right to look, 52, 53

Rima, Barrack, Samandal editor, 202, 209

Rojo, Pedro, 78

Rossetti, Chip, 76, 78n6, 86, 87, 90, 91, 96, 96n12, 99, 100, 100n13; translation of Metro into English, 77, 80, 82, 83, 85, 86, 87, 89–91, 92 fig. 2.4, 96, 99 fig. 2.7, 100, 102

Rota, Valerio, 4n5, 117

Royal, Derek Parker, 9, 49

Sacco, Joe, 70, 71, 72 fig. 2.1, 73–75, 81, 120, 213

Said, Edward, 6n8, 24, 51, 105n1, 105n3

Samandal, 10, 18, 20, 189–212, 214–19; Beirut-based, 191; challenged by Lebanese Catholic Media Center, 190, 203; changes in format, 190; Creative Commons grant, 197; Creative Commons Licensing of, 195–98; fined by Lebanese government, 190, 203, 205; fines paid through crowd-funding campaign, 205; "flippy pages," 191, 215, 216 fig. 5.2; formats, 191, 217, 218; international contributors, 201; Lebanese Civil War impact on Lebanese comics scene, 200; partnered with xanadu*, 197, 198; "The People vs. Samandal Comics," 203–05; promoting dialogue across borders, 201; styles, heterogeneity of, 218; *Topie* volume published in three distinct versions, 209; translation approaches, 209, 212; trilingual format (Arabic, French, English), 189, 206–09, 215, 217; worlding, 190, 194

Samir, 50, 200

Sante, Luc, 24; *Persepolis* to *Maus*, comparison of, 111, 130

Sassen, Saskia, 192, 194

Satrapi, Marjane, 13, 19, 104–16, 118; comparison to Abirached, 136, 137; comparison to David B., 110–12, 114–16, 124; comparison to Spiegelman, 110, 115, 116, 120, 124

Schiffrin, André, 117, 121, 122, 122n6

Schodt, Frederik L., 161–63, 167

Shwandl, R., 91n11

Screech, Matthew, 33

sequence, 91, 93, 94, 96–99, 174, 175, 215. *See also* panels; layout

Shahnameh, 105, 127

Shih, Shu-Mei, 32

Silverman, Kaja, 50

Singer, Marc, 112n8, 113–14, 117, 135

Singh, Anjali, 121, 122–24, 126, 127, 129–30, 134

Sirente, il, 77

Smolderen, Thierry, 36, 37, 84n9

Soumois, Frédéric, 49n24

sound effects, 87–9, 88 fig. 2.2, 102, 146, 181

Spiegelman, Art, 5, 105, 106, 110–13, 115–18, 120, 122, 124, 126n21; literary comics, contribution to development of, 115

Spiers, Miriam Brown, 163–65, 177, 177n36, 181

Spivak, Gayatri, 3n3, 6n8, 18, 46, 105n3, 114, 136, 141

Stanbridge, Nicole, 152, 153

Stein, Daniel, 14, 15

stereotypes, 9, 10, 17, 25–27, 30, 47, 49, 50, 53, 54, 60, 68, 158

Storace, Patricia, 107

Sugar Skull (Burns), 58, 59, 63 fig. 1.2

"Suspended Time Vol 1: The Family Tree" (Kerbaj), 211, 211 fig. 5.1, 212

Swarte, Joost, 6, 56

swiping, 58, 60, 61

System of Comics, The (Groensteen), 73, 94, 171

Tahrir Square demonstrations, 82

Tale of Two Shamans, A (Yahgulanaas), 151, 155, 174; Haida manga advent, 155

tensions (Hatfield), 17, 34, 73, 74, 84, 85, 89, 91–93, 96, 100, 215, 216

the fdz (Fadi Baki), 189, 190, 193, 197, 199, 200, 203, 206, 209, 210; *Samandal* dedicated to proliferation of comic art production in Arab region, 197

38, rue Youssef Semaani (Abirached), 143, 143n41

Thompson, Kim, 120, 121, 135

Tintin (Hergé), 4–6, 10, 17, 18, 23–36, 23n2, 38–68; albums, 4, 5, 10, 32–36, 39, 42, 44–46; anti-Semitism in, 48; Africans, caricatures of, 48, 49, 52–54; *The Black Island*, 59; *The Blue Lotus*, 48; capacity for worlding, 41; colonial gaze, 50; copyrights, 46; dehumanization of the Other, 49; *Explorers on the Moon*, 59; in America, 36, 46, 56; in the Congo, 35, 36, 45–54,

57, 204; *in the Land of Black Gold,* 45; *in the Land of the Soviets,* 30n8, 33, 35, 36, 39, 40, 41, 46; *in Tibet,* 36; legal challenges to, 26, 51, 52, 68; lettering, 44; localization of, 35; neofacism, 48; pastiches and parodies, 55, 56; pirated editions, 46, 50, 55, 64, 66; *Prisoners of the Sun,* 48; racism, 49, 67; *Red Rackham's Treasure,* 30; revisions, 45, 46, 53, 65, 67; *The Secret of the Unicorn,* 30, 60; *The Seven Crystal Balls,* 48; *The Shooting Star,* 48, 59; standardized font, 44; use of captions, 37–39; word balloons, 38, 39

Tintin au Pays des Nazis (Tintin in the Land of the Nazis), 55

Tintinologists, 23, 23n3

TNT en Amérique, 56

Töppfer, Rodolphe, 37, 41

Tornare, Alain-Jacques, 56

Totor (Hergé), 37, 38

Townsend-Gault, Charlotte, 152

translation, 1, 3, 3n3, 4n4, 5, 10, 13, 15–20, 23, 38n17, 44, 50, 51, 66, 68–71, 70n2, 74–89, 88 fig. 2.2; 89, 91–93, 95, 96, 100–07, 117, 121, 122, 124, 133–36, 140–46, 155, 191, 2000, 204, 206, 207, 209–15, 217; cultural, 4n6, 104–07, 109, 120, 123, 132, 133, 165; four loci of, 86; *Samandal,* varying titles for issues of, 210. See also *Metro*; untranslatability

tressage. See braiding

Trivedi, Harish, 15, 16

Trondheim, Lewis, 118

Tuck, Eve, 149, 150

Understanding Comics: The Invisible Art (McCloud), 27, 28, 28 fig. 1.1

Unpopular Culture: Transforming the European Comic Book in the 1990s (Beaty), 115

untranslatability, 4, 6, 7, 9, 10, 18, 75, 79, 155, 189, 204, 206, 207, 212

Valfret, 203, 203n11, 204, 206

Valium, Henriette, 56

Venuti, Lawrence, 3n3, 69, 70, 75, 83, 102, 133, 134; translation does not provide unmediated access to the original text, 133, 134

Vingtième Siècle, Le, 32–36, 38, 38n17, 40, 45. See also *Le Petit Vingtième*

Vortex (Burns), 64

Walkowitz, Rebecca, 3, 82

Wanzo, Rebecca, 3, 9, 17, 24, 26, 29, 49, 53, 67

Wallez, Norbert, 32n11, 35

War of the Blink (Yahgulanaas), 151, 184; experienced as mural, 183, 187; framelines interact with the diegesis, 181; original art displayed at Vancouver Art Gallery, 181

Winkler, Stefan, 77, 78n6, 88, 94 fig. 2.5, 102

Wolk, Douglas, 120 n15; *Epileptic,* reviewed in comparison to *Persepolis* and *Maus,* 112

Wolman, Gil, 17, 17n14

word balloons, 37, 38, 86, 101, 121, 184

world literature, 2, 3, 4, 5, 6, 8, 17, 19, 32, 80, 82, 136, 212, 217; untranslatability, 5n7, 206, 207

worlding, 8, 18, 22, 33, 41, 42, 45, 46, 52, 67, 114, 141, 190, 200, 218; cities as sites of, 194; *Samandal's* grant, 197

X'ed Out (Burns), 58, 59, 64–66

xanadu*, 198; founded in response to 9/11, 197; founded in 2003, 197; nonprofit art collective, 197; partnered with *Samandal,* 197

Yahgulanaas, Michael Nicoll, 16, 18, 20, 153; arrested for Haida sovereignty activism, 150; asserts naming rights as an act of decolonization, 166; creating for his audience, 162; comics, critique of the term, 156, 158; environmentalist, 149; framelines as tool for decolonization, 175; framelines definition, 180; framelines interact with diegesis, 177, 181; framelines vs formlines, 180; framelines vs quadrillage, 175–7; gridding, border thinking as a response to, 174; Haida First Nations member, 149; "In the Gutter," 176 fig. 4.2; Holm, criticism of, 178, 179, 180; Japan, connection to, 157; manga, remarks of the flexibility of the term, 156; manga used as a political statement, 157; sculptor, 150; *terra nullius*, 174, 175; "tradition of innovation," 153; water

imagery and symbolism, 169, 170. *See also* Haida manga

Yang, K. Wayne, criticizes misuse of "decolonization," 149, 150

"The Yellow Kid and His New Phonograph" (Outcault), 37

Yuste Frías, José, 86

Zanettin, Federico, 86, 91

Zinzin, maître du monde (Exem), 56

STUDIES IN COMICS AND CARTOONS

Jared Gardner, Charles Hatfield, and Rebecca Wanzo, Series Editors
Lucy Shelton Caswell, Founding Editor Emerita

Books published in Studies in Comics and Cartoons focus exclusively on comics and graphic literature, highlighting their relation to literary studies. The series includes monographs and edited collections that cover the history of comics and cartoons from the editorial cartoon and early sequential comics of the nineteenth century through webcomics of the twenty-first. Studies that focus on international comics are also considered.

How Comics Travel: Publication, Translation, Radical Literacies
    KATHERINE KELP-STEBBINS

Resurrection: Comics in Post-Soviet Russia
    JOSÉ ALANIZ

Authorizing Superhero Comics: On the Evolution of a Popular Serial Genre
    DANIEL STEIN

Typical Girls: The Rhetoric of Womanhood in Comic Strips
    SUSAN E. KIRTLEY

Comics and the Body: Drawing, Reading, and Vulnerability
    ESZTER SZÉP

Producing Mass Entertainment: The Serial Life of the Yellow Kid
    CHRISTINA MEYER

The Goat-Getters: Jack Johnson, the Fight of the Century, and How a Bunch of Raucous Cartoonists Reinvented Comics
    EDDIE CAMPBELL

Between Pen and Pixel: Comics, Materiality, and the Book of the Future
    AARON KASHTAN

Ethics in the Gutter: Empathy and Historical Fiction in Comics
    KATE POLAK

Drawing the Line: Comics Studies and INKS, 1994–1997
    EDITED BY LUCY SHELTON CASWELL AND JARED GARDNER

The Humours of Parliament: Harry Furniss's View of Late-Victorian Political Culture
    EDITED AND WITH AN INTRODUCTION BY GARETH CORDERY AND JOSEPH S. MEISEL

Redrawing French Empire in Comics
    MARK MCKINNEY